P9-AFJ-774

Fighting for the First Amendment

Frank Stanton, President of CBS.

Fighting for the First Amendment

Stanton of CBS vs. Congress and the Nixon White House

Corydon B. Dunham

Foreword by Walter Cronkite

Westport, Connecticut
London

Library of Congress Cataloging-in-Publication Data

Dunham, Corydon B., 1927–
Fighting for the first amendment : Stanton of CBS vs. Congress and the Nixon White House / Corydon B. Dunham ; foreword by Walter Cronkite.
p. cm.
Includes bibliographical references and index.
ISBN 0–275–96027–7 (alk. paper)
1. Government and the press—United States. 2. Freedom of the press—United States. 3. Stanton, Frank, 1908– . 4. Columbia Broadcasting System, Inc. 5. Censorship—United States. 6. Subpoena—United States. I. Title.
PN4888.P6D86 1997
323.44'5'097309047—dc21 97–17517

British Library Cataloguing in Publication Data is available.

Library of Congress Catalog Card Number: 97–17517
ISBN: 0–275–96027–7

First published in 1997

Praeger Publishers, 88 Post Road West, Westport, CT 06881
An imprint of Greenwood Publishing Group, Inc.

Printed in the United States of America

The paper used in this book complies with the Permanent Paper Standard issued by the National Information Standards Organization (Z39.48–1984).

10 9 8 7 6 5 4 3 2 1

*To those Dutchmen and Englishmen who,
many, many years ago, developed a revolutionary
new technology, the printing press; who published
under license; and who struggled to become free.*

Contents

Foreword

Much is being written these days about the Information Superhighway. It foretells the future of a great new Information Age of unimagined benefits for mankind. But this great advance in our means of communication hardly had appeared over the horizon before the debate began as to how free it should be, whether there should be controls over access to it and the material that could be transmitted upon it.

As this book will make clear, this is a matter in which the American public—indeed, the freedom-loving public around the world—should take a deep interest. Since Gutenberg invented movable type, the generations that have gone before, and those still alive, have witnessed attempts by the powerful to control the masses by controlling what they are permitted to know. In every challenge to freedom of press and speech, it has been made abundantly clear that only an informed public is a free public; that only an informed public can enjoy the benefits of democracy.

This precious inheritance of ours, the constitutionally protected right to know what our government is doing in our name, is under daily attack by those in government who would prefer to do their business in the dark. Some do it simply by classifying as secret many documents that bear no threat to our security but only to slothful or venal bureaucrats. Others make more obvious frontal attacks on the media. Those who defend the people's right to a free press are heroes of democracy.

As President of CBS, Frank Stanton stood up for the broadcast press and resisted government efforts to intimidate it. In 1971, after CBS News broadcast the news documentary *The Selling of the Pentagon* and CBS News was investigated by a committee of Congress with support from the Nixon White House, Stanton fought for the freedom of the broadcast press, even at the risk of contempt of Congress.

The lesson of that fight for freedom is as critical to the future as it was to the development of a free broadcast press in the past. This book informs and alerts us to the power of government to suppress the news, and particularly news about the government itself. It paints an imperative, real-life picture for all who value democracy and the role of a free press. It takes the reader behind the scenes in an extraordinary chapter-and-verse examination of what certain political leaders sought to do at the time of *The Selling of the Pentagon* and what was required of America's broadcast news organizations to resist them. It also shows how some government officials drew back from attacks on the press as a matter of principle. But what counted was Frank Stanton's passionate and courageous commitment to a free press.

History serves dramatically to illustrate the need for continuing public awareness that our press freedoms must be protected. This is vital as we enter the new Information Age with all its promise for us and our descendants. That's why Corydon B. Dunham's book *Fighting for the First Amendment* is must reading.

Walter Cronkite
Anchorman and Managing Editor
The CBS Evening News, 1962–1991

Introduction

As we approach the twenty-first century, most Americans are unaware that the electronic press, which is the public's principal source of news and information, does not have full First Amendment protection.

Congress set criteria for the grant of licenses necessary for broadcasters' use of the electronic spectrum. It then investigated broadcasters' compliance with these criteria. Program content was reviewed by Congress and the Federal Communications Commission (FCC). News reports and documentaries were investigated. The Supreme Court refused to extend to the broadcast press the same First Amendment protection provided to the print press, so the investigations continued.

In 1971, Frank Stanton, President of CBS, challenged the growing congressional practice of investigating broadcast news coverage. This was to become a defining moment for broadcast journalism.

CBS News broadcast a documentary, *The Selling of the Pentagon*, which exposed massive Pentagon propaganda for increased U.S. military power and support of the Vietnam War. The Commerce Committee of the House of Representatives promptly launched an investigation into CBS News. Its Special Subcommittee on Investigations subpoenaed Stanton to produce the "outtakes" (material gathered for the production of the program but not used) so that it could review CBS

News' editorial judgment. Stanton refused to produce them. Certainly such a congressional investigation of a newspaper report about the government would be unthinkable.

Congress believed it had the authority to investigate broadcast news. It also thought the television networks had become too powerful and their news divisions "out of control." At the same time, the Nixon White House was engaged in an active campaign to discredit the networks and news coverage critical of the President and his conduct of the war. It supported the investigation.

After hearings, the Committee voted that Stanton should be held in contempt of Congress. This could have placed CBS broadcast licenses in jeopardy and sent Stanton to jail. The House of Representatives then held an extraordinary constitutional debate of "high privilege" about its power to investigate the electronic press and the standing of broadcast news under the First Amendment.

This book describes the political and private reasons for the congressional and White House actions, the personal objectives and biases, the lobbying and stratagems, the abuses and acts of principle by government leaders and the surprising developments at the last minute in this struggle for broadcast press freedom. The account is derived from extensive interviews with Stanton, White House officials, members of Congress and their staffs, Pentagon officials, news correspondents, program producers, broadcast network and station executives, and members of the print press and industry observers, as well as from Nixon tapes and White House confidential records impounded following President Nixon's resignation.

It shows what it takes to resist the power of the government so that the press may inform the public, and the personal and the economic risks of that resistance. The account also serves as a cautionary note for the electronic Information Superhighway.

The government is moving to establish oversight of much electronic programming content, seemingly with diminished care for First Amendment values. Government proposals to regulate program carriage and "indecency" for cable have already been enacted and upheld by the Supreme Court. Other proposals include mandatory public service announcements; a government formula for the use of time by political figures; and regulations and legislation to make all the electronic media more suitable for children. All these and other proposals would depend ultimately on some central government authority for judgment and enforcement. The experience of broadcasting is informative because it demonstrates the unavoidable loss of speech and press freedoms which follows government oversight.

But the focus of this book will remain on news coverage, the challenges of the Information Age for news and what it takes to resist the suppression of news. The basic questions remain: Was the First Amendment adopted to protect only what is printed or to protect access by the public to all news, information, and opinion, however it is distributed? Will media owners fight for press freedoms?

Stanton's career was marked by a continuing struggle for freedom of information. For example, he not only defied congressional investigation of news judgment at the risk of contempt of Congress, but also secured the suspension of prohibiting legislation to permit the broadcast of the Nixon-Kennedy debates; increased the programming devoted to news and provided free time to the opposition political party to balance the President's use of the airways; and insisted throughout upon the highest standards for broadcast news coverage.

Today, journalists in the electronic and print media voice their concerns about the adequacy of television's hard-news coverage. They also point out that profit objectives may reduce publisher resistance to government interference with press freedoms that are essential to an informed public.

I was active in the defense of the broadcast press as a lawyer and ultimately as NBC's Executive Vice President and General Counsel, with responsibility for government affairs. I was familiar at the time with Frank Stanton's confrontation with the government over *The Selling of the Pentagon*, as well as his appearance for the broadcast industry on other free press issues.

I want to thank particularly Reuven Frank, former President of NBC News, for his time and advice, as well as all those who gave of their time for interviews and suggestions, including Kathryn Silberthau Strom, Esq., Gordon Manning for his vigorous help, and Terry Pietroski and Gert Wieckoski of Pitwick Associates for their help in developing the manuscript. I would also like to thank my wife, Janet, for her support throughout, my son Cory for his enthusiasm and interest, my son Chris for first encouraging me to write this book, and the Woodrow Wilson International Center for Scholars and their intern, Michael A. Splete.

Chapter 1

Congressional Subpoena

On February 23, 1971, a CBS News documentary, *The Selling of the Pentagon*, reported the Pentagon's use of massive propaganda to urge an increase in military strength as well as military solutions for America's foreign policy, including the Vietnam War. A Special Investigations Subcommittee of the House of Representatives Interstate and Foreign Commerce Committee, under the chairmanship of Harley O. Staggers (D-W.Va.), announced it would investigate CBS News and the program.

On April 8, 1971, a little over a month after the broadcast, two members of the Subcommittee staff made a special trip from Washington, D.C., to "Black Rock," the headquarters building of CBS on 52nd Street in New York City. They showed their credentials and asked to see Dr. Frank Stanton, President of CBS.

Since broadcasters are licensed by the federal government, congressional staff are important people. They were shown immediately to Stanton's office on the 35th floor and ushered in to see him. Stanton stopped work and rose to greet them. The two men, James F. Broder and Mark J. Raabe, handed Stanton a subpoena. It stated it was issued under the authority of the U.S. House of Representatives by the Special Subcommittee on Investigations of the House Interstate and Foreign Commerce Committee, which was conducting an investigation into *The Selling of the Pentagon*.[1] They said, "This is it." It called for the production of all material involved in the production of the program, including the film not broadcast, known in the industry as the "outtakes."

Ordinarily, staff members of a subcommittee would have gotten in touch with the CBS Washington office, maintained to represent CBS in the capital and to provide service to the Congress, the Federal Communications Commission (FCC), the White House and other agencies of the government. "I remember saying to them that they came all the way up from Washington to give this to me. You could have delivered it at my Washington office," Stanton says. But obviously a point was being made. An official government presence was being registered.[2]

Starting with the Radio Act of 1927 and continuing under the Communications Act of 1934, as amended, broadcasters had accommodated to considerable oversight by the Congress and the FCC. Unlike the print press, which is free of government interference under the First Amendment, the rationale for government supervision of broadcasters was that they used limited electronic spectrum, which required a grant by the government. Government regulation was needed to prevent one station's signal from interfering with another's. In addition, the government set criteria for the granting and renewal of licenses. Certain types of programming were required for the stations' broadcast schedules, including news and public affairs. The FCC examined the stations' performance at renewal time to see if the statutory standard of "public interest, convenience and necessity" was met. The FCC assessed the licensees' "character" and their compliance with FCC regulations and congressional statutes.[3]

Congress and the FCC had conducted a number of investigations into broadcasters' news operations and news coverage. But Stanton saw this subpoena as different and as posing an issue of fundamental significance for television news. It was a clear and direct assault by Congress on the independence of the editorial judgment of the television press and was directed to a news report on the government itself.

If a congressional committee could review news content and editorial judgment and subpoena outtakes for that purpose, there could be no independent news. The continuing exercise of such government power and review of broadcast news content would not only undermine the freedom of television news, it would destroy its ability to inform the public about the government and government abuse. Broadcasters would become reluctant to report on issues where government or special interests enlisting government support could bring about congressional investigatory hearings into news decisions. The result would be the avoidance of such issues, issues the public needed most to be informed about.

Stanton's immediate reaction was that the subpoena had to be resisted. If that meant a fight with Congress, it was a fight that had to be fought. The decision, he says, was almost instinctive. It came out of his many years of experience with news coverage and past efforts by government to control news judgment.[4]

Press accounts may be flawed in a number of ways. But it is the teaching of the First Amendment that the press is to be protected from government review and government sanction, even if a claim is made of press error and even if error is present. Otherwise the press would be deterred by the potential for error from publishing reports, portions of if not all of which it must obtain from others. Government review and sanctions for error, beyond the private remedies of libel, would necessarily restrict the free flow of information to the public.

It was the experience of the early Americans with English licensing of the press and speech and the experience and writings of English commentators that led to the First Amendment command that "Congress shall make no law . . . abridging the freedom of speech, or of the Press." The alternative, found in many other countries, is a press which reports government-approved truth. This was not the American tradition, nor did Stanton believe it was constitutionally acceptable.

The Chairman of the CBS Board, William S. Paley, was away, Stanton says, and this meant he was able to make the decision he thought was necessary and act promptly. Under his operating arrangement with Paley he had virtual autonomy when it came to news matters. He says he did have some concern that Paley might have said, "can't we find some other way around this," but it was Stanton's decision to make. When informed of the decision, Paley raised no objection. Although Stanton was not certain about Paley's position, he stresses that "There were, to my knowledge, no senior people in the CBS organization working with me who sought me out and said, 'maybe you ought to find some way out.' "

It was not yet clear how serious Staggers was about the investigation. In the Democratic-controlled Congress at that time, the leadership and committee chairmen ran the Congress. They supported each other. While clearly there was government outrage about the documentary, no one knew how far Staggers would go. Perhaps the controversy could be resolved without production of the outtakes and government review.

Having made the decision to resist the subpoena, Stanton met with the Executive Vice President of CBS, Jack Schneider; the head of CBS News, Richard S. (Dick) Salant; the General Counsel, Robert Evans, Esq.; the Corporate Information Executive, Kidder Meade; and the President of the Broadcast Group, Richard Jencks, to work out the public statement of the CBS position. As his daily log shows, the actions were swift.

LOG
4/8/71

10:00	Broder, Raabe (from Staggers' office)
11:14	JAS (Jack Schneider)
11:34	Salant, Evans
11:45	Salant, Evans, Meade
11:50	Salant, Evans, Meade, Jencks
1:00	Lunch: RSS (Salant), RVE (Evans), EKM (Meade), RWJ (Jencks)
3:05	Tel.c. WSP (Paley)
4:04	Meade
4:07	Jencks, EKM
4:13	EKM, RWJ, RSS
4:21	EKM, RWJ, RSS, RVE
5:10	Tel.c. Harley Staggers

When Stanton finally reached Staggers to tell him of his decision, Staggers was low-key, saying, "I think we'll work this thing out all right."[5]

Stanton announced that CBS would not produce the outtakes and issued a statement that was to be its position throughout the subsequent months:

"We will comply with that part of the subpoena which calls for a film copy and written transcript of the material actually broadcast.

"The subpoena also demands all outtakes and other materials used in connection with preparing the broadcasts, but not actually broadcast. It therefore raises an unprecedented issue in the history of the relationship between the Federal government and the press in this nation. No newspaper, magazine or other part of the press could be required constitutionally to comply with such a subpoena. . . . The sole purpose of this subpoena, so far as we can ascertain it, is to obtain materials which will aid the Committee in subjecting to legislative surveillance the news judgments of CBS in preparing *The Selling of the Pentagon.*"

The statement concluded, "We will respectfully decline to furnish to the Committee the outtakes and other materials used in connection with preparing the broadcast, but not actually broadcast."[6]

This quickly became not something that could be "worked out" but a battle of great principle on each side. For Staggers, it was the power of the institution of the Congress itself to investigate matters within its jurisdiction and to protect the public from falsity and distortion on federally licensed airwaves.

There was also an underlying tension from the congressional perception that there had been some shift of power during the late 1960s from Congress and the President to the three television networks which reached millions of Americans every night. Their news coverage influenced public opinion on political issues. Each branch of government looked for ways to contain network power. The experience of the President and the Congress with network news coverage and the antagonism which members of both branches held for the television network news divisions was not only part of the background for the Staggers confrontation with Stanton, it was to play an important role in the positions taken during the ensuing Stanton contempt proceedings.

The view of many in Congress at the time was put most directly by Representative John Dingell, the powerful Democrat from Michigan who believed deeply, as did others in the Congress, in the need to regulate what they considered to be the undue power of broadcasters. In the absence of government scrutiny, broadcasters would run riot with no one "to bid them nay."[7] The personal experience of some members with network news also made them hostile.

When Stanton turned to the Republicans for help, the House minority leader, Representative Gerald Ford from Michigan, said he would like to help but was waiting for word from the other end of Pennsylvania Avenue. By this time, President Nixon's views about the television press were well known, but not the extent of the campaign underway against the networks. It appeared that Nixon and the Republicans would back the congressional investigation.

Stanton saw that if Congress could summon television newsmen before congressional hearings and review their editorial news judgment, there would be no end to it. It could be expected that Congress would do so whenever it was politically popular or whenever the government was criticized, or even just to get a headline. And it would judge "fairness" in governmental terms, not in journalistic terms. Under such a threat of government investigation, the television press from which most Americans got their news would not be able to do its job of informing the public about the government.

The news programs of the CBS Television Network could only reach the public if broadcast by the individual stations affiliated with the network and located in markets across the country. Except for the five owned by CBS, they were independent businesses holding FCC licenses necessary to broadcast in their markets. They were critical to the operations of the network and, under the law, had the ultimate say as to what was broadcast over their facilities.

Stanton recalls, "A couple of affiliates called urging conciliation. I took a positive position with them. I had a feeling that if I had said, 'I wish there were something that could be done,' they would have offered to help work it out. But, my immediate staff took my position and whether they necessarily agreed with it or not, they certainly were loyal and strong."

Thus, the stage was set for a major congressional test of television's First Amendment protection. At that time no one anticipated how difficult this struggle was to become. To succeed, Stanton had to stand successfully against both the power of the Congress and the Nixon White House.

Chapter 2

The Selling of the Pentagon

The program opens with a film showing infantry storming across a field. Roger Mudd, a CBS news reporter, is heard saying this battle is not being fought in Southeast Asia but is rather "a battle in salesmanship." It is *The Selling of the Pentagon.*[1]

The maneuvers shown are being conducted somewhere in the Carolinas. The camera pans, and you see they are being performed in front of a grandstand filled with people.

Mudd reports: "Nothing is more essential to a democracy than the free flow of information. Misinformation, distortion, propaganda all interrupt that flow. They make it impossible for people to know what their government is doing, which, in a democracy, is crucial. The largest agency in our government is the Department of Defense, and it maintains a public relations division to inform people of its activities."

The Pentagon Public Affairs Division would "spend more than $30 million that year, more than ten times what it spent just twelve years ago." [This was only the tip of the iceberg. It was later reported as more likely to be $190 million.] Mudd makes the charge that the money is spent "not only to inform but to address issues of war and peace.

"We selected three areas for our concentration, direct Department contacts with the public, Defense Department films and the Pentagon's use of the media—the press and television. . . . We sought no secret files, no access to classified documents and looked only at what was being done in public."

The program showed one of the many military demonstrations carried out on Armed Forces Day every year at a number of bases. "The cost of the ammunition alone is $2 million." At the end of the demonstration, in what is called "mad minute," all kinds of heavy and light weapons, everything from tanks to rockets, blaze away in a thundering display of firepower. In the bleachers the audience cheers. Young children turn away from the sight and hold their ears against the noise.

After the demonstration, the public goes out on the field to look at the weapons. The children get a chance to see them up close and play on them.

Mudd continues with a segment on military advocacy of foreign policy. [This was to become one of the main points in controversy, since the military is supposed to implement foreign policy, not to lobby or engage in public appeals for particular positions.]

> *Mudd*: The Pentagon has a team of Colonels touring the country to lecture on foreign policy. We found them in Peoria, Illinois, where they were invited to speak to a mixed audience of civilians and military reservists. The invitation was arranged by Peoria's Caterpillar Tractor Company, which did $39 million of business last year with the Defense Department. The Army has a regulation stating: "Personnel should not speak on the foreign policy implications of U.S. involvement in Vietnam."

The program shows an auditorium filled with an attentive audience, and then the Pentagon presents what had for years been a U.S. belief—the "domino theory."

> *Colonel John A. MacNeil*: Well, now we're coming to the heart of the problem—Vietnam. Now the Chinese have clearly and repeatedly stated that Thailand is next on their list after Vietnam. If South Vietnam becomes Communist it will be difficult for Laos to exist. The same goes for Cambodia, and the other countries of Southeast Asia. I think if the Communists were to win in South Vietnam, the record in the North—what happened in Tet of '68—makes it clear there would be a bloodbath in store for a lot

of the population of the South. The United States is still going to remain an Asian power.

Mudd: Over the years, the Colonels have travelled—at taxpayers' expense—to 163 cities and spoken to 180,000 people. In a question and answer period, they promote American presence in Southeast Asia. . . .

General Lewis Walt: We fought them up on the DMZ, we fought them across the Lao border, we fought them down south across the Cambodian border. But they're trying to keep the war going on—why? Because they think that we're going to give up and pull out before the job is done. That's what they've been told, that's what they read in our newspapers and our magazines.

Mudd: Tonight, like any other evening, there are between six and ten Pentagon speakers appearing in public. With military transportation at their disposal, they traverse the country shaping the view of their audiences. For years, General Lewis Walt has been the Marine speaker most in demand.

General Walt: This is what's kept the war going on. If we could have had the entire American nation in back of us, all of our Americans in back of our Armed Forces in South Vietnam, this war would have been over a year and a half ago. [Applause]

Mudd: At a St. Paul, Minnesota shopping mall, an Army display emphasizes power, a recurrent theme in their programs.

The program shows a display of military equipment emphasizing massive firepower.

Mudd: The Army Exhibit Unit has been to 239 cities in 46 states and has been seen by over 20 million people. The cost to taxpayers: $906,000 a year.

Thunderbirds are shown flying over in dramatic formation. They are reported to have flown "108 exhibitions last year in front of six million people." Supposedly the demonstrations will attract volunteers. Mudd says, "what it really is is an elaborate commercial for air power."

Green Beret troops give a demonstration of hand-to-hand combat, including the use of karate, knives and headlocks. The film then shows the children in the audience going onto the field and imitating what they have just seen. They go to the heavy weaponry and pretend to fire.

The program points out that each year the Pentagon runs a guided tour for thousands of VIPs and community leaders with red carpet treatment. It puts on demonstrations of military maneuvers and shows the latest in equipment. Generals and other military officers are on hand to answer questions and discuss the American military. The groups see air lifts of thousands of troops. They see demonstrations of helicopter transportation and firepower.

Some of those given the tour were interviewed:

> *Robert Greenhill*: I think the message I would take back is that we have a first-class military operation led by first-class leaders.
>
> *Willard Dover*: I think the message is that you can be proud of your boys in the service.

An investment banker says: "I can see from this tour that Fulbright and Proxmire statements are baseless . . . if more people could see this you would see less carping." [At the time both Senator J. William Fulbright (D-Ark.), the most outspoken Senator against the Vietnam War, and Senator William Proxmire (D-Wis.) had raised questions about the strength and training of the military.]

An Army film shows a man sloughing through the mud and water, in combat. The voice-over says, "there are those at home demonstrating, having abandoned the fight against communism." Scenes are then shown from a Defense Department film narrated by Jack Webb, a television star from the popular television series *Dragnet*. Last year, Mudd reports, "52 million Americans saw Pentagon motion pictures, 45,000 public gatherings viewed them and at least 356 commercial and educational television stations have presented them as part of their public service broadcast time."

Mudd continues, "An official Pentagon regulation states propaganda has no place but in preparing this broadcast we looked only at products of the last decade after the thaw in cold war politics." Well-known journalists and movie stars served as narrators for the films.[2] John Wayne made a film about the U.S. presence in Vietnam (over a thousand prints of the film were circulated). In the film he says the communists are overthrowing the South Vietnamese government to secure their own revolution and have killed thousands of South Vietnamese civilian leaders. A military spokesman says that the communists in China are bent on taking over all of Asia; there are also communists in Cuba, and it is essential that America builds up its military power here and overseas.

In the Pentagon's most ambitious film, *Red Nightmare*, Jack Webb describes a communist scheme to take over the United States. The hero of Webb's film dreams that his town is invaded by communists and, with remarkable ease, is quickly subverted. The only American not subverted is placed on trial and convicted for crimes against the State. The film was first released in 1962 and then again in 1965. According to Mudd, "nine hundred prints of this film are now in circulation."

Mudd reports: "The Defense Department believes that the best way to save Americans from a red nightmare is by films like these. The films contain a high proportion of propaganda, distributed during Kennedy, Johnson and Nixon administrations. It has been more than a decade that peaceful coexistence policy replaced the early warriors, but the film makers of the Pentagon still are on the old themes."

Mudd reports that the Pentagon machine has another function with the largest and most penetrating of all contacts through the media, including newspapers, magazines, and radio of any American organization.

> *Mudd*: The vastness of the Defense establishment confronts a reporter with an almost impossibly complex task. Pentagon stories develop in many other ways besides formal briefings, but the sheer size of the building itself remains bewildering. Often it is impossible to get to a news story, even when the story does not involve national security, until the Pentagon chooses to announce it.
>
> Going into and out of the 30,000 Pentagon offices each day are 200,000 phone calls and 129,000 pieces of mail. But very little of this communicating is done with the press. We asked the man in charge of all Pentagon public relations, Assistant Secretary of Defense, Daniel Henkin, about the press and its coverage of the Defense Department.

[And then, in an interchange with The Honorable Daniel Z. Henkin, Assistant Secretary of Defense (Public Affairs), which was to become the center of the government's investigation of CBS News, Mudd asks:]

Mudd: What about your public displays of military equipment at state fairs and shopping centers—what purpose does that serve?

Henkin: Well, I think it serves the purpose of informing the public about their Armed Forces. I believe that the American public has a right to request information about the Armed Forces, to have speakers come before them, to ask questions, and to understand the need for our Armed Forces, why we ask for the funds that we do ask for, how we spend these funds, what are we doing about such problems as drugs—and we do have a drug problem in the Armed Forces. What are we doing about the racial problem in the Armed Forces, and we do have a racial problem. I think the public has a valid right to ask us these questions.

Mudd: Well, is that sort of information about the drug problem you have and the racial problem you have and the budget problems you have, is that the sort of information that gets passed out at state fairs, by sergeants who are standing next to rockets?

Henkin: No, I wouldn't limit that to sergeants standing next to any kind of exhibit. Now there are those who contend that this is propaganda. I don't—do not agree with this.

Mudd then asks a *Washington Post* Pentagon reporter whether the Pentagon is successful in its propagandizing efforts. The reporter says it is, and that it is impossible to counter the Pentagon because of the enormous size of its effort and the number of people working on it.

When asked about the need for stories on weapon development, the reporter says, "if the weapon is going to be described in public as it was in 1969 and 1970, along with the sales job to get the anti-ballistic missile defense approved, it should be described accurately. The point here is that because the technology is reachable, that there will always be the pressure to build it. The danger to the U.S. in all this is that weapons are inexorable and they're imperious, and only public challenges and public resistance can keep technology from running us right onto the road of Armageddon."

Mudd: Each year, 12,000 radio and television tapes are mailed to 2,700 radio stations and 546 television stations. Over two million printed releases are sent to 6,500 daily and weekly newspapers. In these releases, medals, promotions and re-assignments are emphasized.

Tolbert [former military public information officer]: There are hundreds of weeklies and small dailies in this country that live on what we call the hometown release, where the Army, Navy and Air Force maintain hometown news release centers, and are just spewing this stuff into these newspapers who accept it willingly and who print it . . . the community press which is extremely important to this country, is giving a free ride to a military story.

Mudd quotes one speaker as saying, "I'm one of those who believes that the most vicious instrument in America today is the network television." Mudd points out that the Pentagon uses sympathetic Congressmen to appear on the air to counter what it regards as the anti-military tilt of network reporting. War heroes are made available for taped TV reports for the home districts of pro-Pentagon politicians. Representative F. Edward Hébert, Democrat of Louisiana and the Chairman of the House Armed Services Committee, is pictured in such a report. He asks Major James Rowe, a Green Beret and former POW, what keeps the Viet Cong fighting. Rowe replies, "the support that the VC receives from the United States is the only thing that keeps them fighting." Hébert asks Major Rowe for his reaction to a recent peace rally.

Major Rowe: I walked up and I heard one of the speakers yelling "down with imperialism." . . . I heard the same things from the Vietcong except there it was in Vietnamese and here it was in English. And I . . . walked through the crowd, and I saw VC flags flying from the flagpole of the Washington Monument . . . I saw American flags with the stars removed and a peace symbol superimposed. I saw the red flag with a black peace symbol on it and then I heard one of my Senators say we're here because we cherish our flag. And the only thing I could think of then, Sir, was, what flag does he cherish?

Chairman Hébert: Let me congratulate you, please sir. It's an honor to have you on this program with me and I only wish to God we could have more people wearing the uniform privileged to speak as you have spoken because the silent majority will and must be heard.

Mudd: The war is covered extensively not only by the civilian press but also by the Defense Department's own camera crews in

Vietnam. Their product is distributed to America's TV stations and networks.

A military cameraman, an Air Force sergeant, speaks about his assignments by the military to make it appear the South Vietnamese were doing much of the fighting:

Demitor [Pentagon film producer]: In many stories that were filmed in Vietnam we staged a number of stories of the Vietnamese. We were propagandizing the war and an example of it was a story titled "U.S. and South Vietnamese forces patrol enemy infiltration routes." We went out with the Vietnamese in the Riverine patrol, went down the river until we found an area that was suitable for our landing. Because I knew it wasn't an actual combat situation I had no fear—I was off the boat on the land before the Vietnamese infantry came up, so that we could get a shot as the boats came onto the shore. They proceeded inland about three quarters of a mile or half a mile while we were getting shots of them running through the rice paddies. They didn't fire any shots. There were no traces of Viet Cong.

We were told, when we had a sufficient amount of footage exposed, to tell the Vietnamese and they would turn around.

The sergeant goes on to say that then the American forces took over conducting the actual military attack. None of this was publicly shown but what was shown was the Vietnamese in their staged assault.

. . .

Mudd: Defense Department information machinery is well established in Vietnam, where a special language has developed that takes some time to learn. "Protective reaction" means the United States resumed the bombing of North Vietnam. "Selective ordinance" means napalm. "Defoliation" means nothing will grow there any more. A "civilian irregular defense group volunteer" is a mercenary. "Population resettlement" means getting villagers out of their villages, and "Military Assistance Command Daily Press Briefing" means this scene right here, which is popularly known among newsmen in Saigon as the Five O'Clock Follies.

Jack Tolbert describes how he had been able to manipulate the information flowing out from the battle scene.

Mudd: As a public information officer, what effect do you think incidents like that have on a democratic society which is supposed to enjoy a free press?

Mudd had asked an important question. The answer was to draw very little public attention.

Tolbert: Well, I feel that the military information arm is so vast, has been able to become so pervasive, by the variety and the amounts and the way and the sheer numbers, it's able to present its viewpoint to the American people. I think this attitude it was able to develop allowed Vietnam to happen. Had we not been able to convince the American people prior to Vietnam that a military solution was a correct solution, without a doubt and not to be questioned, we couldn't have had a Vietnam. I feel that if we allow this pervasiveness to continue, that frankly it could lead us to another Vietnam.

Mudd concludes: "We have reported tonight only a fraction of the total public relations apparatus belonging to the Pentagon and supported by taxpayers. Indeed, the news restrictions on the current invasion of Laos raise the question whether the public's right to know is being served or thwarted.

"On this broadcast we have seen violence made glamorous, expensive weapons advertised as if they were automobiles, biased opinions presented as straight facts. Defending the country not just with arms but also with ideology, Pentagon propaganda insists on America's role as the cop on every beat in the world. Not only the public but the press as well has been beguiled, including at times, ourselves at CBS News. This propaganda barrage is the creation of a runaway bureaucracy that frustrates attempts to control it.

"Last November 6, President Nixon sent this memorandum to executive agencies, criticizing what he called self-serving and wasteful public relations efforts. He directed an end to what he described as 'inappropriate promotional activities.' The President specifically ordered, in his words, a curtailment of 'broadcasting, advertising, exhibits and films.'

"Just since the memo was written the Army's Golden Knights, a parachute team, have performed for the public in Nevada, California, [and] North Carolina. Other Army exhibits have travelled to 59 different locations. Air Force displays, like this Hound Dog-Quail missile, have appeared in at least 36 shopping malls and municipal centers, since the memo was written.

"We went back to the Pentagon and asked what effect the Presidential directive would have. We were told there will be cuts in personnel, not activities. There may be some disagreement, of course, over just what constitutes an 'inappropriate promotional activity,' but to date not a single activity shown on this broadcast has been eliminated.

"Tomorrow morning, according to Defense Department schedules, there will be an Army show pushing the ABM in Mountain View, California; an Air Force missile will turn up in Houston on Friday; the Pentagon's travelling colonels will be in Hampton, Virginia, March 8; and next week fifth graders at the Hill Elementary School in Davidson, Michigan, will get to see the Navy's propaganda film on Vietnam.

"This is Roger Mudd for CBS REPORTS."

CBS said the documentary provoked a widespread response. It was "predominantly favorable," but the response of the Nixon administration and other public officials was "sharply critical."[3] The program came about because the head of the CBS News division, Dick Salant, who had been a lieutenant in the Navy in World War II, had seen an NBC News program about the military and wondered why the Pentagon was using taxpayer money to make promotional films. "If the Pentagon finances a multi-million dollar press agent job on the civilian population, he thought it worth the telling," the *New York Times* reported. CBS was undergoing a cost profit squeeze that might have dictated against "antagonizing elected or appointed bureaucrats. But Mr. Salant went ahead. The public should know about it."[4]

Certainly the hostile reaction from some was prompted by the belief that the networks were undermining public support for the Vietnam War effort. *The Selling of the Pentagon* was the latest in what was thought to be biased, if not unpatriotic, network coverage of the war. The producer, Peter Davis, insists he was not doing a program about the military but about the Pentagon and those running the Pentagon's propaganda efforts.[5] The military saw no such distinction, nor did its supporters. The Chairman of the House Armed Services Committee, F. Edward Hébert, was to say, "I think it was the most horrible thing I've seen in years. The most—the greatest disservice to the military I've ever seen on television and I've seen some pretty bad stuff."[6] *Barron's*, the financial magazine, attacked the program essentially for being unpatriotic, criticized the editing, and urged a review of CBS broadcast licenses.[7] A *Washington Post* editorial criticized the editing. Its own television station, WTOP-TV, broadcast the program and criticized the *Post* editorial, as did Dick Salant and Reuven Frank, head of NBC News.[8]

Vice President Spiro Agnew, who had served previously as the spokesman for the Nixon administration in attacking the networks, criticized the program as "disreputable." In a speech on March 18, 1971, he called it a "subtle but vicious broadside against the nation's defense establishment." Stanton called Agnew's speech a "vivid example of the traditional conflict between Government and the free press which has marked this country's history. CBS does not claim any immunity from criticism. CBS does not claim to be infallible. But the Vice President's indictment is mistaken. . . . 'The Selling of the Pentagon' has been praised by distinguished Americans from all walks of life. It has also been criticized. But we believe that it is an important and valuable job of journalistic investigative reporting."[9]

Because of the criticism by Chairman Hébert, Vice President Agnew and Secretary of Defense Melvin Laird, Stanton decided to rebroadcast the program and to give the critics an opportunity to comment on the program in conjunction with the broadcast itself. *The Selling of the Pentagon* was rebroadcast on March 23, 1971, from 10:00 to 11:00 P.M. When originally broadcast, CBS gained a 15 share of the viewing audience, while the NBC movie *Eye of the Cat* got a 29 share and the ABC drama *Marcus Welby, M.D.* got a 48 share.[10] The CBS documentary was seen by 7,690,000, viewers while *Welby* was watched by more than three times as many people. The repeat of the program got somewhat higher ratings because of the publicity surrounding it. Then, from 11:00 to 11:15, CBS carried a postscript from the leading critics and a brief CBS response:[11]

> *Mudd*: The most prominent critics have been Vice President Agnew, Secretary of Defense Melvin Laird and F. Edward Hébert, Chairman of the House Armed Services Committee. Bob Schieffer interviewed Mr. Hébert on the CBS MORNING NEWS.
>
> *Schieffer*: Mr. Chairman, what did you think of the program, "The Selling of the Pentagon"?
>
> *Hébert*: I haven't got the time to tell you. I think it was the most horrible thing I've seen in years. The most—the greatest disservice to the military I've ever seen on television, and I've seen some pretty bad stuff.
>
> *Schieffer*: Why do you think it was so bad?
>
> *Hébert*: Well, it's very easy to tell why it was so bad. It was, I

think, one of the most professional hatchet jobs, and a splendid professional hatchet job. For instance—this is an old technique that you know as well as I know—this is nothing new to us, but to the unsuspecting viewer it's something that they accept as being fact. . . . But the script that's in the commentator's hands absolutely destroys what has just been seen, by the use of nice little words.

For instance, there's a fire power demonstration . . . and it says, "That's the new way our wars are being fought"—I'm recalling from memory—"That's the way our wars are being fought but not in front of grandstands." Why, that little word, that's a very cute word. The use of these little words and innuendoes are the things that are the vicious, the devious things. And that's what I objected to.

For instance, they presented me—in the clip on me—that clip was obtained under false representation from my office here, it was obtained under the representation it was to be used as a POW documentary. And it turns up here, in this film, as though the Pentagon had used me as a patsy to take a major role. . . . The film was part of a show—and I used the word "show" advisedly—for presentation of a bimonthly program that I've had in New Orleans over WWL for years and years and years—and WWL pays for it. . . . [But the documentary says] "the Pentagon gets pro-Pentagon politicians and makes war heroes available to them." Now, this is the damndest lie and the damndest misrepresentation of a fact that I've ever seen. And it is a misrepresentation. That's what I object to. And this is through—practically through the whole film.

Hébert's anger was, indeed, one of the things that led him in the beginning to ask Chairman Staggers to conduct an inquiry. It was to persist. Peter Davis insists that the film was not obtained under false pretenses.[12] Hébert did think he was portrayed in a way that made him look bad. There had been debate within the CBS News division about the use of this clip, since Hébert was not part of the Pentagon. But it did illustrate the point that the Pentagon made war heroes available for use by supporters in Congress, and Hébert was one such supporter. The postscript continued:

Schieffer: Well, is there a propaganda machine over there these days, Mr. Chairman? . . .

Hébert: I think the Pentagon is trying to sell the best bill of goods it can. And what do you want them to sell, communism? Do you want these people to go over there and tell you that Hanoi's right?

Schieffer: Mr. Chairman, you're not trying to tell me, are you, that this documentary . . . was an un-American act?

Hébert: Wittingly or unwittingly, however done, consciously or unconsciously, deliberately or not deliberately, it is one of the most un-American things I've ever seen on a screen—on a tube. I'm not saying they did this deliberately. I can't read a man's conscience. I can't know what's in a man's mind. I'm not saying that. All I can do is judge the product. And the product was a non-American activity. That's what I'm saying.

Mudd: Secretary of Defense Laird was also critical. He, too, was interviewed on the CBS MORNING NEWS. . . .

Kalb: Well, we know that Vice President Agnew has called it "disreputable" and Congressman Hébert had called it "un-American." Do you share those reviews of the documentary, sir?

Laird: Well, I believe that there probably could have been a little more professionalism shown in putting the show together . . . this particular program has indeed helped us because of the very unprofessional type of work that was done in quoting a colonel out of context completely. He was using a quotation and the words were put in his mouth. . . .

Mudd: The most highly-placed critic has been the Vice President. He has levelled five different attacks on the broadcast, the most widely-reported in Boston last Thursday night.

[A clip of one of Agnew's speeches showed:]

Agnew: The news organization that makes such charges should itself be free of any taint of misinformation, distortion and propaganda in its own operations. [Sustained applause] In this regard, it is the CBS Television Network, not the Department of Defense, that leaves much to be desired in terms of "the free flow of information." [Sustained applause]

Mudd: In his speech last Thursday, the Vice President did not specify any "misinformation, distortion and propaganda" he had found in "The Selling of the Pentagon." He did, however, call it, quote, "a subtle but vicious broadside against the nation's defense establishment." . . . Mr. Agnew was asked about his criticism of CBS at a news conference in Boston the next morning, and he was more specific in his attacks on "The Selling of the Pentagon."

Agnew: With regard to "The Selling of the Pentagon," it's important to note that there was quite a bit of cut-and-paste done in that documentary, where the speech of the Colonel, for example, was—portions of that were extrapolated that occurred during possibly a half an hour talk and run together as though they—the sentences followed one another. . . . My purpose was simply to tell the American people and to show them through uncontroverted evidence based on substantial and complete investigation that they cannot rely on CBS documentaries for facts. . . .

Reporter: One man's cut-and-paste might be called another man's editing. Can you cite to us any specific inaccuracy or attempt to mislead in the film "Selling of the Pentagon"?

Agnew: [different statements] were run together as though it were a continuous thought . . . and that really wasn't so. I can give you one more off the top of my head. There was a quote by one of the speakers for the Pentagon, a Colonel, the words were something to this effect. I don't think this is the accurate phrasing, but the words were to the effect that if Laos, that if South Vietnamese went Communist, Laos would of necessity go Communist, too. The makers of the documentary let those words come out as though they were uttered, conceived and in every respect the property of the Colonel who made the statement, whereas actually he was quoting, at that point, Prime Minister Souvanna Phouma of Laos, who made this statement himself. . . .

Mudd: We have listened to rebuttal and criticism of our broadcast. . . . Here to reply is Richard Salant, President of CBS News.

Salant: No one has refuted the essential accuracy of "The Selling of the Pentagon." You have seen and you have heard Pentagon activities for yourselves: the manipulation of news, the staging of events and the selling to the public of the Pentagon's points of view. None of our critics has said that these things didn't happen or weren't done—and so the validity of the broadcast stands unscathed. . . . Another charge you heard was that we edited the statement of one of those traveling colonels. We were supposed to have left out the fact that he quoted Souvanna Phouma. I've examined the transcript of the Colonel's statement and it is difficult to tell where Souvanna Phouma left off and the Colonel started. At any rate, when we checked back to the original magazine source we found that the Colonel was paraphrasing this statement from Souvanna Phouma in *U.S. News and World Report*, November 6, 1967: "Should South Vietnam become Communist—that is to say, should all of Vietnam become Communist—it would be difficult for Laos to exist. The same goes for Cambodia, the same for other countries."

The Colonel lifted that statement to make a Pentagon point; he embraced it and simply used Souvanna Phouma as his authority. But the Prince said something else the Colonel omitted. In that same interview Souvanna Phouma gave a warning about going into Laos which the Colonel did not quote: "We are all seeking a limit to the conflict. . . . Therefore from a military point of view this barrier would not be effective. And from the political view, on the international scene, the barrier would not only extend the conflict into Laos, but perhaps even to Thailand."

On March 24, Vice President Agnew went after the CBS rebroadcast and the postscript. He accused the network of "deliberately publishing untruths" and said he was "totally dissatisfied with what CBS characterized as a rebuttal on the part of administration officials including myself." When interviewed by an editorial panel of the area's top news executives, Agnew said that while he was given the right of rebuttal, he was not allowed to decide what he could say. "They edited some of my previous remarks and [remarks of] other administration people and showed the ones they wanted to show."[13] White House Director of Communications Herbert G. Klein added that while he did not "concur in all phases" with Agnew's attack on news reporting by the television networks, he agreed that the program "was not a fully balanced documentary."[14]

Chairman Hébert reiterated his charge that he was misled in supplying film to Davis and said that Davis was guilty of a "vicious fabrication." He asked Stanton to broadcast his "earlier lengthy televised criticism of the program" in full and without editing "in the spirit of fair play and my right to dissent."[15]

The substance of the program—that the Pentagon was deliberately and officially engaged in improper propaganda activities—was not addressed. An editorial in the *New York Times* on March 24, entitled "Politics in the Pentagon," said the problem was not the Defense Department's flamboyant tactics in advertising its skills with arms and men and not the profligate spending of taxpayers' money on publicity sideshows and expensive lobbying for the favors of American business leaders: the problem was that such activities "regardless of their style and substance, run counter to the principle of democratic government." It called the Pentagon films exhibited before military and civilian audiences an insult to the nation's intelligence and an "appalling breach of faith." *Red Nightmare*, which purported to describe a communist takeover of an American town, and *Road to the Wall*, which showed an enemy intent on conquering the world, were "a throwback to the hysteria of the Cold War era. . . . They resemble in technique the worst output of totalitarian propaganda. . . . Even if appeals to fear and hatred were not repulsive in themselves, they would still clash head on with the vital doctrine of a nonpolitical military." The *Times* concluded it was "intolerable" for public relations colonels and other officers on active duty to tour the country to tell the American people what policies they ought to support or oppose in Indochina or anywhere abroad or at home. When the Armed Forces by pressure of propaganda arrogate to themselves an activist role in the "design of national or international strategy, free government is undermined." This was an issue "at the core of civilian control of the military and of government by an elected leadership accountable to the people."

In the months that followed, there was little public or government criticism of the Pentagon's expenditure of millions of dollars in propaganda. There was no investigation of the Pentagon's advocacy of foreign policy. There was little done to change the Pentagon's public relations apparatus or its activities. Public attention was shifted from what was said in the program to how it was said.

Chapter 3

Staggers' First Hearing on the Subpoena

On April 8, Harley O. Staggers (D-W.Va.) formally opened the Subcommittee hearing on the subpoena and the question of CBS' production of CBS files, program outtakes, and other material.

Staggers was not an ideologue, nor was he hostile to the press. He held a safe seat in West Virginia and was the Chairman of the House Interstate and Foreign Commerce Committee because he had seniority. He was a warm and effective politician, personable, with a slightly ruddy, cherubic countenance and a fringe of white hair. He affected a "country boy" manner, but much of this was no doubt genuine and natural to him. There was no television station in his home district.

He had grown up in Keyser, West Virginia, a town of 6,000 which depended for its welfare on the B & O Railroad. As a youngster he had a job as a railroad "call boy," going from door to door to summon the railroad workers to position the engines on a large turntable when the trains arrived at the railroad yard.

He had been elected sheriff, served in the Navy in World War II, campaigned for congressional office and, once elected, served for many years. He was an agreeable go-along, get-along Congressman, with a lovely wife and six children. He was deeply and genuinely religious.

He wore out three Bibles during his tenure in Congress and opened or closed many meetings and even personal encounters with a brief prayer.

His main interest was the railroad system that served the coal industry in West Virginia. But his Committee oversaw every business activity in the country—and abroad—that touched on interstate and foreign commerce. And while he was seen as a weak chairman, on any question involving the power of the House he felt strongly and could count on the support of the other powerful committee chairmen as well as the House Speaker, Carl Albert (D-Okla.).

Broadcasting magazine wrote that Staggers "has suddenly placed himself at the center of a huge and bitter fight over the First Amendment (although he rejects that characterization of the issue). . . . 'What is at stake,' he says, is 'deception'; the First Amendment has 'nothing to do with it.' He is determined to obtain passage of legislation that would make illegal what he considers to be fraudulent practices by broadcasters. If their freedom to edit as they choose is unchecked, Mr. Staggers warned in a CBS News interview, then 'Big Brother' has arrived. . . .

"The man appears uncomfortable with controversy. Little in his background or make-up would lead him to seek it. But to Harley Staggers . . . there is a moral question posed by the activities of broadcasting's giants, and it has nothing to do with constitutional subtleties. He has perceived an act to be evil, and he will have none of it. It is as simple as that. 'We just want to be sure,' says the chairman of the House Commerce Committee, 'that people don't do the wrong thing.' "[1]

He was briefed for the April 8 hearing by the Subcommittee staff, which had experience from previous investigatory hearings with questions of deception and with outtakes. While he knew what he wanted, he was not an expert in the field of communications.

The announced purpose of the legislative inquiry was to investigate whether there was "deception." If the audience thought it was seeing an actual interview when in fact it was watching a scene created by a program editor, an arrangement and combination of questions and answers that could give a misleading impression of the substance or the manner in which the interview was actually conducted, the public would have no way of knowing it was watching a fabrication. The Subcommittee and the staff believed the hearing could be used to stop the potential for such deception. If television network news was engaged in an improper practice, this hearing would expose it. Further, legislative measures might be adopted to require disclosure of the fact that the film shown had been edited.[2]

To settle this issue, the Special Investigations Subcommittee and, in turn, the full Commerce Committee needed to see the program's outtakes and how the editing was done. The narrow question then was: Could the Committee subpoena material which CBS had, but which it did not use in the broadcast, to determine for itself whether or not the impressions created by the program were fair and accurate? Thus, the editorial judgment of CBS News in the selection of material to be broadcast and in editing questions and answers would be reviewed. This was the compelling reason for Stanton's refusal to produce such material, since that would submit the editorial judgment of CBS News for government review.

Staggers had not hesitated to use his investigative powers in what some saw as a coercive manner in the past. Only the year before, on the day of the retirement of Rosel Hyde, who was Chairman of the FCC, Staggers had subpoenaed him to appear and produce documents withheld by the FCC as part of a pending adjudicatory proceeding. He coerced their production through the threat of contempt proceedings.[3]

Staggers turned to William Springer (R-Ill.), the ranking minority member of the Special Subcommittee, for his help. Springer had a good reputation as a legislator. He was a loyal Republican and upheld the traditions of the House. Springer played a special role in the work of the House Commerce Committee. He was brighter than Staggers and worked well with him. For example, when Staggers made a presentation to the House Rules Committee to take a Bill to the floor for a vote, if he got into trouble with the Committee he would let Springer help him out and explain the details.[4]

Springer had participated in the Special Investigations Subcommittee's previous investigations of television news. He did not believe the First Amendment applied to the television press. Staggers said to Springer: "I am going to need your help on this." Springer agreed to give it. He also agreed to deliver the Republicans. He had the "green light" from Nixon.[5] Although the Democrats controlled the House, Republican support would be essential if any significant number of Democrats split away from Staggers—and some liberal Democrats might do so on the war issue or the First Amendment issue. Many Republicans supported Staggers and viewed Springer as their point man on the Subcommittee in the fight with CBS.[6]

The other members of the five-man Subcommittee followed the lead of the Chairman and acted as a united whole. They were Representatives James J. Pickle (D-Tex.), Leonard R. Blanton (D-Tenn.) and Richard G. Shoup (R-Mont.).

At the start of the hearing, Staggers said the Subcommittee had general jurisdiction and power to conduct investigations and consider the adequacy of laws and regulations applicable to those in commerce. From broadcasting's inception, Congress had recognized the medium as affecting the public interest because it used a limited spectrum, not available to all.

He then addressed the basis for review of broadcast news content: "Whether certain technological advances and/or the employment of certain production and editing techniques . . . and other practices by networks . . . have given rise to the need for new laws for the protection of the public—through disclosure requirements or other suitable means." He said information had now been received about misleading practices affecting purportedly genuine news programs and documentaries, including staged events presented as though they were real, rearrangement of the sequence of events, mismatching responses given during interviews or other distortions of an actual event filmed by the camera.

Staggers used three examples of earlier investigations of news programs to buttress his position: a CBS Chicago station broadcast entitled *Pot Party at a University*, which had involved a staged pot party at Northwestern University; a CBS News documentary, *Hunger in America*, which had mistakenly described malnutrition as the cause of a particular child's death; and CBS' *Project Nassau*, a program about gun-running and the possible invasion of Haiti, which was never broadcast.

In answer to the CBS claim for First Amendment protection for news outtakes, Staggers had a ready answer. The report of the Subcommittee following its investigation of *Project Nassau* said, "Fraud and deception in the presentation of purportedly *bona fide* news events is no more protected by the First Amendment than is the presentation of fraud and deception in the context of commercial advertising or quiz programs."

Staggers added that "the original, uncut and unedited material must be examined." He said, "Our purpose is not to look into whether CBS has been biased against the Department of Defense." He concluded, "Again I stress that it is not this subcommittee's function to sit in judgment of the viewpoints expressed in television news or documentary programs. We do not have, nor do we seek, authority to curtail the presentation of controversial issues or unpopular cases or personalities. It is this subcommittee's view, however, that the American public is entitled to know whether what it is seeing on the television screen is real or simulated, edited or unedited, sequentially accurate or editorially rearranged, spontaneous or contrived."[7]

The Subcommittee had also subpoenaed outtakes from the nature program, *Say Good-Bye,* broadcast on NBC. If the Subcommittee could find a practice of distortion by the networks, there would be greater justification for congressional action. Staggers also thought this would show the Subcommittee was not out after CBS alone and would provide a kind of investigatory "balance."[8] But this program had not been produced by NBC, but by Wolper Productions for Quaker Oats. The advertiser had bought time on the network for the show with its commercials. The program showed a hunter shooting a mother polar bear from a helicopter, her little cub left alone and stranded. It was a moving criticism of such hunting but not a "news documentary." The polar bear shown in the film had in fact been shot with a tranquilizer gun for the program and promptly recovered and lumbered away.

NBC responded to the subpoena it received by turning over to the Subcommittee the time contract with Quaker Oats and Wolper and the film as broadcast. Since it had nothing to do with producing the program, it had no outtakes. On learning the facts about the program's production, NBC had issued new guidelines to require more disclosure in the future for such programs produced by others. But NBC did not face the issue presented for CBS. NBC's Washington lawyer, Howard Monderer, Esq., delivered the film and the contracts to the staff, as requested. Upon his arrival, the Subcommittee subpoenaed him and swore him in as a witness. When it was established that NBC had no outtakes, he was asked whether NBC would produce outtakes if it had them. Monderer would not agree with the proposition.[9]

The CBS Deputy General Counsel, John D. Appel, Esq., accompanied by Lloyd Cutler, Esq., of the law firm of Wilmer Cutler & Pickering, was then sworn in and submitted a letter from Robert V. Evans, Esq., Vice President and General Counsel of CBS. He declined to produce the outtakes and submitted legal opinions for the record claiming First Amendment protection. Appel asked the Subcommittee to reconsider the issuance of the subpoena for outtakes because of its intrusion into CBS News' editorial judgment, which he contended was protected from such inquiry by the First Amendment.

The Chairman and then Mr. Springer both argued strenuously that there was no First Amendment protection for such material. The Chairman gave CBS ten days within which to reach a final conclusion. It was clear that all members of the Subcommittee believed the subpoena should be honored and CBS would have to produce the outtakes for the Subcommittee's review.[10]

The broadcast industry was, for the most part, still just watching. Indeed, there was some division in the industry. An informal poll of individual stations disclosed "substantial support for the views of Vice President Agnew and the Department of Defense in their criticism of *The Selling of the Pentagon*." The random consensus was that New York executives "do not speak for all broadcasters." It was also reported at the time that the President of the National Association of Broadcasters (NAB), Vincent Wasilewski, in a speech on broadcast matters, "touched only lightly upon the maintenance of journalistic independence of broadcasting and apparently for diplomatic reasons."[11]

The subpoena did prompt a response from the print press. The American Society of Newspaper Editors (ASNE) sent a telegram to the House of Representatives denouncing the subpoena of the background material for the documentary. ASNE agreed that every news report can be judged for accuracy and fairness as published. "It disagrees totally with any attempt to pry into newspaper's, broadcaster's or any other journalist's private files to judge editing." It viewed the Subcommittee action as "a dangerous and unwarranted intrusion into journalistic freedoms." The Chairman of the Freedom of Information Committee of Sigma Delta Chi, the professional journalist fraternity, denounced the subpoena as "repugnant." A broadcaster should not have to edit with one eye on the film and the other over his shoulder. The Association for Education in Journalism called it an "unwarranted interference." The President of the Associated Press Broadcasters Association also criticized the subpoena. The National Academy of TV Arts and Sciences said, "Every medium of mass communication is threatened by this attempt to have government sit in judgment."[12]

The *Washington Post*, which had originally criticized CBS for improper editing, said the subpoena was "unwarranted" and a "substantial threat to the news media in this country." It said, "CBS deserves to be judged on what it put on the air, not on what it collected and discarded along the way."

Its editorial noted that the program had provided a public service. The subpoena, however, would have a "chilling" effect. "It would mean any newsman who said anything critical about any governmental official could be called on the carpet to explain how he reached that conclusion. . . . Indeed, the final stop on the road down which Mr. Staggers has embarked is complete governmental control of the content of television news and public affairs programming."[13]

As the seriousness of the Subcommittee's intention became more widely known and Stanton informed news organizations what he believed was at stake, Stanton began to pick up more support. Elie Abel, Dean of the Columbia University Graduate School of Journalism, said that Stanton "was right" and he should resist the efforts of a group of politicians to impose on the media a "federal standard of truth." The National Citizens Committee for Broadcasting, a critic of commercial broadcasting practices, filed a petition on March 29, asking the FCC to issue a ruling that "a broadcaster's criticisms of the government will in no way jeopardize his license to operate over the public airwaves."[14]

Herbert G. Klein, President Nixon's Director of Communications, privately urged Nixon not to support the Staggers' subpoena. At an ASNE news conference held with Nixon, Nixon defended Agnew's past charges against the networks. "Some of his criticisms . . . in terms of some network press coverage, if you look at them objectively, you just can't quarrel with him." Nixon was asked about the subpoena and did not support it.[15]

The government made some adjustments in its position. On April 9 it announced that the Defense Department had made some reforms in the military's public information program, saying, "times have changed and we try to learn from them." Daniel Henkin ordered commanders to stop glamorizing judo and other types of hand-to-hand combat in open house demonstrations on military bases. He ordered a review of films that the Pentagon made available to the public to weed out those reflecting outdated foreign policy concepts. Jerry Friedheim of the Pentagon noted that the 1952 movie *Red Nightmare* was "produced during the cold war, at a time when the nation's foreign policy was different, at a time when we regarded the communist bloc as a monolith."[16]

Controversy in the television business is desirable if it stimulates a large audience, if it is controversy about entertainment programs or professional athletes or celebrities or, for that matter, news programs. But some advertisers do not want to be associated with controversy and often withdraw from programs they think will offend viewers. Broadcasters have to be concerned over the possible loss of advertising revenue. It is their only source of funds, and such revenues support the entire program schedule, including news programs.

When pressed as to whether the dispute over *The Selling of the Pen-*

tagon might affect its revenues, CBS said it detected no sign of an advertiser reprisal as a result of the program or its news coverage generally. It reported that sales for the fall were as brisk as ever. Leonard Goldenson, President of ABC, which was gaining in the competitive race, told his board of directors that on a recent visit to the White House, "President Nixon went out of his way to compliment the fairness of ABC News." He said that ABC was using this to good effect with advertisers. Jack Gould of the *New York Times* reported that it was no secret that Mr. Goldenson and ABC executives had suddenly been entertained by key figures in American industry, if only in part because ABC enjoyed the pleasure of the White House.

But network revenues were not the only concern. Gould reported that "In Washington journalistic circles not involved in broadcasting, it is common knowledge that many politicians want 'to get' CBS." He noted that after CBS refused to answer the congressional subpoena and there was a conflict between CBS and the government, there was "apprehension" on the part of CBS-affiliated stations. Only five of the 204 stations had sent messages of support. Beyond that, he pointed out, "Their income, many executives believe, is the core of the dilemma of electronic journalism. The threat of loss of a federal license to individual stations means possible jeopardy to revenue running into the millions."[17]

John J. O'Connor, television critic for the *New York Times*, pointed out that this program would not have gotten nearly so heated a response from a predictably irate government if it had appeared as an article in a newspaper. When there is an investigative piece, the reporter proceeds on the premise that there may be something that should be exposed. "If something is found and it doesn't provoke shrieks about distortion and prejudice from the object under attack, he hasn't written much of a story." In the case of television, this was even more explosive because of the emotional impact on the viewer and the size of the audience. As many as 40 million people might watch a provocative news documentary.

O'Connor also pointed out that the print press has long "fought for their rights under the first amendment" and "solidly established those rights in the courts." Government officials are hesitant to battle the print media. Broadcasting stations, however, are licensed by the government. He wrote, "The basic danger was pinpointed by Clifton Daniel, associate editor of the *New York Times.* 'The exercise of that [government] authority carries with it the temptation to decide not only who may broadcast but what may be broadcast. If we are to preserve freedom of speech and of the press, that temptation must be resisted.' "

But, O'Connor noted, that temptation was not being resisted.[18]

The Peabody Prizes for television excellence, administered by the Henry W. Grady School of Journalism at the University of Georgia, are usually awarded for programs after the calendar year ending December 31. The Peabody organization realized that awarding its prize for *The Selling of the Pentagon* a year later would be a meaningless gesture. It advanced the date of the award. *The Selling of the Pentagon* was awarded a special Peabody Prize on April 21 and hailed as "electronic journalism at its finest."[19]

On April 25, the *New York Times* pointed out that Staggers had maintained throughout that "broadcast media did not have the same rights as printed media because they are licensed by the government." But Stanton saw that the issue once joined had to be fought out. "A contempt citation could precipitate a legal battle that could go all the way to the Supreme Court. 'I'll see it through,' he said. 'That's the kind of harassment that could drive us up the wall.' "

Stanton's refusal to produce material needed for the government to review the program created great risk for CBS. Stanton was facing charges that CBS had engaged in deception, was irresponsible and biased and now contumacious. Many thought Stanton should find some prudent way out. The forces against him were too great and the risk too high. But Stanton believed in press freedom, and he was going to fight. The determination to do so, he says, came from years of experience with government attempts to influence news coverage and from his belief in independent news service as one of broadcasting's most significant contributions to the public.

Chapter 4

Stanton: The Broadcast Executive

Stanton's decision to resist the Staggers subpoena was almost instinctive. He had contributed to the development of the CBS News division and had a long, personal knowledge of Washington and the inner workings of the government.

Stanton had grown up in Dayton, Ohio. In his home town, the Boy Scouts movement was active and he became an Eagle Scout. In his senior year in high school he was president of his class. As an undergraduate he ran for student body president of Ohio Wesleyan. In his sophomore year of college he became scout master for a church in Delaware, Ohio. "I guess I was eager to do that kind of thing. I remember going to Helsinki as a representative of the State of Ohio at a youth conference. It was an exciting thing for a boy from Ohio."

After graduating from Wesleyan, he earned his Masters degree and then a doctorate from Ohio State University with a thesis on industrial psychology. With this background he went to New York in 1935 and applied for a job at CBS. His polling knowledge and research interest appealed to CBS and he was hired. Years later he was described in the press as having earned a reputation as the "boy wonder of broadcasting." He was to display an uncommon durability in an industry known for its rapid turnover of executives. He weathered the transition of broadcasting from the age of radio to the age of television. And he weathered the Chairman of the Board of CBS, William S. Paley, who over the years had strong ideas about entertainment programming, entertainment talent and broadcast executives. While Paley was Chief Executive Officer and oversaw entertainment programming, Stanton provided the day-to-day operational leadership. CBS became the most successful television company in the nation's history. It achieved a high level of profitability with high standards set by Stanton.

Stanton's personal willingness to confront the problems he saw was "just part of what I thought I should do." When pressed for events in his younger years that might have reflected a willingness in his character to "fight the good fight," he remembers that while he was in graduate school he discovered that the undergraduate fraternity of which he had been president in his senior year had engaged in some form of anti-semitism on the campus. He says it was a Methodist school and there weren't very many Jews in the student body, but this problem had come up and "I had concern about it and wrote to the national headquarters. When they took no action, I resigned from the fraternity. They told me I couldn't resign; that once you were a blood brother, so forth, all that crock. I did resign. There were eight of us in my class. When I did it, I let my brothers, so to speak, know about it and hoped at least one or two would support me. Not one of them did. I was persona non grata because I had resigned. You could say, why did I do that? I had gone against the grain. I guess it's because I thought it was the right thing to do. My parents had said that if you believe in something, 'you get out there and do it.' "

When first employed at CBS, his work was primarily audience research, finding out what audiences were watching CBS and other programs and their size. "I remember when 'The War of the Worlds' with Orson Wells was broadcast on CBS radio which said men from Mars were landing on earth. I was living in Jackson Heights at the time in Long Island and immediately came into the office. I knew there was going to be a lot of flak about that program. I wanted to get into the field the next day with twenty-five hundred personal interviews to find out first of all whether people heard it, and if they heard it, whether they believed it to be happening, or whether they were willing to accept it as the Halloween prank that Orson Wells deemed it to be.

"The research showed that most people saw it for what it was. In the first place, most people didn't hear it. But those who did hear it, looked at it as a prank and accepted it that way. Now, we were never really sure whether they were going back and saying, 'Oh, well, I did know at the time.' And, as we defended ourselves, both in Washington, and with the public, I leaned heavily on the research that I had done immediately on the morning following the broadcast. But we did find some interesting things. One man in New Jersey said that he thought that the men from Mars were really invading down around Princeton, and that was going to spare him a lot of trouble, because he had falsified his books, and now he wouldn't have to worry about it."

Audience research was in its early stages in broadcasting and little used. But gradually its value, particularly with advertisers, was recognized by management, although entertainment and news executives did not embrace it. Ultimately Stanton built a department of research that numbered at one point as many as 105 professionals. He also worked with Paul Lazarsfeld of Columbia University, who was interested in audience research, to develop a methodology for reliable broadcast ratings.

His rigorous training in polling and its interpretation taught him the value of careful attention to the facts. Stanton came to upper management's attention because of research he did that led to challenging an FCC finding against CBS. It was clear to Stanton that the FCC engineers' methodology was seriously flawed. "So I wrote a memo to Paul Kesten, executive vice president, and said one of the things I think we ought to do is to take one place and make an example of it to show how faulty the audience survey is on which this whole case against us is premised. We did that and it showed the FCC error." But while CBS management was impressed, the FCC was not. It would not even let Stanton testify. "The chief FCC engineer said, 'This witness is not an engineer, he's not a lawyer, therefore, he can't be heard!' And I said, 'Well, doesn't what the audience says have some bearing?' But the FCC took the position, 'Absolutely not! It's what the engineers say and it's what the lawyers say.' " Stanton was kept off the stand. It was to be for the last time.

"I appeared at another hearing, because somehow, the fact that I took the heat, and didn't run for cover, impressed the senior people at CBS, and one vice president came down and said, 'Didn't that scare you?' And I said, 'No, you just sit there, and those guys put their pants on one leg at a time, the same as I do.' And he said, 'I would be terrified to be the witness.' Anyway, as time went on, every time there was a little heat, they'd say, 'Get Stanton to be the witness.' "

Stanton's experience with research then led to his working with the head of the news operation. "In the early days, Ed Klauber was the operating chief of news at CBS. He had been an editor at the *New York Times.* He was an iron man, very tough, very bright. Very imperious. He must have been a very difficult editor at the *Times*—smart, knowledgeable, never wasted a word. I had very few encounters with him but he got interested in political research. He got me up one day on a one-on-one meeting. I had never been in his office before, and he said, 'What do you know about these election surveys and predictions?'

"When I first came to New York to do research for CBS, Gallup was the only professional that I could identify in the Madison Avenue hierarchy. And I got to know him. And then I got to know Roper and, indeed, in 1936 spent a lot of time with Roper going over his figures because he was sticking his neck out early on for *Fortune*. So when Klauber asked me about this research, I could speak firsthand about what was going on. He was very disdainful about research for ratings. For him, you did the program and the hell with whether it got a rating. But by this time everyone else lived by them. In radio, they were called the Crosley ratings. But Klauber came out of the news room and the news room didn't pay any attention to ratings. They reported the news. What the public wanted to hear was not their credo. In fact, they sort of wore that professionalism on their sleeve. Ratings were for the front office and circulation. Of course, that's changed now.

"Klauber quickly got interested in how the surveys were done and how the questions were formulated. It was a very sensible and true look at the approach to ratings and at public opinion polling. So I had a connection with him which no one else in the company had. No one else cared that much about getting into it. In fact, my belief in research caused a major split with Ed Murrow on the question of polling early on in his career. Ed Murrow said, 'There's nobody going to go out and ask questions unless I go out as a journalist. You can't do it this way!' We never did heal the breach.

"Today, audience polling is widely used. But it hasn't changed the journalists' approach that much. I'm struck by just that fact. You watch the talk shows today, and there are a number of them. You have all these journalists who show up once a week for a round table discussion and they are always saying, 'Well, the public thinks this, and the public thinks that, the public's not going to accept this,' and you wonder, aside from the people they run into and I'm sure there's some insulation, how do they get 'the public's view' like that, as opposed to their own sense of it?

"At the same time, inside the administration, they are using polling techniques very well, and very sophisticated ones, I'm sure. The administration polling gives them a much better idea probably of what the public's views are than the journalists we tune in to watch. The government now has gone overboard on polling, in my opinion. And a lot of businesses, too.

"I don't think you can substitute polling for leadership. And, if you're going to wet your finger and stick it up to find out whether you should get out in front on something, you can't get that out of polling. You also have to know how to use it.

"Certainly, in campaigns now, in addition to presidential campaigns, in gubernatorial, Senate, and House campaigns, they all use polls, and you have the sinking feeling that it's the finger to the wind as opposed to seeing the need for leadership on an issue."

During World War II, Paley went to a government information post in London. Stanton stayed at CBS and became one of the two or three men who ran the company. "During the war years I spent three days a week in Washington on assignments there for the war effort, largely in the Office of War Information; and four days a week working almost around the clock at CBS.

"Three of us ran the company. Joseph Ream, who was then General Counsel, had station relations and several other departments under him. Frank White, who was the Chief Financial Officer, had a number of the operating divisions under him. I had the company-owned stations and sales. Paul Kesten, who was an Executive Vice President, had program responsibility and to the extent he didn't get involved during the war years, I had the program department as well. We worked very closely together so that each one knew generally what the problems were in the areas managed by the other two. It was a committee kind of management brought about because we were short of manpower and everything else.

"The three of us gave a reception for Paley when he came back, to which we invited all the department heads and so forth. And Paley came in uniform and he was the hero of the evening. As the reception wore on, Paley came by and he said, 'Are you going to be in the office tomorrow?' Now this was a Friday night, and I said, yes, I would be. Saturday and Sunday were days in the office just the same as the other days. And he said, 'Let's have lunch.' Later that evening in talking with Paul Kesten I said, 'I guess we're having lunch with the Chairman tomorrow.' And there was a long pause and he said, 'Well, perhaps you are but I'm not.' And I felt like I had stepped up to something I shouldn't have said. And he said, 'Where are you having lunch?' and

I said, 'I suppose someplace in the city.' 'No,' he said, 'I think he's having the lunch out at his place in the country. Do you know how to get there?' And I said, 'I don't even know where it is.' It turned out it was out in Manhassett, Long Island.

"I got there at the house and I'd never been there before. I spoke to Paley and met Mrs. Paley and it quickly became evident there were at least a dozen or as many as fifteen people there—all friends from the area—relatives and so forth, including many of whom I had heard about but never had met. And we went in to have lunch. It was pouring rain. At the end of the lunch, Paley said, 'I sort of feel like I'd like to take a walk. Does anyone want to take a walk with me?' Well, I figured that if there was ever a cue, that was it and I said, 'I'd like a little a fresh air.' And we went out and he said, 'Let's go down by the pool.'

"Now it's raining like cats and dogs and we ran down to the poolside where there was an umbrella over a little table and we sat down and he quickly came to the point. He said, 'I don't know what I want to do now that I'm back. But I'd like you to become president and run the company.' And I said, 'Mr. Paley, you hardly know me.' He said, 'I know enough about what you've done and I'd like you to become president' and I said, rather quickly, 'What are you going to do?' And he said, 'I don't want to be pinned down, I don't know what I'm going to do, I want to be free to do what I want to do but I want you to take over the company.' I thanked him but told him that I'd like to think about it because this was a change in my schedule that I obviously hadn't anticipated and I'd like a little chance to think about it. He said, 'How much time do you want?' and I said, 'Let me talk with my wife and I'll get back to you within a week.' And he looked at his watch and said, 'Well, I guess we'd better go back in.'

"We went up to the house and we went in the back door and he said, 'Well, then, you'll take care of the announcement on Monday.' And I said, 'Mr. Paley, I thought I had. . . .' 'Oh, yes,' he said, 'Well, take your time and I'll hear from you.' And that's the way it was left.

"And I think that was the first weekend in September and I never saw him again until Christmas Eve. I didn't know what had happened. I knew that he was getting a divorce. I knew that he was out in California. I heard that he was in and out of the office but I never saw him. At that time I was Vice President and General Manager of the Company so it didn't change my duties within the company but it left me in a bit of a quandary.

"On Christmas Eve, working as I did right up to the last minute, I was leaving around 5:00 and the elevator doors opened on the executive floor and Mr. Paley got off the elevator with a very attractive young woman and they were both carrying Christmas boxes. He acted surprised and obviously I was surprised. He greeted me warmly and introduced me to the lady he had brought in and he said, 'How are things going?' and I said, 'Pretty well. I rather expected, you know, we'd be talking.' 'Oh', he said, 'You want to do it right now?' And he said to the lady, 'Do you mind waiting out here?' and dumped her with her packages and his packages in the reception area. We walked into the office and I led off by saying, 'I can only assume that you've had second thoughts about our conversation and if that's the case I understand.' 'Oh no,' he said, 'I've just been waiting to hear from you.' So I said without any further preliminaries, 'I'm ready to go ahead.' There was no discussion about salary, no discussion about contract, nothing. It was just that I consented and that was that and that's how I became president." Stanton was 37 years old.

"At the first Board meeting after the first of the year, the Board elected me President. There was no discussion about my role or what Paley was going to do. He had told me quite clearly he didn't want to be burdened by any details or explanations. So I took him at his word and I thought if you had to run the company, you ran the company.

"Programming was the driving force for the network, not just for CBS; it was true for NBC too. It was clear to me that if you had the programs, obviously you got the audience. If you got the audience, you got the advertisers. And if you had those two, you got affiliates because in those days there was switching among radio station affiliations. NBC had the top fifty kilowatt (high power) clear channel stations and we had some fifty kilowatt stations that weren't clear channels and we had a lot of regional and local stations which were not as good in terms of power performance. We were very vulnerable competitively.

"The important thing was to put the emphasis on the programs. This was something that I had observed secondhand in Paley's philosophy and certainly in Paul Kesten's, so it wasn't an original thought with me. If you're going to build a company, you've got to be sure the product is right. And, Paley was the expert on programming. There was no question about that.

"I had said to Paley I thought that Paul would have been a better person than I as President, when the offer was made to me and he said, 'Yes, but Paul's health is not good and he doesn't want to continue.'

Paul's health was not good. There were days when his arthritis was so bad he couldn't open the door in his office. I put on door knobs that had arms on them so that he could use his elbow to open the door. So I knew that he was frail and his health wasn't good. Paul did continue for a short time while I was President, but then stepped out."

As Chief Operating Officer, Stanton soon ran the company as a whole. This included the network, affiliate relations, sales, engineering, the owned stations, news, sports, corporate information and Washington relations. Stanton was to have this multifaceted job under Paley in one of the country's most prominent industries for many years. Ultimately CBS became number one in audience and revenue, and that continued for many years. Stanton demanded much of those who worked with him, as he did of himself. And CBS was by any measure a great company. Those who worked there began their sentences with the phrase "We at CBS . . . ," which reflected the pride Stanton instilled in his employees. Some saw it also as a bit arrogant. But CBS did an absolutely first-rate job.

Stanton lived for CBS and its world of broadcasting. "My wife and I didn't entertain at the house. If we had a dinner or wanted to entertain people, we always went out. The house was ours and she didn't let a lot of outsiders in. That's all there is to it. She was very well read and read five newspapers a day. She had excellent judgment and was a great help to me. I told the Chairman of the Finance Committee of the Board which we used as the Executive Committee, when we were talking about succession and what would happen, that if anything happened to me the first person you have to sit down and talk with is my wife because I've told her my plans. I wouldn't dare tell anybody in the company because it would leak. So, if you need to know my thinking, get a hold of her because she is privy to everything. That came about as a result of our sitting down every night and closing down the day, generally about quarter of one.

"I got the *New York Times* delivered to the house and I never went to bed or turned off the light really without scanning it for the next day. It gave you a little bit of a fix for what was going to happen. Keeping your lines open, not only to sources of information, but the other way around of having people know what's going on is, I think, the responsibility of somebody in the hierarchy. I tried to do that.

"I had two people I saw primarily, George Rosen, who was then the editor of *Variety* on broadcasting and Jack Gould at the *New York Times.* They would have a lot of questions about little things and if I knew anything about it, I tried to give them the background on it. Every Saturday, I spent an hour with Jack Gould to make sure that he understood the background of things. We had long phone conversations about what was going on. A lot of the stuff I gave to him was off the record or not for publication. Out of that relationship grew the idea that he would be a good man to have on my staff and I hired him. But, it didn't work out and he went back to the print world. Rosen and I had lunch at the Carlton House on Madison Avenue almost every Saturday except in the heat of the summer and it was sort of a routine affair. He wrote his Wednesday stuff over the weekend."

Stanton was interested in the program side even though this was really Paley's area when he was active at the company. Stanton hired Arthur Godfrey for radio although Paley didn't like him. (Godfrey was an enormous hit for many years.) Stanton on his own committed millions to hire Jackie Gleason, which had to be done on the spot and without Paley having any knowledge of who he was or any advertiser on board to sponsor his program. (Gleason also was a tremendous plus for CBS entertainment programming for many years.)

At one point Stanton also got closely involved in the sports department, which was a new experience for him and not what his reputation suggests would be of great interest to him. But he went at it, as he did everything else. "We bought the Yankees, because Paley wanted it. We didn't lose money on it. If you took the investment and the tax advantages and so forth, we didn't lose money. But we lost character with some of our peers. I went up to Boston at Fenway Park and met with all the owners of the clubs because there was a question about whether they would let us buy the Yankees. I said I wanted to meet with the owners to let them know that we didn't have horns. And they sat around this big table at Fenway Park starting about 10:00 in the morning. I was in front of that group, except for a few times when they met in private, from 10:00 in the morning until almost 4:30 in the afternoon. And we needed one more vote because all kinds of things came out in that meeting. They thought there was some mysterious thing we were going to do with baseball and television.

"And you know I was too effective that day because we got that vote. Gene Autry, the entertainer, was very close to CBS because we had a lot to do with him in CBS Radio and, of course, he received enormous income from CBS Records. Then ultimately he got into television and he owned stations which were all on the CBS network so there was an affinity with us. Gene had said to me in the morning,

'Now this is going to be alright. Don't worry about it. I've talked with some of my friends and you've got the votes.'

"I think that it's wrong for a broadcast corporation to try to get into that kind of business because it's just a different business, that's all. That was a mistake—oh, boy—what a mistake that was. Jim Burke, who ran Johnson & Johnson, came up to see me one day from New Jersey and Jim said some of the members of his Board think we should use some of our money to buy a baseball club. And I said, 'Jim, don't even finish the sentence—don't do it.' I saw Jim years later and he got up and was telling stories and he told that story. He said how I spared them getting into the baseball business. Can you imagine anybody in the pharmaceutical business getting into baseball?"

Paley never entertained Stanton in his home after their initial luncheon. He invited Stanton, but for various reasons Stanton always declined. He says it was to keep his relation on a professional level and he did not want to get that close to Paley. It would have made his life far more difficult and the running of the company more complicated. Stanton and Paley were very different and made an unusual but highly successful combination in an intensely competitive, high-profile, influential industry. Paley traveled in the most glamorous social circles. His wife, one of the famous Cushing sisters, was known as the "perfect" Babe Paley. Another sister was married to Jock Whitney and they lived close to each other on Long Island's wealthy North Shore. Stanton did not travel in those social circles and did not want to. He was much too busy with the company and his own intellectual interests. The "outside" world was Paley's job. Stanton did not think he could be both the inside man and the outside man, except for his heavy Washington and affiliate schedule.

Sally Bedell Smith has written, "Theirs was a relationship built on convenience and necessity: each instinctively recognized that his own weaknesses were the other's strengths. Over the years, they were amiable and rivals by turns. They were wary of one another, each privately disapproving of how the other lived. Without their shared devotion to CBS, Paley and Stanton might well have disliked one another. Each used the other for his own ends. Stanton wanted operating control of CBS, and Paley wanted someone to operate it for him while he maintained ultimate authority. For all his absenteeism over the years, Paley tried to keep Stanton under his control. To Paley, Stanton . . . could be counted on always to do the correct thing. Paley also knew that the work stimulated the midwesterner, almost to the point that he could not get enough of it. Stanton's seven-day work weeks more than matched Paley's abundant energy in the early days of CBS. . . .

"Stanton could not understand Paley's ability to drift in and out of the company, and his unwillingness to bear down in a sustained way. And Paley was bothered by Stanton's unflappability. . . . Stanton seemed to wear his integrity too conspicuously on his sleeve for Paley's taste. But most of all, Paley believed that Stanton did not know how to live. To Paley, Stanton was hopelessly square."[1]

Paley was interested in broadcasting because of its power and newness, furthered by the excitement of the entertainment industry. His field was programming, and when it suited him, in the early years, he was good at selecting what would work for the audience. That was his major and important contribution to CBS and placed the network out in front for many years, especially after his skillful raid on NBC's talent, which included Jack Benny and others.

His mother had told him, "never to do anything you can hire someone else to do for you."[2] So his life was making decisions about CBS in areas that interested him and of social gentility, art collecting and travel to resorts and his homes in Long Island, Jamaica and Lyford Cay—extraordinary, beautiful residences. At the same time, Paley had trouble dealing with anything that implied he was not the chief of CBS. Since he was often absent and had, in fact, made Stanton president and turned the operating control of the company over to him, Stanton, in the public eye, held the presidency. This was ultimately to be a source of irritation and considerable embarrassment to Paley. Paley was Chairman and Chief Executive Officer and the broadcast industry and Wall Street knew this, but Stanton was most often publicly in the forefront on broadcast issues. Also, Paley was not about to give the ultimate control of the company to someone else, as he was to demonstrate later by rotating presidents at CBS following Stanton's departure.

In 1966, after Stanton had run the company for many years, Paley told him he would be made Chief Executive Officer, and Paley said he would remain Chairman and concentrate on planning. In an extraordinary balk, on the day of the CBS Board meeting Paley decided to back out. He told this to Stanton on the way to the meeting. "It was one of the most dramatic things I ever saw," recalled Dick Salant, who as a corporate Vice President served as secretary to the Board. "The only way you could ever tell that Frank Stanton was angry was when the back of his neck was red. That day it was flaming. Afterward I asked Frank what had happened and he said, 'Bill couldn't go through with it.' "[3]

Stanton continued to lead as he always had. This was true also in Washington, D.C., where Paley was not comfortable with the confrontations common to that community. Stanton excelled in this part of his job and was conscientious in his pursuit of it. The other networks were also active in lobbying and dealing with the great variety of issues raised by broadcasting and station licenses. These ranged from restraints on political coverage to the place of sex and violence on television; from restraints on ownership of stations to arrangements with affiliated stations; from the use of frequencies for black and white television and then for color; and FCC and congressional actions permitting the development of broadcasting but seeking to keep the networks from having too much power in an industry which had such wide access to the public through entertainment, sports and news.

The CBS Board had confidence in his management. While Paley believed CBS could stay with radio, as did many broadcasters, Stanton urged the Board to invest in black and white television to compete against RCA, which was making money from both sets and broadcasting. It was expensive and Paley was reluctant. But the Board and Paley finally agreed. "When color emerged, Kesten tried to derail General Sarnoff's efforts to go to electronic color. He came up with a mechanical color disc and really hoped to stay with black and white. But I went in the opposite direction."

Stanton used his standing to promote the development of the CBS News organization. News was a critical part of the broadcast service. Television stations and the networks who supplied much of the programming used by stations were required to provide news and public affairs programs to the public as a matter of national policy. In awarding and renewing licenses, the FCC placed emphasis on the amount of time a station allocated to news programming. In addition, many broadcasters believed in the value of their news service.

In 1935 Paley had brought Edward R. Murrow to CBS and had great respect and affection for him. But after Murrow, Paley appeared to lose interest. Stanton says, "At CBS, Ed Klauber was the guru, if you will, of the news. He was a very strong person on the news side. Much of the company's position in the early days of news such as 'The World News Roundup' came from things Ed Klauber pushed. The man who is neglected in the history of CBS as far as news is concerned was Paul White and above him, and right outside of Paley's door, was Ed Klauber.

"But he was a difficult man. So difficult that people said that executives wouldn't venture out of their office without putting their hat on a cane and sticking it out to see whether it got shot off. During World War II, news was so important to the company that we took the five minutes before 9:00 every night and Elmer Davis, who had come from the *New York Times* to CBS, gave a wrap-up of the news up to that particular point. No one else took the heart of the evening and gave five minutes to news. That was Klauber. A lot of this rubbed off on me. When we were a three-man committee running the company, and when I became president, the development of CBS News was a personal commitment.

"Ed Murrow and I had joined the company almost the same month in 1935. A lot of the radio program schedule was made up of straight talk. The job that Ed had was getting interesting talkers and speakers. He was not a news man. He was in Europe at the outbreak of the war arranging interesting talks. Because we were shorthanded he was pressed into using a microphone. Of course, his broadcasts from London became a great service. When he was at CBS Radio, or in those days the Columbia Broadcasting System, he had nothing to do with the newsroom. He was the director of talks.

"As part of our effort to reinforce our position in the world of news and public affairs, we published a booklet in a *Reader's Digest* format once a month of the outstanding talks we had broadcast, because at that time and today as well there is a respect given to black ink on paper. We tried to take advantage of that by showing we not only did this on the air, but 'Read what we did.' We got a lot of people wanting to get on that list. We sent it to every Congressman, every mayor, every important educator. We had a fantastic mailing list. That was to support the image we were building that we had a leadership position in the field of information.

"Elmer Davis and Eric Sevareid had never done any broadcasting. They came from print. They were selected because they were good journalists. I was in audience research and I was roped into getting a group of people to listen to Sevareid read the news. He did a test broadcast, so to speak. They were very critical and they said he didn't speak clearly. Sevareid said he didn't think he would ever make it in television. 'With radio, I've got the microphone, I write the material, I know what I'm talking about. There's nobody in the control room.'

'Now,' he said, 'there are lights, guys running around with cameras. I can't do it.' And I had to tell him that this was the way news was going to move and he had to get with it. The position that Ed Klauber and Paul White and Ed Murrow took was, 'the guy knows what he's talking about.' And that was the way we built the news division, with news people who knew something—not people who were just attractive faces. They were the hard core of our television news."

Stanton insisted that good reporters and commentators were brought on and supported by CBS. "Later on when Ed Murrow finally got into television and developed *See It Now*, he didn't want to work with the television division. So we had three divisions. It was a joke in senior management that we had a radio division of news, we had a television division of news and then we had Ed Murrow. Later, we had a television division of CBS news and a radio division of news and a *60 Minutes* division."

By this time, Stanton had become a leading spokesman against government restraints on television news. In August 1954, Stanton arranged the first network editorial. It was one of his early efforts to open the airways to more news coverage, which meant in this case taking on the Senate for barring radio and television journalists from the floor when a committee was debating whether or not to censure Joseph McCarthy. Stanton called for television to have the same right to cover the news as the print press.[4]

In 1957, Nikita Khrushchev, the leader of the Soviet Union, escalated the Cold War with threats that the Soviet Union would bury the United States. CBS wanted him to appear in an interview on *Face the Nation*. Stanton supervised the negotiations. Afterward, President Eisenhower and Secretary of State John Foster Dulles criticized CBS for allowing a Soviet official to appear unedited on American television. This came as no surprise to Stanton, but he believed the public should learn of the Soviet leader firsthand, and television could uniquely do that.

In the press there was widespread praise for the interview, and Stanton responded to the government's criticism by taking out a full-page advertisement in the *New York Times*, lauding CBS' journalistic enterprise. Stanton also defended the interview in an address to the National Press Club in Washington. Initially, Paley said little about the broadcast. "I got the idea he wasn't happy, but he was always careful in how he exercised his displeasure. He wouldn't say he was angry," Stanton says. "As the praise in print picked up, he was happier by the hour." In the end, Paley backed up Stanton by issuing a memo to the CBS organization, calling the interview one of the most outstanding broadcasts ever carried on radio and television. That fall the Radio and Television News Directors Association gave Stanton an award for this achievement.

One of the decisions of which Stanton is most proud is his appointment of Dick Salant as President of CBS News. "I discovered Salant when I was in the color television fight and he was working then at the Rosenman law firm. I went to Ralph Colin [one of the firm's senior partners and a member of the CBS Board] and said that I was so impressed that I'd like to consider bringing him in as my assistant. I hired Dick and he was right with me all the time. I came to depend on him so much in terms of understanding the problems of news from a policy point of view.

"News was volatile and had public interest significance. It reported directly to me. When I announced Dick's appointment as head of CBS News, Walter Cronkite, Eric Sevareid and Charles Collingwood came to me and seriously questioned it because Dick was a lawyer, not a journalist. I told them that Dick was a man of public affairs, knew what was going on in the world. He had received distinguished awards at Harvard for writing. Of course they did not know him as I did. I asked them to wait to see what kind of job he did. In a very short time, they were big enough to come back and say, 'You were sure right.' From that point on, Dick was perfect.

"The first time around when I appointed Dick I have no recollection of Paley having any position about it. In fact, I remember he said to me one day, 'Who is this Salant?' He thought that Dick was a gutsy little tiger and there were times when I think Dick felt Paley was sort of compromising and Dick in effect called him on it and this was not received well by the emperor. Dick and I would occasionally have a meeting with Paley and I could feel Paley tightening up because Salant was too independent and too smart. A lot of men are nervous when somebody is smarter than they are and Dick was just that smart and had the courage to speak his mind."

During this period, Fred Friendly wanted to be head of News and was working on Paley. Stanton says, "When Paley said, 'Fred's the kind of guy we ought to have in News,' I took a very cautious, negative attitude and said that he had great talent but I didn't think that he would be the man to set policy. But I could see that the day was going to come when I had to face up to making a change, because Paley could just not stand Salant. Paley finally expressed his dissatisfaction to me about Salant and said we should make a change. After all, he was the Chairman and I had supported Salant for all those years. Every time I did it was tough. I thought it was going to bruise Dick but I thought our relations were such that he would understand, and he did.

"I wanted Salant back as my assistant; there were plenty of things for Dick to do. I never disclosed to him the Paley role but Dick was smart enough to know he was not Paley's favorite. The Company had grown and we were in books and magazines and musical instruments and so forth. The demands on my time took me more and more away from the core business of broadcasting, and more particularly away from news. We had seven operating divisions and I couldn't have seven people reporting to me. So I then set up a broadcast group, a publishing group and so forth. And I put at the head of the broadcast group, the man I thought would someday probably move into my chair, Jack Schneider.

"And, then of course Friendly got off the reservation. Friendly's gripe was that I had appointed Jack Schneider as the head of the broadcast group and made him responsible for a lot of the things I had been doing. He objected to reporting to Schneider. I was aware that some in CBS News didn't like the idea that news didn't get right to the top of the company whenever it wanted to.

"At one point we were covering some Senate hearings that had to do with the Vietnam War. After the first day or so, they were not worthy of live coverage. Schneider didn't want to be in there full time with cameras. Friendly took the position that the network had to carry those programs live and threw down the gauntlet. He also said that he would not report to the group head. He had to report to me. My door was always open to anybody who had a justifiable complaint. So I saw Fred. And he said those programs had to be on live. The fact is, they were dull.

"Schneider, who did not favor Friendly, got him over to talk with him about the coverage. Friendly told Jack he wouldn't accept that from him, he would only take that from Stanton. Then Friendly came in and laid down the law to me. He said, 'If you don't do this I'll resign.' Friendly and I had had a long talk on a Friday afternoon and I said to Fred, 'You want to resign, but why don't you think about it over the weekend and we'll talk again on Monday.'

"Fred came in on Monday morning and during our conversation, my secretary came in and said Mr. Gould is outside and says that it's very important that he see me. And I said to Fred, 'What the hell does Jack Gould know? Does he know that you are having this conversation?' 'No, no, nothing about it.' So I said, 'Excuse me just a minute and I'll step out to see Gould.' I knew Jack Gould very well and if Jack told me it was very important, I respected it. So, I went out to talk to Gould and he brings Friendly's letter of resignation out of his pocket and says, 'Do you have any comments about this?'

"I went back in and I said to Fred, 'Jack's got your letter of resignation. You told me that nobody knew about this.' 'Well,' he said, 'I was just talking with Jack about it.' That was a miserable day. That was about 11:30 and just before I was going to lunch I got a call from his lawyer, saying that he had to come over and see me right away. He came over and said to me, 'Fred is sorry for what he has done. He understands that he can't behave this way' and so forth. And I said, 'No way I'll take him back in that position.' And he said, 'Fred can handle Jack Gould, he can get the letter back,' and I said, 'I know Gould is too good a journalist to ever let a thing like that happen.' So, that was a terrible, terrible day."

Friendly has written that he was going public because Schneider was, that CBS had an announcement already prepared and that he did not release his resignation letter until after the CBS announcement was "already on the wires." He writes that when he reached Paley, the last thing Paley said to him was, "Well, if you hadn't put out that letter, maybe we could still have done something."[5]

Stanton recalls that Schneider offered Gordon Manning, who was in charge of hard news, the overall job as head of CBS News but Manning wouldn't take it. Stanton says, "Fred had exacted a promise from Manning and Bill Leonard, who was then head of documentaries and soft news, that neither would take the job if it were offered to him because Fred wanted to be reappointed by Paley. But Paley was not there. He was never on the scene in all the crises I had. Paley was always in Europe or somewhere else. It did make it easier for me because it gave me a free hand." And Salant, in whom Stanton had the utmost confidence, was brought back and remained head of CBS News for many years.

Stanton believed strongly that if there was any difference in views between Paley and himself, it should never show, and he did not confront Paley or comment critically about him in front of anyone. He was a loyal number two man, and this was understood and accepted by everyone at CBS. Some executives saw that if Paley was wrong or too rigid on an issue, as he sometimes was, they could take the matter up with Stanton, who could review it privately with Paley behind the scenes and perhaps improve things.

Stanton's belief in the importance of news, however, was such that on at least one occasion he argued with Paley in front of a few of the senior executives. The season's new program schedule was being put together and Paley announced that he had had enough of *Marcus Welby, M.D. Welby* had become an enormous ratings hit on ABC television, which at that time was the number three network and struggling to make its mark. While the program did have good production values, its success was partly the result of the fact that the other two networks, CBS and NBC, were running news in that time period. *Welby* had no competition.

Paley said that in the new season CBS should schedule entertainment for that time slot instead of news. Stanton explained that although everyone could understand the problem that *Welby* presented, he believed if news was pulled from that period, an equal amount of time should be found elsewhere in the prime time schedule for equivalent news programming. Given the firmness of his statement, Paley agreed.[6]

For a time in the 1950s, CBS was the news leader. But then under Bob Kintner, President of NBC, Bill McAndrew, President of NBC News, his assistant, Julian Goodman and NBC News producer Reuven Frank, NBC News took over with Chet Huntley and David Brinkley paired on *NBC Nightly News*. Frank writes, "Don Hewitt, who at one time or another produced both the CBS Evening News and CBS's convention coverage up against Huntley and Brinkley where they were most successful, would later say, 'They came at us like an express train.' They carved a hiatus in CBS News's half century of complacency. . . ."[7] For as many as ten years, NBC's Huntley-Brinkley report in the daily network news lineup was far and away the most watched television news program in the United States. Huntley and Brinkley knocked out Edwards at CBS. Cronkite took his place. In 1963, CBS expanded Cronkite's evening news program to a half-hour. NBC followed suit.

NBC had a runaway sweep of audience and received critical acclaim for its coverage of the Democratic and Republican conventions. In 1964, when Senator Barry Goldwater won the Republican nomination, NBC attracted a larger audience to its Republican convention coverage than CBS and ABC combined. Only a fifth of the audience watched something other than NBC. Bill Paley thought the problem was Cronkite and intervened to replace him. Robert Trout and Roger Mudd became the CBS anchors for the subsequent Democratic Convention, but NBC was still the wide leader. During one hour of the coverage the ratings service showed NBC with 84% of the audience.[8]

Then, when Brinkley refused to cross a picket line set up by striking workers at NBC, the *CBS Evening News* pulled ahead of NBC. Stanton says, "For all the troubles that we had in becoming a competitive force to NBC, it was a challenge. It was fun. And we tried to use all of the skills that we had to make sure that people knew what we were doing. The entertainment side was obviously the locomotive that pulled our whole company. It was doing fine. We knew our news was good, but we had to get more people to recognize it or to turn to it. You couldn't change a second-rate show into a first position by promotion. You could get people maybe to sample it once. But once they saw it, if they didn't like it, nothing was going to get them to watch it."

In those years there was a willingness to invest in news, even though it was a loss operation. There was a sense of public service. Stanton says, "The decision to do what's right for news coverage for the viewer starts at the top. That isn't something you can delegate—that's right at the top. And that comes about from the leadership of any organization. It is based on the character of one individual, granted that he associates himself with people who share that feeling. Where does that come from? I can't say. But I certainly recognize it in other people."

At this time, the network news divisions at NBC and CBS were also producing a large number of documentaries. "Documentaries enabled us to open up an issue at length. They were a great service," Stanton says. "But there is a real cost involved. We not only had the cost of the news program, but we lost income from the entertainment programs we pulled out of the schedule. A significant hour documentary in those days usually cost about $600,000 out of pocket. That didn't include the staffing. The loss in terms of commercial income by not having sponsorship revenues from the entertainment programs it replaced was significant. Beyond that, there was a third factor, and that is, when you break your program schedule and put a documentary in, the audience generally leaves you in large numbers, and you're left with low circulation. The programs that follow are also adversely affected.

"Many affiliates said, 'We don't need these documentaries. If you guys from New York want to have them, go ahead. But we don't need them at all.' We had to do a lot of persuading to get our affiliates to carry them. But it's something that should be done. It's that need for getting the issue out in the open which the documentary does well. If a documentary was really on an issue of importance, that meant there was going to be some reaction. Some of it negative. Something of that issue is going to be controversial. One of the guideposts for us was that a documentary had to be fair. It couldn't take an editorial position. It had to explore both sides or many sides of the issue.

"The News documentary had to be supported in two ways, a statement to the News division and in the budget review which allocated money for the documentaries. That meant that the corporation was putting its heavy hand of approval on that program. To take an hour out of prime time even once a week was a significant commitment. To the credit of the advertisers who joined us in sponsoring these documentaries, most of them were enlightened to the extent that they realized they were walking into a thicket patch and that they might be associated with a program that created problems. And most stayed with us."

The CBS annual report for 1961 led off with a report about CBS News and its expansion. After describing the radio and television news coverage and specials produced over the year, the report noted that CBS News had produced 55% of the entire schedule of the CBS Radio Network and more than 17% of the entire CBS Television Network schedule. This reflected a 40% increase in regularly scheduled information programming. Major expansion was planned for domestic coverage, with the addition or the creation of five new regional bureaus. The division's report said, "It is the conviction of CBS News that its function is not to substitute conclusions of its own for those of the viewer or listener; rather, all the significant facts and viewpoints should be presented in order that the viewer or listener can make up his own mind on a fully informed basis. . . . The keystone of CBS News policy continues to be accuracy, objectivity, fairness and balance."

Stanton was strict about the standards for news coverage and its special standing in the eyes of the viewer. "The real problem that I saw in the mid-fifties and maybe earlier, was that everything had to be well-prepared. If it appeared there were sound effects or applause for a speaker that was being covered in the news, and in fact there wasn't any, that would not be allowed. We were scrupulous in applying standards to news, because of the juxtaposition of the news to entertainment. You could slide off an entertainment program where you had entirely different standards, and in fact, where you could have fiction as well as reality. But when you came to news, there had to be a fire wall there, or a break, and a different set of standards went into effect.

"In an effort to make that fire wall obvious to the viewer, I said at one point after color came, 'let's keep our news in black and white, because this will say to the audience, this is the real thing.' Obviously, I didn't succeed in my idea, or in implementing my idea. We did some testing and the affiliates were so eager to have color, and they were going to have color on their news whether we had color on ours or not, and so, it was an empty gesture. But it was one of our efforts to put a neon sign around it and say, 'This is News!'

"Now you have Hollywood-produced entertainment news pieces where you cannot distinguish between fiction and news. That's too bad in my opinion, in the sense that the world of make believe will be more difficult to separate from news reality. With electronic or computerized graphics on entertainment programs coming over into the graphics on news, it just means one more thing that frames news in a way that it might be misinterpreted as being entertainment and not news.

"If you're going to have a continuing relationship with your audience, it seems to me you have to have certain fundamental concepts, and one of them is, they look to you as being a responsible purveyor of information. It's a very awkward stance, because you have, cheek by jowl, the responsibility on the news and public affairs side, and no holds barred, virtually, on the entertainment side. You have to try to make sure visually, as well as morally and clearly, one is news, and the other is entertainment. If your audience is going to come to you and stay with you on a regular basis, I think they've got to learn that they can depend on you for information, and that is all part of the concept of responsibility."

Gordon Manning, Vice President and Director of News at CBS News and head of CBS hard news during much of this period, earned an outstanding professional reputation. He believed strongly in news integrity and defended his correspondents against government and private pressures. He says, "The editor's chief allegiance must be to the viewer. The man or woman serving in that capacity must constantly keep that goal in mind. The editor is responsible for the implementation of company guidelines and its budget and operational orders. And at the same time the editor must monitor the work of the editorial staff, insisting on fair and accurate work delivered to deadlines. The editor is the 'Horatio at the bridge' of any news operation, an essential middle man to ensure the end product is in keeping with company policy and in the best traditions of American journalism. But the chief obligation is to the public."[9]

Chapter 5

Stanton in Washington

Stanton's association with presidents and congressional leaders, his management of CBS for many years and his reputation for probity were to help his challenge and make it difficult for Congress to view it as an act without principle.

Stanton had been the CBS spokesman in Washington for many years. He was one of the industry's most respected leaders. He had worked hard to establish good relations with presidents and members of Congress. He saw this as an important part of his job as a network broadcaster. Not only did Congress have legislative oversight of broadcasting, networks had to be concerned about adverse legislation which might harm their service. FCC commissioners also were important decision-makers on a large number of network and station economic and program regulatory issues.

The White House was not only part of the networks' news coverage, it determined much of what access broadcasters had to impending national events and policy. It could also establish national communications policy. For many years, because of his professional standing and because he was highly respected, Stanton was welcome at the White House. But his relationship there varied depending on the president.

Stanton's earliest White House visits were with President Harry Truman. Leonard Reinsch, who was head of Cox Broadcasting, had helped Truman as the Vice President with advance work and speeches over the years. He called Stanton one day and asked to meet him in New York, where CBS kept several hotel rooms for affiliates and clients. Stanton says, "Leonard walked in the door and said, 'Is this room secure?' I said, 'I operate on the premise that nothing is ever secure.' We went into the bathroom, turned on all the faucets and with the shower curtains dripping and all the faucets running, I said, 'What is this?' Leonard said, 'I have just been with Vice President Truman, who has met with the President down in Warm Springs. He thinks that Roosevelt is going to die. He looked to be in terrible shape. Truman is very concerned and wants to be clued in on what is going on in the country, what is going on in the government. Roosevelt didn't spend much time with him and Roosevelt's staff spent no time with Truman, apart from maybe looking down on him. He was an outsider and no one ever told him anything.' Leonard asked me if I would meet with Truman and I said at some point perhaps I could.

On the following Tuesday, Roosevelt died. Stanton says, "I was in the office and a call came through at eight o'clock, saying the White House wanted to speak to me. I said, 'No, no, not me, they are trying to reach CBS News.' The operator said, 'This call is for you.' So I took the call and it was Leonard Reinsch who said, 'Can you be at the White House tomorrow morning at 7:30?' My two senior associates were away. I was there trying to hold together the CBS Radio operations covering Roosevelt's death. I said, 'I really can't do that. I am having a terrible time here trying to keep CBS together to cover this.' And again Leonard said, 'Can you be here at the White House tomorrow morning at 7:30?' Finally I said, 'Leonard, where are you calling from?' And Leonard said, 'I am calling from the Oval Office of the White House and President Truman is sitting here next to me.'

"The next morning, I walked into the Oval Office and President Truman said, 'I understand you are a knowledgeable fellow. I've got to make two speeches. One to the Armed Forces and one to a Joint Session of Congress. I want you to go in the other room and help me write those speeches.' I said, 'Well, you know, that is not exactly my role,' and Truman said, 'I need your help and I would like you to go in there and help write those speeches.' Truman was very direct, very blunt and so in I went and started to work. In the course of it, as the morning wore on, people would come in with notes and Truman would get up and walk out and come right back. Once he walked out and turned around and came right back and I said, 'That was quick.' Truman said, 'That was Morganthau [Roosevelt's Secretary of the Treasury], who came in to offer his resignation and I accepted it.' And he sat down. It was just as quick and as direct as that.

"Mrs. Roosevelt had wanted all of the small keepsakes that had been on Roosevelt's desk to be kept and not lost. They had all been taken off the desk and put on the window sills and then the desk had been removed to be shipped off to Hyde Park. And here was the new President of the United States and he had no desk. Truman said that there was a desk that was in the White House during the War of 1812 and when the British burned the White House, a knee hole in that desk had been burned. 'I would like to get that desk. Let's see if we can find it.' "

So, after dinner, Stanton and Judge Rosenman, one of Roosevelt's confidants, got a flashlight. "We proceeded to go through the White House looking for that particular desk and ultimately we found it. The desk was brought down and put in the Oval Office and used by Truman thereafter." Stanton says with considerable emphasis and respect, "Truman knew a great deal about American history. He was very bright. Many wondered how Roosevelt had reached out to pick him, a relative unknown.

"On another occasion, when I was in the Oval Office, Matt Connelly, the Press Secretary, came in and said, 'the Russian Foreign Minister was on his way to San Francisco to sign the United Nations Treaty and the question is, should he stop here to see you before he goes on out there to sign it?' And Truman said, 'Well if he doesn't stop here and see me, he is not going to San Francisco.' I said, 'Isn't that a little harsh to the Foreign Minister?' And Truman said, 'Wait a minute' and he called in his assistant again and he said, 'I'll tell you what, when he comes here, after he sees me, you tell him we are not able to fly him to San Francisco. He is to take the train.' And Connelly nodded and walked out and I said, 'Gee, that is very tough. Why are you being that tough?' And Truman said, 'I want him to see this country, how big it is.' And that was that. He was very direct.

"Truman immediately removed all the Roosevelt people. They had not been helpful to him," Stanton says, "and treated him as an outcast. He wanted his own people. His staff consisted of six people. That was it—six staff—that is all he had. And he would meet every morning with them as to what was going on. Truman had not been in the

White House that much and he told me that until he had become President, he had not been upstairs in the White House. He had heard Roosevelt's radio press conferences but had never seen how they were conducted. I suggested to him, 'Shouldn't you get some idea of what is going to happen, what the press is going to ask you, the kind of questions and all that?' And Truman said, 'Do you think I should do that?' And I said, 'Yes, I would.' So we gave Truman a sort of practice briefing session on what the press conference would be like.

"As it happened, this was right before his first press conference. Several of us were sitting with Truman behind his desk, talking to him, as the doors opened. I got up and started to move forward and Truman said, 'I want you here with me.' And I said, 'This is something I really can't be helpful to you with. At this point, I have got to be on the other side of the desk.' And Truman said, 'I would really rather you stayed with me.' And I said, 'No, I really have to be on the other side of the desk.' " While he could be of help to the new President, and as head of CBS part of his job was to maintain relations with the President, Congress, the FCC and on down, Stanton believed when it came to news coverage he had to be objective and "on the other side of the desk." The press conference was well received. Members of the press liked the new President's directness. At the end of the press conference, they burst into applause.

Stanton says, "I did a program analysis of his State of the Union Address. You could see where the interest lagged and where it picked up. I unrolled a chart on his desk. I said, 'Here is where the audience went up, and here is where the audience went down.' Truman was absolutely fascinated. The morning after Truman did a talk, I sent him a report on his audience. He was a very canny guy. I didn't have to punch any holes for him to see.

"The first Presidential television press conference by President Eisenhower was recorded on film. The film could be used only if Jim Hagerty, Eisenhower's press secretary, approved it. But it was a start."

Stanton had his first dealings with John F. Kennedy when Kennedy ran for President. For many years, Stanton had sought to have Section 315 of the Communications Act, the "Equal Time" law, changed because it effectively prevented the broadcast of presidential debates. It also restricted broadcaster discretion in news coverage. Stanton made many Washington appearances urging its repeal or modification, but there were those in Congress who were concerned that a broadcaster could favor one candidate over another unless the law prohibited it.

Section 315 provided that if a station allowed a "use" by one candidate for federal office, it had to provide an equal opportunity to all other candidates for that office. It sounded fair, but in practice it provided a shield for incumbents seeking reelection. For example, in a presidential campaign there may be more than 20 declared candidates, most of whom have no constituency or chance of being elected. If a broadcaster put on a major party candidate in a debate or otherwise, all the others would be entitled to the same amount of time.

The networks had offered time, free, repeatedly over the years to both major parties, if they would only repeal the restraint in the law so that the public could see the two presidential candidates debating live on television and hear them live on radio. For example, NBC had offered eight hours of an expanded *Meet the Press.* CBS and ABC had made similar offers. Stanton gave South Carolina's Strom Thurmond, the 1948 Dixiecrat Presidential candidate, assurances that substantial third-party candidates would also receive equitable coverage. All to no avail.

In the 1950s Robert Sarnoff, then chairman of the board of NBC, and Stanton repeatedly urged this on Congress. Stanton did a guest column in the old *Herald Tribune* for John Crosby in 1952. "I devoted that column to a plea for opening up Section 315 for debates. I struck out, without any question. Nobody wanted to.

"I went to Eisenhower and to Stevenson in 1952 and offered prime time periods to debate the issues. Stevenson embraced it, understandably. I talked to the man who was running the campaign for Eisenhower, Ben Duffy. I went down to his office and he said, 'Why should we stoop to debate this Governor of Illinois?' I tried to jog him a little bit and tell him that this is the way you get out votes and true democracy, and so forth. He certainly didn't give me any indication that he would go to Ike and say, 'I recommend,' but he did tell me that he'd put it to Ike and see how Ike would react. Eisenhower through his campaign manager turned it down. He wouldn't have any part of it.

"Then I waited for the next round, and of course the next time around, Stevenson still wanted to do it but of course, by that time, the General was president and he wasn't going to have any of that. So we were out of business. I didn't get it in 1956." Then in February 1959 the FCC decided the Equal Time statute should be applied to all newscasts. In Chicago, where there was a local campaign underway, news reports had shown Mayor Daley welcoming the President of Argentina, opening the March of Dimes campaign and making other appearances. Lar "America First" Daly, a perennial candidate for office who campaigned dressed in an Uncle Sam suit, asked for Equal Time. The FCC granted it. Because of other possible requests under this new decision, broadcasters promptly withdrew invitations to senators and other officials where campaigns might be underway.[1]

Congress immediately revised the law to exempt regular news programs from the statute. Incumbents returned to the air. While broadcasters urged complete repeal, particularly to permit the broadcast of presidential debates, Congress would not do it. Incumbents have an advantage from regular news coverage and at this time few already in Congress would vote to give challengers time to debate them.

"In 1960, Eisenhower was not running for reelection and the field was open. Senator John Pastore [Chairman of the Subcommittee on Communications of the Senate Interstate and Foreign Commerce Committee] was holding a hearing about requiring broadcasters to give free time to leading candidates. I made a proposal that each network give a certain number of hours for the candidates to use as they saw fit. No CBS News, no NBC News in it at all.

"At the hearing, Adlai Stevenson was one of the first witnesses. He was a very strong witness. He had charm and was seen as having sound advice. He read a telegram he had received from a viewer who said it's worth getting free time, but he loved the *I Love Lucy* show and he didn't love Stevenson. I think there was something in it that said 'drop dead,' too. Stevenson read that and brought the house down.

"Our General Counsel at that time, Leon Brooks, and I were sitting in the back of the hearing room. During the hearing no progress was being made for lifting 315. I said to Leon as I was getting up to go forward to testify, 'what could we suggest that would give it a break?' Leon said, almost as an afterthought, 'well, you might ask for a temporary resolution.' I never heard of that before.

"On cross examination, after I hadn't made any progress on my direct testimony, I threw out the debate proposal and said, 'give us a chance to try it out.' Senator Pastore asked, 'How would you do it?' I said, 'With a temporary resolution,' and he said, 'Maybe we ought to talk about that.' That was right at the end of my testimony, so I made a bee line into his office afterward to see what I would be able to pick up. He was receptive to the idea and he and Senator Magnuson took me to lunch.

"Lyndon Johnson had said to me one night at a reception, 'See that guy over there [Sen. Warren Magnuson (D-Wash.), Chairman of the

Senate Interstate and Foreign Commerce Committee]. That's the man you're gonna have to work with. Go on over and introduce yourself.' Maggie was short and broad. That was the first time I'd met him. After that, I entertained him frequently in New York and saw him in Washington. So I kind of got the impression that in the Senate, I had the two most important guys on my side, Magnuson and Pastore.

"When Magnuson and Pastore took me to lunch, they asked, what did I have in mind? So I said what I had always said, that we would take prime time and make it available for a debate in some form. I also said that I didn't mean just to confine this to the President and Vice President. There was no reason that you shouldn't do it for congressional campaigns and senatorial campaigns and Pastore jumped straight up out of his chair.

"I remember the scene in the Senate dining room. He said he would never support that idea. He didn't want some young law school graduate from Harvard coming down to Rhode Island and debating him. And so I quickly said it didn't have to be for the Congress. The most important offices in the land were the President and the Vice President. It was important that the public get some feel for them. So then, they calmed down.

"It was that luncheon that paved the way. They asked if I had any language in mind on the resolution. I said no, but would have some down immediately, which of course we did. This wasn't a last-minute idea. I had taken it to our affiliates in either 1950 or 1951 and said I wanted to help enlist their support for it. And, I think I got almost an unanimous affiliate vote in favor of it.

"Pastore said, 'How do you know they are going to debate if we do this? Why should we get all upset and get this legislation approved? It was a temporary resolution and hadn't been written yet. Why should we do all the work when you don't even know that your candidates are willing?' So, I went over to see Nixon and I went over to see Johnson. But first I had to get House approval.

"Oren Harris (D-Ark.) was the Chairman of the House Interstate and Foreign Commerce Committee. We had a little difficulty there. We were up against the date of the 1960 Convention when we were trying to get this legislation through and had to move very fast.

"Gene Autry was the guy who pulled it out for that one. I called Tom Chauncey in Phoenix. Chauncey was a partner of Gene Autry. They owned the CBS Phoenix station. I knew that Gene was close to Sam Rayburn and so I asked Chauncey to ask Gene and Gene called

Rayburn. The Speaker sent word for me to come down that day at one o'clock, and I was there. So was Oren Harris. Rayburn got right to the point. He asked Harris, 'Do you have the votes?' Harris looked at me and I said, 'Yes we do' and Rayburn said, 'Put it on the agenda.' Boom. Walking over to Harris' office, Harris was worried he might not have the votes. Oren said if we didn't have the votes it would be his neck with the leader. They put it up for a vote and it passed. This was not because Rayburn thought Kennedy had the nomination at that time. Mr. Sam was for Lyndon. But Lyndon apparently never communicated to Rayburn his opposition to debating, even though they were very close.

"Had Johnson communicated that reservation, Rayburn would not have put it on the agenda. If somebody had zigged instead of zagged, it would have made the difference."

Herb Klein says his original instructions from Nixon were to dodge around and cite Section 315 and avoid the debates. Klein writes, "We had agreed that we would tepidly support the effort by the networks to suspend Article 315, which demanded equal air time for all recognized candidates."[2] There were then about fourteen active candidates, other than Nixon and Kennedy. Stanton says, "Klein had been saying that Nixon wouldn't debate. But when I went to see Nixon, Bob Finch, an assistant close to Nixon, came out to see if he could help. So I told him I was trying to find out whether Nixon would debate. He said, 'No doubt about it. He's a great debater.' He didn't say he'd mop up the opposition but that was the sense of it and I said, 'Well then, there is no question that I can represent to the Committee, if I get a hearing, that you're willing.' He said, 'Absolutely, no question about it.' And I knew right then we were through with the conversation.

"I went to see Johnson about the debates and I told his secretary when I got to his office I hoped that I'd have a chance to speak to the Senator and she said, 'Go on in, he's got somebody in there with him, but he won't mind.' I couldn't see who it was, I could just see the back of heads and Johnson saw me and in his rather indelicate way, said, 'What do you want in here?' So I told him what I wanted and then he adroitly said, 'Well, why don't you ask Jack?' And that's the first I knew it was Jack Kennedy who was sitting there. Jack got up and we shook hands and he was very friendly, and Johnson gave me my opening by saying, 'Ask Jack,' and Jack said yes, he would, and I could tell that Johnson was about ready to cut my throat. I had put him on the spot because at that point they were both jockeying for the nomination."

Klein explains that everything about television debates was new. The print press was to have no significant role in the debate and no one knew what to expect from television debates. Klein writes that he rode over with Nixon to the first debate. Nixon had been ill. "I thought he looked bad wearing a shirt which was too large, but it seemed like no time to disturb the candidate with such impressions. He was tense and silent. I briefed him on the procedures which would follow our arrival at the studio, and left him to his own thoughts. . . . The producer was Don Hewitt. . . . Hewitt later told me and Frank Stanton, the CBS president, that he was worried about Nixon's appearance."[3] Kennedy looked tanned and appeared healthy. Nixon looked pallid. Klein says Nixon would not permit make-up. He had a "fear that if he did use make-up, he wouldn't look macho enough." Kennedy had embarrassed Humphrey in a Minnesota appearance about Humphrey's use of make-up and Nixon wasn't going to get caught in that.[4]

Klein writes, "As I watched the debate from the studio, appearances did not strike me personally as did contrast in style. I was more worried about the fact that the Vice-President was defensive and the initiative in the debate had been with Senator Kennedy. . . . [After the debate] I think he felt he had done well, and none of us disillusioned him that evening." Later Nixon realized he had made a basic mistake. He wrote, "I spent too much time on substance and too little time on appearance. . . . Where voters are concerned . . . one TV picture is worth ten thousand words."[5]

After the first debate, which took place in CBS-Chicago, Stanton says he went down to the studio floor to congratulate both the participants but was told Nixon had left immediately after the debate. When he went in to see Kennedy, who was speaking on the phone, Stanton thought he looked pleased at the result. Kennedy then introduced Stanton to a man standing in the shadows in the corner, Mayor Daley. As both were leaving, Daley said to Stanton, "I was just going to go along with the Kennedy campaign, but after seeing the debate, I'm going all out to help elect him."

As others have pointed out, Stanton says, "The interesting thing about that first 'debate,' because it sure wasn't the ultimate debate but it was a start in that direction, was that the next day people who only heard it on radio thought Nixon had taken Kennedy and, of course, I saw it in the studio and didn't have that impression." Reporters at the scene say they thought Kennedy won.

Klein writes, "History always will remember the classic Lincoln-Douglas debates, but the debate which reached the largest percentage of the American population and which had the most dramatic impact was the first 'joint appearance' of Nixon and Kennedy."[6]

Originally, five prime-time periods had been set aside for the debates. After four debates, Nelson Rockefeller urged Nixon to continue on for the fifth, as did others. Klein says the press reports unfairly favored Kennedy and Nixon tired of the debates. He did not continue.

Stanton pressed on. He says: "There were a couple of time slots that were still available where we could have put more debates and I thought it would be a good idea to get the Vice President in one of those slots. Jack Gould or somebody had called me and was talking about it and I said I thought it would be a good idea to have the last debate with the Vice Presidential candidates and he wrote about that. Johnson was in North Carolina on the campaign trail when he saw this come through on the tape and he called me and said, 'I am not going to debate Cabot Lodge [the Republican Vice Presidential candidate] and I'm telling you right now lay off and don't give any more of these interviews.' I said this would be a wonderful break for Johnson personally and would be good for the whole democratic process; not only to see the President but to see the Vice President because he would be president if something happened to Kennedy. Oh, he gave me hell for bringing that up. I think it was the United Press who called him in the Carolinas and asked him to comment and he was angry as he could be with me for putting him on the spot. I remember precisely where I was in my house when that phone call came through. I was in the front room at my desk when my wife told me that Johnson was on the other line and I didn't even need the phone to hear him." After the election, Stanton pressed on.

Stanton says, "The networks in the past had offered the major parties blocks of time but they left time on the table. They didn't use it because they wanted to use it their way, and didn't want to use it in a fair way, in my opinion. In the best of circumstances, I think parties ought to be organized some way to have access to the air on both sides to really focus on the issues.

"I proposed that in the next campaign, starting with the Labor Day weekend, on that Sunday night, we would have a stand-off between the two major candidates. The host would explain that we were giving time every Sunday night at 9:00 for an hour for the two Presidential candidates to take a single issue and hammer it out. And on the final night, the final Sunday before the vote, the two candidates could summarize the campaign as they saw it. So we would focus the campaign that way. Kennedy had told me he wanted to debate in 1964. We had Senate support lifting Section 315. Oren Harris had agreed he would hold hearings quickly and get the thing through the House so we could start planning. After Kennedy was assassinated and Johnson was sworn in, I was at the Mayflower Hotel when Johnson called me and said to come out to the House. 'Let's have dinner. I will send a car for you.' I was standing outside at the Mayflower when the Secret Service and police outriders pulled in. Then his car. I got in and he poked me in the side and said, 'Forget about the debates. I'm not going to do it.' "

Stanton recalls why he pressed so consistently for repeal of 315. "I believe it goes back to the basic feeling that I had that we had to utilize the media to the ultimate in terms of keeping the public informed. I felt that you had to get out there and expose the issues and the candidates. I wouldn't deny the candidates spots if that's what the candidate wanted. But I wanted the right to take the two leading candidates and bring them up in front of the camera, or the microphone, and let them talk out their issues, and let the journalists cross-examine them. I thought it would be good for democracy."

In 1975, FCC Chairman Richard A. Wiley, who believed in such debates, led the FCC to rule that broadcasters could cover presidential debates as "bona fide news events," exempt from the Equal Time statute. Senator John Pastore, Chairman of the Commerce Committee's Subcommittee on Communications, sent word of his opposition to such a decision, but Wiley persisted. He also sought some bipartisan support and persuaded James Quello, a Democratic Commissioner, to join the Republican majority. On the night before the vote, Pastore called Quello and urged him not to join Wiley, but Quello saw the value to the public and went with Wiley. The vote was 5–2.[7] That enabled the broadcast of Presidential debates in the 1976 election. (Gerald Ford was thought to have lost the debates in 1976 because of his statement that he did not think the European countries behind the Iron Curtain believed they were dominated by the Soviet Union.)

Someone other than a broadcaster had to arrange the debates for them to be "bona fide news events," and the League of Women Voters conducted the debates to the exclusion of broadcast journalists' arrangements. Today, broadcasters can legally arrange debates but a Presidential Commission has taken the lead.

The Kennedy administration had its own agenda for the broadcast industry. Kennedy selected Newton Minow, who had worked closely with Adlai Stevenson for many years, to be the Chairman of the FCC. Stanton says, "I wanted to get as close to the new chairman of the FCC as I could, as early as I could. I looked upon this as part of my job. I called Leonard Reinsch and told him I'd like to meet Minow. The arrangements were made. I went down to the Statler Hotel and had breakfast with Minow the morning after the Inauguration. He told me that he had been offered two jobs in the administration. One was in the Department of Justice and the other was the Chairmanship of the FCC. He said, 'I know nothing about your business,' and I said, 'Why did you take the FCC job as against the other?' Since Minow was a lawyer I thought professionally he would go the other way. He shook his finger at me and he said, 'Television's role is the most important thing in the world today—to educate the children of tomorrow. That's what we've got to do.' So I knew at the beginning that we were in for trouble. Now he did respect up to a certain point, the Constitutional freedom that we had. But not much. So I was not surprised at the 'vast wasteland' speech."

In one of his first acts as Chairman, Minow made a speech at a convention of the broadcast industry, lambasting the broadcasters for failing to live up to their obligations to the public to provide quality programs. He said as he looked at the broadcasters' programming, he saw only a "vast wasteland." Some broadcasters felt it was more a publicity stunt than an effort to open up a productive dialogue with the already heavily regulated industry. The speech was to become famous and established Minow's reputation among opinion makers as a champion of quality programming.

Stanton says, "Minow had White House help on that speech. I don't think the world knew that at the time. It was fashioned and crafted at the White House. That's why I tied so much significance to what he said and I took him on and tried to join issue with him. I think it was really Bobby Kennedy more than Jack who felt that the industry ought to be brought up short for not having done enough for the public. I'm quite certain Jack had other things on his agenda but Bobby had that on his agenda.

"I think, in a sense, that's traceable in Bobby's case to his wife. She took out after me one day when I was having lunch at a restaurant on 56th Street and she had the table right next to me. Without any hesitation at all she just moved right in on me and my guest and she gave me a lecture, to the amusement and amazement of the people around.

She made the same charge, that we'd let the children of the country down by not using television to educate them."

Cronkite writes that politicians' attempts to control television have led to some unfortunate confrontations. In the Wisconsin primary in 1960, Kennedy was persuaded to appear on the CBS election night coverage when the viability of a Catholic presidential candidate was still being tested. In the course of the interview, "I naturally asked his opinion of how the Catholic and non-Catholic vote was going.

"He was obviously upset by the question, and only later did I learn that his campaign manager, brother Bobby, claimed he produced Jack for our broadcast on condition that the Catholic issue would not be raised. I was never informed of such a promise. . . . I would not have agreed to it anyway.

"Soon thereafter John Kennedy called on CBS President Frank Stanton to complain about our coverage with a warning whose implication was unmistakable. He reminded Dr. Stanton that if elected president, he would be naming the members of the Federal Communications Commission to which CBS was in many ways beholden. Dr. Stanton courageously stood up to that threat, as he did on so many other occasions in defending television's free press rights."[8]

The networks' coverage of the assassination of President Kennedy was seen as a particularly sensitive response to the public need of the moment. Only national television could so unite and tune into the feelings of the public at such a time of national mourning. Stanton immediately pulled all commercials from the CBS system. Robert Kintner, President of NBC, did the same. Although Stanton believed background music was not appropriate for hard news coverage, he commissioned specially composed music to be played during that day. But audience reaction was quite negative and the music was dropped. Internally, Stanton was chided for having spent such a large amount of money that was then wasted. At the same time, there were viewers who called to object to the loss of their favorite soap operas.

In the 1960s, television was still a new medium and there was no manual to consult on such occasions. The network chiefs had to feel their way in deciding how best to serve the public need. That they were successful on that occasion has been recognized and applauded in the years since, as the management of television at its finest.

Stanton first met Johnson when he was still in research. Stanton says, "I was working through lunch at my desk. We had frosted glass bank partitioning, so that you could see the person's head passing by but they could not look in very well. I saw this tall man moving back and forth and he heard me in my office, opened the door and stuck out his hand and told me who he was. It didn't mean anything to me then. At that time, Lyndon Johnson was still in the House of Representatives. He said, 'Your friends down on the 12th floor tell me that I have to get the Research Department's blessing on my radio station before I can get on your network.' Very personal, My network! And I said, 'What are you talking about?' And he said that he and his wife had a station down in Austin, Texas, and did I know where Austin, Texas was? I said yes, I did know where it was. It was the state capital and it was my business to know where it was and I named the county. And, that impressed the hell out of him. 'But,' he said, 'You haven't got very good coverage in my county, or in my city.' And I explained I thought we had reasonable coverage. I had the map of Texas. San Antonio was down here, and Dallas was up here, and Austin was here, and the circles just kiss at Austin. It was a weak signal, but we'd been getting by. But we could use his station. So, I gave him encouragement, and I said, 'I think you ought to pursue this, and when it comes up for vote, I'll tell them the same thing I'm telling you.' Well, of course the Station Relations Department went right to the top of the company and said I had no business screwing up their negotiations, because I gave him a card that I shouldn't have given him. But, I was naive, and I didn't know what the hell I was getting into. That's the first time I met Lyndon Johnson.

"Well, of course he just stuck on me like a leech, and he got the affiliation. Only a few advertising accounts wanted to add Austin, so he'd call me up and say, 'How do we get that Texaco Company on my station?' And, I would tell him what I thought might be useful in the way of a sales presentation. And he built a good little business as an 'Optional Station.' As I got to know him better, he'd say, 'Let's have a meeting. Bird and I want to have a meeting with you on Sunday morning.' And I'd go down, and he'd spread out all his financials on the living room floor. And he and I'd get down on the floor and go over the figures on what his costs were and what his sales were. And Lady Bird would sit on the settee, listening, and being very attentive, and we'd maybe spend a couple hours at that, and then I'd have a bite with them, and I'd hightail it back to New York.

"After he became President, he invited several of us over one night for a drink. He was sitting at his desk that was on blocks of wood. I looked at it and I said, 'Mr. President, here you are leader of the world's greatest country, and you haven't got a desk that . . .'. And he said,

'Fix it!' And I said, 'Well, how much freedom do I have?' He called in somebody and said, 'If Frank wants to do this, make sure he gets what he needs to do it.'

"It was a desk that had been made in the carpenter shop, at the Senate Office Building. He wanted it for sentimental reasons because it had been his desk when he was the Majority Leader in the Senate. It was an indifferent piece of furniture. I redesigned the base and put a caned screen in the front of the knee-hole to hide the gear on the floor and it needed a new base to raise it for the President's height. When I got the pieces I needed, I had to remake the base and do it on a day when he wasn't going to be there. I told Johnson I had the pieces ready and could bring my workers down with me, but I would need the better part of a day to install the new parts. He said he was going to be in New York on a certain day and if it was convenient could I come down.

"So I took a draftsman, a cabinet maker and a finisher with me. We got to the White House, finally got the proper passes, got up to the White House door and the Secret Service came and took all the stuff away. It was raining. I thought the finisher was going to have a stroke, because they carried these nice mahogany pieces of desk out in the rain. They took them someplace to x-ray them to make sure there weren't microphones inside. I didn't get them back until 11:00.

"About noon, I was down on the floor, trying to look at what we could do about accommodating the change before we'd even turned the desk fully upside down, and his secretary came in and said, 'The President is calling.' So, I took the call on the floor on my back, and Johnson said, 'What are you doing for lunch?' And I said, 'Do you know where I am?' And he said, 'No, where are you?' And I said, 'I'm under your desk!' He had forgotten. He was calling me up in New York, wanting me to come over to the Waldorf to have a sandwich. It was crazy! But, fun! Then we had to turn his desk upside down. That upset the things down in the basement. All the bells went off. And the guards burst in with drawn guns.

"Johnson could be very crude. But he had this political thing at his finger tips. He managed to get the Civil Rights Bill passed which was extraordinary for its time. It probably would not have passed had Kennedy been in office. The last chapter hasn't been written on what he did in office, because too many people see the crude stories and don't see what he did. He came in and picked up Kennedy's legislative program.

"He knew the Congress like the back of his hand. Down at the ranch, he had phones on almost every tree, and right there beside the phone was a list of all the members, and he could go right out and check them off. At the pool there was a phone literally in the crotch of the tree, and he had a pad of the Senate. And he'd call in, and he'd say, 'This is what I want you to do.' I was there. I saw him do it. I know he had the same kind of phone in his bathroom at the ranch and at the White House. He kept track of those guys and he knew all their foibles. And he'd say, 'You're not going to vote for me? What about that situation with so and so?' And that would do it. Congressmen were not that independent. They didn't have their own fund raising back then.

"I was too close to Johnson. He thought he owned you. He didn't own me. He was trying to. And I had to watch that all the time. As for news coverage he didn't like, he understood the separation of church and state. But, he still didn't like it. And he'd climb all over me. Around 7:35, if that phone rang, Ruth would say, 'Please don't take that call, or we'll never get back to dinner until 10 o'clock.' He'd get on the phone, chew me out, and say, 'Don't you love me anymore? Are you trying to screw the American people and misinform them?' He could be very vile. And then he'd say, 'What are you doing this weekend? Come on down and spend the weekend with Bird and me and relax. You're working too hard!'

"He wanted me to take jobs down there, and my wife said, 'If you want to take it, you take it, but I'm staying here.' One time, he had me down on a Saturday afternoon. I forgot what it was about. We walked into the cabinet room on the way into his office from the Rose Garden and McNamara and Rusk were sitting there, I guess it was prior to a cabinet meeting. Johnson introduced me to them. I knew McNamara. I didn't know Rusk. And as we went out of the room, he said, 'Now Goddamn it, this is where you oughta be!' He had offered me jobs before and I had steadfastly said no. And of course, these men were no dummies, and they heard that. McNamara was on the phone to me at home that night saying, 'What was this all about?' I knew Bob from his days at Ford and I said, 'Relax, there's nothing to it. He's trying to twist my arm to come down.'

"I wasn't qualified for what he wanted me to do, anyway. He said one time, 'I'm gonna move McNamara out of the Pentagon into HEW. How much do you know about the Pentagon?' And I said, 'It won't work!' He said, 'Why not?' I said, 'I didn't serve in the military.' 'Well, why the hell didn't you serve in the military?' 'So,' he said, 'we'll keep Bob in the military, you take HEW.' And I said, 'I don't know anything about HEW!' At that time, it had the biggest budget in the whole government. And then he said, 'Dean Rusk is not very well. He's been sick and nobody knows it, but I might lose him. Why don't you go over and become Under Secretary of State, and I'll move him?' All in one conversation. Crazy!

"Once when I was chairing a board meeting for Rand out in Santa Monica. He got me on the phone and said, 'How soon can you go to Vietnam?' And I said, 'I'm out in Santa Monica.' He said, 'Fine, you've got a head start.' And he put three of us together; I guess I was the lead dog, along with the editor of the *Denver Post* and the staff officer of the Associated Press. We didn't meet until we got to Vietnam. He had told each one of us, 'I want to find out what the hell is going on. I want you guys to find out.' And he gave us a piece of paper that said we could do anything we wanted to do. And of course, it was chaos. General Westmoreland wanted the three of us to stay in his quarters. We decided that we couldn't have a free hand getting information if we were going to be with Westmoreland. Westmoreland did one hell of a job of trying to convince us of what was going on.

"We broke up and each of us took a different sector. I took I Corps, which was right up against the border, and Westmoreland gave me, I think it was called a T-39, Saberliner. It held a pilot and a co-pilot with maybe two other seats. We were going so high, and I said, 'What is the altitude?' And, no more than I'd said that, but shrapnel blasted outside and the pilot said the Vietnamese were on to the fact that we were up there.

"We went down to the Mekong Delta one afternoon to try to talk to some of the troops down there. We were in two planes. We lost one plane. We didn't lose the passengers, but we lost the plane. They were flying an evasive course, and got caught. That was a scary trip. And we had no cover at all. I had this little note from Johnson. But it wasn't a bullet-proof vest.

"The CBS correspondents in Vietnam, when I showed up, said, 'What the hell are you out here for?' I said, 'Well, we've got a lot of people here and we're spending a lot on coverage, and this is very important.' I'd like to see the circumstances under which you're working.' They didn't know what I was doing out there, and Charlie Collingwood said to me, 'You'd better wear a different set of clothes, or you will wind up dead.' It scared the hell out of me.

"We came back after a week. We couldn't talk in Vietnam. We weren't secure enough, so we went into a hotel in Tokyo, and spent a day comparing notes, and trying to decide what we were going to tell Johnson. Then we flew to Washington, and gave him our impressions.

He said, 'I want you to go over and tell Bob McNamara about it right now.' He called McNamara and told him, 'I've got three guys coming over to see you. They just came back from Vietnam. I sent 'em there, and I want you to talk to 'em.' He didn't say who we were, or anything. We pulled up in front of the main entrance to the Pentagon. With a Presidential car, we didn't have any trouble getting there. Standing on the steps to greet us were Bob McNamara and his Deputy Secretary of Defense, a lawyer from Cravath, Ros Gilpatrick. We had a long meeting with them.

"I had told Paley that I had a special job to do, and I'd tell him about it when I came back. And, of course, he was dying to find out what was going on. But he was very bitter about it. If there was anybody in the United States of America who would have loved to have been asked, it was Bill Paley.

"I told Johnson one time, if he was interested in watching the evening news, 'you can't watch it on one set, you get three sets, and get a clicker that will kick up the sound on any one of the three.' 'Fix it!' You know, he was always saying, 'Do it!'

"One day I was getting dressed in Blair House, he put me in all kinds of places, and he was there sitting on the bed, and I was putting on my clothes—there was no privacy with the guy at all—and I guess I put my shirt on first, then put my pants on. 'Oh,' he said, 'One of these Goddamn easterners that put your shirt on first. Down our way, we put our pants on first.' I sat in his bedroom with him enough that I think I knew an awful lot about what was going on. But he had, for a person who accomplished so much, between the Vietnam War and his preoccupation with the Kennedys, an unhappy time.

"In hindsight, I probably shouldn't have been as close to him as I was. But the pressure of the Presidential office is such that you don't want to be uncooperative. If I had applied the same rules to myself that I applied to the journalists, I should have stepped back because of the possible conflict for our news coverage. But I wasn't doing any reporting and it did help me know what was going on in Washington. It was a difficult situation."

In fact, Stanton was criticized by some of the senior news people at CBS for his closeness to Johnson, but he did what he thought was necessary. He says he counted on his tough-minded friend Salant to warn him if at any time his association with Johnson was compromising CBS News.

Stanton made no headway with Nixon on a personal basis, nor did most other network executives. Stanton says, "In 1960, I spent a number of hours one afternoon with Nixon. I was seeking to arrange the Nixon-Kennedy debates and I asked if I could see him. He invited me to lunch and when I arrived at his apartment, all his lieutenants were there, Haldeman, Ehrlichman, Klein and others. He excused us from what was obviously a skull practice and took me to the Links Club for lunch.

"He was very concerned about Rockefeller running and kept asking me what I knew about that. I did not know but would not have told him if I did since it wouldn't be appropriate for me to be getting in the middle of that. He then talked for about four hours about the world picture as he saw it, what he expected would happen and what would not happen in various parts of the world. He talked about his Moscow trip and a number of the issues facing the country. I sat and listened. It was a tremendously impressive display of his knowledge and awareness of what was going on. Had a record been made of what he said at that luncheon, the public would have seen a different Nixon in 1960 than what they saw later in his campaign. He could be both impressive and friendly in one-on-one talks and he certainly was that day." Nixon maintained his distance, however, outwardly displaying neither friendliness nor hostility in meetings over the years which Stanton attended.

Stanton spent a great deal of time on the Hill. He says he believes during the 1950s and 1960s he was on a good footing with the Senate and House Commerce Committees. In the House, "my dealings with Chairman Staggers were good and my relations with Springer [the ranking minority member] were good. I would stop in to see them when I was down in Washington. It was part of maintaining the relationship.

"Staggers was not much in the way of meetings. I would pay a courtesy call. Springer was genuinely interested in broadcasting and coming from Illinois and the center of the country, he had an interest in the growth of the network and how we picked our stations and so forth. So did Manny Celler who was head of the House Judiciary Committee. God knows why, but he was particularly interested in some of the area around West Virginia. If you gave them facts, they came to rely on you. If you were trying to talk to them about a bus line, forget it. But television had sex appeal.

"You have to turn the clock back and realize that a lot of these conversations with members of Congress took place at a time when television was a mystery to all those people. They didn't quite understand where it was going and what it could do. Not unlike what people are now saying, 'What's this Information Superhighway going to be?' They're uncertain. People felt that way about television.

"Thoughtful congressmen wanted to know what it was going to mean in terms of education, for example. Some of them had great ideas that the television set would turn out to be a classroom. It didn't happen, but you sat and talked with them and told them how developments were coming. There was a great interest in the sheer statistics of television; who owned the sets and where they were located. In the very early days you would take the late afternoon train to Washington, and seeing antennas all along the railroad track, you'd say to yourself, 'how can these people afford television?' If they're grabbing at television, this is something that's coming from the bottom up, because Park Avenue didn't have any antennas. And you'd talk with these guys about those anecdotal experiences and then, of course, the statistics of broadcasting were in my back pocket because that was my formal job. And I could tell them what was going on in their areas about the growth of television and what television stations were doing.

"I had on my wall a map of the United States—it covered the whole side of my room. And I had a long line from my phone. And if somebody called me and said they had a letter from somebody in this district, I'd say, 'What county is it?' And, by that time, I was up looking at the map. And I'd say, 'Well that's so and so county, right next to wherever.' Now I didn't say, 'look, I've got a map right in front of me,' but I was familiar with the neighborhood, so to speak. Well, they thought that was pretty hot stuff, you know, and advertisers did too. Advertisers would call. Some weren't very systematic about the statistics of the industry. But they'd get a complaint from a client about coverage and I'd get over to the map and start talking about the location. That was a tool of the trade. You had to know this.

"In those days I didn't talk with Congressmen about issues that involved us, necessarily. It was just a folksy kind of exchange because television was the new kid on the block and they wanted to know about it. I remember taking Earl Warren, when he was Governor of California, up to one of our studios to show him just the backroom, so to speak. Well, this was a real treat for him and I asked him if he wanted to have a look at the studio. Well, 'Certainly.' He didn't know what he was going to see but when he got in there and saw how they pushed the buttons, he was fascinated. These guys were interested. And I had a medium or a new toy, so to speak, to show them. You don't have that now. Now you've got maybe a computer to show them.

"There was considerable interest in the dress of the women on television because this was the first time a lot of people saw the kind of styles that were being exhibited in fashion magazines, if you took fashion magazines. But, in some of those communities, the circulation of *Vogue* was nil. But here the fashions were seen right on television and it was dazzling and dangerous. I remember one guy one night at a little dinner saying to me, 'how do you keep the camera from showing too much?' It was an interesting period, no question about it. Nothing anybody was able to talk about opened up vistas the way talking about television did. Going from listening to seeing was a fantastic leap. The print people never wanted to talk about it because it took the ball game away from them. But it was enormously important in social and cultural relations to be able to see what was going on. And if you were down in the back country and you could watch these things—well, this was something nobody ever dreamed about before.

"Every time I took a visiting dignitary into the CBS Grand Central Studios and showed them around, it was interesting to see how they immediately translated what they saw in terms of their interests. Educators saw it as education, architects saw it another way, everybody saw it a different way and they wanted a piece of the action. They weren't quite sure how, but they wanted to get into it.

"And religious leaders. I remember I had a couple of leaders in one of the denominations at a dinner and in the course of the evening we got around to talking about television and I said, 'Would you like to see the studio?' Well, they didn't want to stay in their chairs. I took them to the studio and one of them said, 'We could reach our congregation through the medium.' I can't think of anything else in my lifetime that had the kinds of appeal that television had. There was also a sense of quality that was brought to the creation of television at that time and these are all the reasons why I always said that it was a stimulating job."

Some in government felt they should make sure this potential power wasn't going to be abused. Stanton points out, "They had to think in those terms because no one knew just what this new medium was going to do. Elected officials saw immediately their image on that screen could win or lose for them. It could make an enormous difference."

By 1971, television had become more of a known factor. It had been regulated for many years and was generally accepting of regulation by the FCC and oversight by congressional committees. Stanton's defiance of the Staggers Committee challenged this practice and the interests of powerful government institutions. The ability to distribute news was certainly significant. But the television networks had no political base, no constituencies in the usual sense of voters supporting a congressman or a president. Stanton was entirely knowledgeable about the vulnerability of the networks and the workings of government. What the networks did have in dealing with the Washington community was the possible support of their affiliated stations. These stations were close to the elected officials from their communities. Their local news and public affairs coverage were important to officials running for elective office.

The networks' relations with their affiliated stations were of commercial importance to both the networks and to the stations. The television networks delivered their programs by long distance telephone wires to local stations in their markets across the country to reach their audiences. If a network program was not broadcast by the affiliated station to the local community, the program would usually not be seen in that market. The networks provided the programs free to the affiliates and paid millions of dollars to the affiliated stations to carry the programs. With the vast audience—in the tens of millions—reached by this system, the networks were able to sell this viewership, together representing usually over 90% of the viewing audience in prime time to advertisers who wished to place commercials in the network programming.

The affiliates were not mere distributors, but as the point of entry to the market played a role in what was broadcast. Under the Communications Act and FCC rules, the affiliates had the final say on what was broadcast over their stations. All this gave them a voice on network policies. At various conventions and other occasions, the affiliates could make their views known. These were important occasions in the network-affiliate relationship.

The owners of the broadcast stations across the country that became network affiliates in order to receive the network service of entertainment, sports and news programming were usually not from news backgrounds. Many could probably be considered small businessmen. Their experience was often in sales and advertising and their success depended on staying responsive to local tastes and views. This was their guide for programming, including clearing network material and selecting their own local news and entertainment programming.

Stanton could not count on automatic support from the affiliates for his stand against Staggers or President Nixon. Not only were affiliates independent businesses, but, at this time, many of them, particularly affiliates in the midwest and the south, did not like the tone of the network news. At one point, the CBS-affiliated stations held a meeting in Chicago and the owners of several stations strongly indicated a lack of sympathy with the policies at CBS News. Indeed, the Nixon administration saw that a natural alliance could be established with station managers who did not like the network news. It could bring pressure on the network news from these powerful economic partners to help in presenting Nixon views to local station audiences. One broadcaster in Texas quoted Herbert G. Klein as saying, "the local station was doing an excellent news job and asking why it relied on CBS News."[9]

A number of affiliates complained to the network managements about liberal bias on the part of the network reporters and anchors. Reuven Frank writes of the May 1970 closed-to-the-press session at the NBC affiliate convention as one impassioned "attack on NBC News: for lack of objectivity, for opposing the President, for favoring war protestors, for presumption, even for low integrity. What had started with Agnew's Des Moines speech [attacking the networks] was reaching a new level. . . . By the time of the NBC meeting, many of the affiliates, well-to-do businessmen whose profits depended on federal licenses, were preparing to bail out, some of them agreeing with the White House, some merely fearing it. . . . The general complaint was that we were one-sided in covering the war and the protest against it, that we had ignored the other—that is, the President's—position."[10]

Herb Klein's delivery of President Nixon's message to that spring's convention of the National Association of Broadcasters (NAB), which praised local broadcasters and their stations and pointedly ignored the networks, was seen by many as reflecting the administration's views of who were the good guys and who were the bad guys.[11]

The affiliates had political clout. Representatives and Senators back home who wanted favorable coverage for reelection listened to them. Were the affiliates actively to oppose network interests, this could lead to serious problems in Washington for the networks' legislative and regulatory interests. And the stations were no patsies for the networks. They knew how to use their power. They were not supporters of the networks for the sake of being blindly helpful. They pursued their own interests, sometimes concurring with the networks and sometimes not. Nixon's rapport with affiliates presented the networks with the problem of sorting out how much affiliate objection was on merit and how much from political bias on the right or White House pressure.

After *The Selling of the Pentagon*, one CBS affiliate was reported to be trying to get stations to leave CBS.[12] Dick Salant believed the Agnew message and the Klein message were simple: If the affiliates didn't bring the networks into line, the stations would face government retaliation in Washington, something no station would want.[13] Klein defends the message he gave, saying, "I was invited out to make a speech at the NAB and the year before I had said something good about network news and the next year, I wanted to mention that the local stations were doing a great job. They were expanding, they were doing more news."[14] And this was true. But others in government were urging the affiliates to complain to the networks. License holders who supported network news realized their stance was not likely to be favorably viewed. Stanton comments, "I find the White House protestations of innocence hard to accept because the signs were to the contrary. Look, if I had been in their shoes I would have worked that side of the street a lot harder than they did."

The Staggers Subcommittee was doing what it thought was required for the public interest. Under such a rationale, government officials with great power move to do what they see as appropriate. They may be acting with the best of intentions, but they are the government's intentions.[15]

Again and again, history shows the tendency of members of the government to restrict the airways or "shape the news" to meet their objectives, usually their political objectives, rather than opening the airways to greater public information and debate.

Stanton says, "My philosophy over the years has shifted more and more. If there's a fault, I'd rather have the fault be on the side of too much information, than on the side of protecting the public. And, I think the freedom to get it all out in the open—disclosure—solves an awful lot of problems. And, that's not an easy course to implement with government or even with journalists."

Chapter 6

Congress and Television News

When Congress passed the Radio Act in 1927 and the Communications Act in 1934, the grant of a license to broadcast gave stations the exclusive right to use a limited resource, the broadcast spectrum. In this sense, Congress believed it "created" broadcasting. A station was a "trustee" and required to operate "in the public interest." The FCC regulated broadcast operations under this statutory mandate, and failure of the station to perform in accordance with FCC requirements could warrant the loss of its license when it came up for renewal or if attacked on particular grounds.

The Supreme Court had upheld a number of FCC regulations dealing with station ownership, networking, affiliate relations and programming. In the 1940s, the FCC adopted the Fairness Doctrine, which required licensees to present controversial issues of public importance and contrasting views on those issues. Under this doctrine, the FCC reviewed broadcast news when complaint was made to determine if contrasting views were adequately presented. The FCC could require additional programming, in effect, if it determined such was required to meet the FCC's determination of "fairness." The FCC also adopted rules granting a right of reply to those attacked or criticized in a station's programming.

In 1969, the Supreme Court held this FCC regime was constitutional under the First Amendment in its *Red Lion* decision. The conservative Rev. Billy James Hargis criticized Fred Cook, a liberal journalist, in program time he bought on the Red Lion radio station in Pennsylvania. Cook asked for free time to reply and the station refused. The FCC held that this violated its rules, and this decision was upheld by a unanimous Court. The Court said that broadcasting was different from print: the broadcast spectrum was limited, not all who wanted to could broadcast and FCC regulations would create robust debate on controversial issues. The decision thus established significantly less protection for broadcast speech and press than the freedom afforded print.[1]

In 1971, the House Commerce Committee did not doubt its power to investigate broadcast news. Communications legislation and decisions of the Supreme Court were legal authority for such an investigation, and Congress had conducted investigations into news coverage for some time. All this set the stage for its investigation of *The Selling of the Pentagon*.

Earlier investigations had shown how Congressional staff could readily find wrongdoing. Congress had required the production of "outtakes" and used them to reach adverse findings. For example, the House Commerce Committee's Special Subcommittee on Investigations under Chairman Staggers had investigated television news coverage of the 1968 Democratic National Convention in Chicago. Basically, the charge was that the networks had exaggerated police beatings of demonstrators, distorting the news, and had shown police violence, but not the provocation that caused it.[2]

This investigation continued for a number of months. Dozens of witnesses and thousands of documents, including outtakes, were subpoenaed and produced for the Investigations Subcommittee. Its report on July 23, 1969, concluded that the Subcommittee had the necessary authority to investigate the editing of television news.[3] The report said it would be possible to conclude that the networks had deliberately sought out for interview those with known biased feelings against the conduct of the convention but noted, "such a conclusion is, of course, of necessity, extremely subjective." The staff investigated "prejudicial" selection and editing. It looked at outtakes to determine whether the networks had "deliberately withheld" material which would have been derogatory to demonstrators. The investigators said they found such material in the outtakes but they also found material which was critical of police conduct. They concluded: "There were incidents shown on the videotape and film, but not over the air, which arguably could have presented a different picture of the convention than the one that was actually conveyed." They said, "Crowds were shown in violent and ugly moods. Police were shown being stoned and pelted with rocks and bottles. Obscene signs and language were discernible, both of which might have diminished any sympathy felt for the demonstrators by the average viewer." The staff did find that "the out-takes were not uniformly favorable to the police." The staff then concluded that "A review of the material left the investigators with the impression that significant out-takes contained a predominant amount of material which would have been unfavorable to the demonstrators."[4]

The staff saw "bias" in the news based on the staff review of the coverage and the outtakes. It said that there seemed to be "substantial evidence of animosity by members of the television news organizations against the Democratic Party, or at least against certain of its prominent members, and the administration of the city of Chicago." The only extrinsic evidence of animosity cited was the claim that the newsmen had wanted to stay in Miami, where the Republicans had met and were angry about the move to Chicago and the restrictions they found there. The staff said it "reviewed the television news coverage, both broadcast and out-takes, and has spoken with people who were witnesses to the disturbances in downtown Chicago. It does seem in retrospect that the picture presented over the networks did not place sufficient evidence before the public as to the nature and motives of the demonstrators."[5]

The staff found "prejudicial editing," but identified no clearly supporting particulars. "To be specific, there appear to be questionable uses made of film editing and electronic intercutting techniques. In general, the public should probably be given more of a disclosure as to when these potentially distorting techniques are being employed in presenting television news."[6] It noted, however, the difficulties involved in attempting to verify an allegation of prejudicial editing. In an examination of editing, it was very difficult to determine what the truth was in such a matter because it was such a judgmental question.

The staff also found "unfair juxtaposition and intercutting of live and taped material." This was based on an interview conducted by CBS with Mayor Daley in the convention hall. Daley was shown giving assurances to the viewers that everything was well in hand downtown, and obstinately denying undue force was being used. At the same time, voice-over accompaniments and two film scenes were shown of troops with bayonets and menacing police. It was true, but the staff thought it unfair.

Those who worked on the report point out its continuing significance. These same questions will be faced in the digital transmissions of the future, since electronic intercutting techniques are similar to the editing of videotape and film.[7]

The staff paid no attention to the testimony of the news people who felt that the convention coverage did generally convey "the essence of what was going on in Chicago," given the restraints imposed on them by the city government. The report stated at the outset, "No attempt has been made to investigate the very substantial and significant charges that the Chicago Police or Democratic Party Officials . . . attempted to intimidate and obstruct the work of the newsmen." It said the remedy for that lay elsewhere. It looked to the Communications Act and avoided "entering into any discussion of such matters as unjustified police aggression and harassment directed towards newsmen."[8]

The staff made recommendations. The most detailed had to do with editing and intercutting: "On the one hand, the first amendment would appear to preclude any attempt to prohibit or to seriously interfere with this type of activity. [The Staggers Subcommittee was later to disavow this.] Moreover, the editing and selecting process is a practical necessity if news events are to be presented in the limited time available during the typical television news program." The staff concluded that the editor is in a position "to condense and splice together an event so as to, for example, make events which transpired over a lengthy period of time appear to have taken place within a few minutes. In the process, a distillation or distortion of reality may take place whereby the information received by the viewer, although based on reality, has been given a bias or coloration which reflects more the prejudices and opinions of the director or editor than it does the actual event itself." The report suggested that when using edited videotape or film, a legend reading "Edited Material" should be displayed on the screen: "This would not preclude the broadcaster from engaging in the editing process, but it would alert the viewer to the possibility that the sequence of events which he is watching may not represent the original sequence, but rather a condensed, and possibly rearranged, version thereof."[9]

Journalists saw a different picture than the Subcommittee staff reported. NBC News anchorman David Brinkley tried to explain that "We showed what we could, that our locations were circumscribed and what we showed was unedited." NBC News President Reuven Frank wrote that in Chicago in 1968, "union telephone installers had been on strike since May. It was they who would install our cable and connections. Without them there could be no live television coverage. . . . Also the 'counter culture' had targeted the Democratic convention in Chicago for a massive demonstration against the Vietnam war, and the city was having an attack of nerves." Daley called the union and the company to his office and an agreement was reached to restore live coverage for the convention while otherwise the strike would continue. "There would thus be live pictures, but only from the hall." Daley was sure he had kept the protestors off television.

But, the demonstrators, "knowing where the mayor and the Chicago police had situated the mobile units—there and nowhere else—came to them. . . ." These units could record pictures on tape which could then be taken and fed to the network. "When the turmoil reached its climax, that is exactly how the pictures came to be shown across the country and became part of the permanent recollection." At one point while proceedings at the convention were going on, tape had arrived from outside the downtown hotels showing "running and clubbing and bleeding, confusion and violence." As the person in charge of news coverage on the spot, Frank writes, "I decided that what was happening at Michigan and Balboa [streets] was truly part of the news of the Democratic convention, and I would have to fit it in. . . .

"There were no cameras in the Hilton lobby or near the hotel restaurant called the Hay Market. Bystanders and some demonstrators fled police and tear gas to seek refuge in the restaurant; police pushed some through a plate glass window; other police ran into the restaurant randomly clubbing those inside. We saw none of that; we read about it in the next morning's newspapers. What occurred away from the cameras was worse than what we showed. . . . Most of the horrors testified to later at the commission of inquiry were in fact not seen on television, police shouting 'Kill 'em! Kill 'em!', or clubbing kneeling young women and well-dressed middle-aged bystanders. But what we did show sickened those who watched, and they hated us for showing it to them."

Frank concludes that Daley's "allegation that we had not shown provocation, the complaint most widely echoed in Congress and by the public, was simply not true. For example, the tearing down of the American flag, the provocation he most often cited as ignored by us, was shown not once but three times, and several of our reporters, at different times, had talked about how the demonstrators had set out to goad the police." The transcripts showed "that of the thirty-five hours, exactly sixty-five minutes was devoted to the demonstrations, including twelve minutes of tapes shown a second time."

Frank was aware that there would be "a season of unprecedented trouble with Congress . . . we must have made it up. . . . Congressional Democrats feared that what was seen on television might cost them the presidential election and damage them individually in their districts. Indeed it may have. Nor was hostility to the networks confined to Democrats. Republican whip Leslie Arends proposed that the House investigate 'the role of the networks in our national affairs and just how these federally licensed activities ought to be allowed to get into the business of influencing the public.' That was stating it plain, right down to the magic words *federally licensed*."[10]

The National Commission on the Causes and Prevention of Violence also conducted an investigation, leading to the Walker Report, entitled "Rights in Conflict." This blue-ribbon commission reviewed 3,437 statements of eyewitnesses and participants, 180 hours of motion picture film and 12,000 still photographs. This exhaustive study concluded there was not news distortion or bias. In fact, it found a "police riot." Frank points out that the Walker Report said what happened was "largely what the networks had reported at the time, dismissing as insubstantial the claims that the police had been unbearably provoked." It was clear from the Walker Report that the Chicago police had lost control of the demonstrators and of themselves. "Television, it said, may have made things worse, and there may have been too little analysis of the protest groups." In contrast, the report called the police violence "unrestrained and indiscriminate."[11]

The FCC, which also conducted an investigation, found no distortion, deception or bias. In a policy adopted by the FCC at the suggestion of its then General Counsel, Henry Geller, Esq., the FCC said it would not attempt to find bias from the review of coverage itself. This was too unlikely to yield a sound judgment. The FCC would act, however, if there was extrinsic evidence of distortion or bias, beyond the coverage itself. Since they found none, they did not act.[12]

But by the time the Walker Report and the FCC decision were issued, it didn't make any difference. Those who thought the networks were biased and had been unfair still thought so. Most believed pictures of Chicago police clubbing the country's young people to maintain order at the Democratic convention were distorted and had hurt the Democratic Party. Michigan Democratic Congressman John Dingell called the coverage "biased" and "irresponsible."[13]

Stanton recalls the only potentially difficult situations he ever had with the CBS affiliates were over the coverage of the convention in Chicago and the Vietnam War. "The affiliates thought we had exaggerated the problems in Chicago. They didn't meet with us on the basis of wanting to declare war or threaten us in any way. But there was enough serious talk about whether we had it right. The fact of the matter is, many of them hadn't heard or seen the thing themselves. They were talking about what other people were saying about it. I went out to Phoenix, Arizona where there was a meeting of the Advisory Board and we took the tape of that whole thing out there with us and we went through it. It was a very long session." And Stanton was satisfied the affiliates could see CBS had done a fair job.

The Staggers Investigations Subcommittee could point to several other earlier investigations. In 1959 it had investigated the network quiz show scandals and legislation was passed to prevent the rigging of quiz shows and improper influencing of material on the air.[14] In 1968, the Staggers Subcommittee investigated a news documentary, *Pot Party at a University*, broadcast on November 1, 2, and 3, 1967, by the CBS-owned station WBBM-TV in Chicago. The program was presented to show the use of marihuana on university campuses. The hearing took five days, with approximately 30 witnesses to consider whether the licensee station had improperly participated in a crime (i.e., the procurement and use of marihuana). The Subcommittee report concluded that the licensee contrived the filming of *Pot Party* to enhance its news ratings and was guilty of "staging."[15]

This time the Subcommittee said the First Amendment did not exempt the station from its responsibility to operate in the public interest; but this time, the Subcommittee was also dealing with the commission of a crime. A subpoena had been issued for outtakes, but they had been disposed of in the regular course of business and therefore were not available when the investigation began. Stanton was required to testify at this proceeding and his position was: "We stand by what we had on the air and that is the thing I think we should be judged on and not what is on the cutting room floor."[16]

The FCC had also conducted an investigation of the staging charge in *Pot Party*. It accepted the position advanced by Stanton that the program itself should be judged by what was aired and it imposed no rules directly relating to maintaining outtakes. But it did give the CBS station a short-term license renewal—18 months instead of 36—as sanction for the station's misconduct.[17] The Staggers Subcommittee disagreed with the FCC decision. Its report stated, "By inaction, the Commission has accepted Dr. Stanton's position that the fairness of a news presentation should be judged exclusively on the material broadcast without reference to film footage which had been excised by editorial cutting. This position is contrary to the public interest. It deprives the Commission and other duly constituted public authorities of the most important evidence for ascertaining if a news program has or has not been slanted by a licensee."[18] Thus, the precedent for committee review of outtakes to judge editorial decisions in a news program was confirmed again by the Staggers Subcommittee.

The Subcommittee staff recommended legislation "to prohibit falsification in news broadcasts . . . to make the commission of a crime by a licensee . . . sufficient cause for revocation." It would have required television station licensees to retain all outtakes for inspection "by duly constituted public authorities."[19]

A Subcommittee on Department of Agriculture and Related Agencies Appropriations of the Committee on Appropriations investigated the CBS News documentary *Hunger in America*, which described the hunger of many Americans despite a number of government programs set up to help deal with this problem. The program used San Antonio, Texas, for one of its examples. The farm groups which had been criticized, and Democrat Henry B. Gonzalez, who represented San Antonio, which was seeking to attract tourists to a fair there, attacked the program as erroneous in reporting the death of a child from starvation when this later proved not to be the case, although there were children dying from malnutrition. The FCC also investigated.[20] Representative Gonzalez was to continue to criticize CBS for this program during the investigation of *The Selling of the Pentagon*.

There was a long, extensive congressional hearing on CBS News' efforts to investigate a case of gun running by a group which also was planning the possible invasion of Haiti. The Commerce Subcommittee report was highly critical of the network's participation in *Project Nassau*, even though CBS had maintained contact with the federal authorities, had withdrawn, and did not produce or broadcast a program.[21] This report was to prompt intense congressional concern. Many felt that CBS was improperly engaged in activities that could affect U.S. foreign policy in the Caribbean and elsewhere. The staff report also gave the impression that CBS had funded the group seeking to invade Haiti. Although this was not true, in the words of one observer, it was the feeling in Congress that "the networks had no sense of responsibility. They were out of control." The Subcommittee's report was often mentioned as showing a need to rein in the network news divisions at the time the Staggers Subcommittee was investigating *The Selling of the Pentagon*.[22]

As an institution, the Congress is not a ready bulwark against press regulation. Congress generally supports regulation, and commentators note that the only apparent purpose of many of the congressional hearings was to provide a forum for the criticism of broadcast editorial practices that were beyond its powers to reach.[23]

Moreover, in 1971, when Stanton faced the Subcommittee over *The Selling of the Pentagon*, he was up against an antagonism which stemmed from anger over news coverage of the Vietnam War, the Chicago convention, a specific television news report or a general dislike of the television press. But above all, the issue was one of power, the perception that distribution of information was power and the Congress was not about to let the networks continue on the course it seemed they were on. The Nixon White House felt even more strongly on this point.

Chapter 7

The White House

It is not the purpose of this book to recount the history of Nixon's political career or his relations with the press generally. But what was to become a campaign against the television networks to influence broadcast news coverage was part of what Stanton faced during the Staggers congressional contempt proceeding.

When Nixon was Dwight Eisenhower's Vice Presidential candidate, he was accused of having an improper political slush fund. He received no help from Eisenhower or the Republican National Committee when the press went after him, but he used a television speech to defend the fund as legal and saved his place on the ticket. He saw that television could reach over the heads of his opponents and the print press to reach the public directly.[1]

In 1966, in a statement after his defeat by Pat Brown for the California governorship, he criticized the print press but praised television. "I think it's time that our great newspapers have at least the same objectivity, the same fullness of coverage, that television has. And I can only say thank God for television and radio for keeping the newspapers a little more honest."[2]

In his 1968 campaign for President, he concentrated on his "television image." Print reporters were "left out" and he was successful in taking that image directly to the people through television.[3] Nixon wrote in his memoirs upon his election as President, "I considered the influential majority of the news media to be part of my political opposition. . . . I was prepared to have to do combat with the media in order to get my views and my programs to the people.[4]

He appointed Herbert G. Klein as Director of Communications for the executive branch. Klein had been a professional journalist, former head of the conservative Copley Newspapers' Washington bureau and a member of the American Society of Newspaper Editors. He was a long-time Nixon aide and was to coordinate all administration comment for the press. Ronald Ziegler became "Press Spokesman."

Nixon said he neither read the newspapers nor watched television, and relied on news summaries prepared by the White House staff, Patrick Buchanan and others. Handling the television press and its coverage was a White House preoccupation. Constant efforts were made to gain more favorable coverage through organized comments, criticism and complaints.[5]

The networks were accustomed to complaints from all parts of the political spectrum—it went with the territory. But while the correspondents were kept insulated from this pressure, management had to respond to it. When the government called with a complaint, the networks could not simply hang up, as the print press at least liked to say they did. For television management, dealing with the government was clouded by concern over broadcast licenses and the threat of adverse government legislation and regulation.

Complaints from presidents were often delivered in no uncertain terms. President Lyndon B. Johnson, for example, would call the network chiefs directly and often to complain in the most intense way. Gordon Manning, the head of CBS hard news as Vice President and Director of News, recalls the need for resistance to Johnson's efforts to remove CBS reporter Morley Safer from coverage of the Vietnam War.[6]

George Reedy, Press Secretary to President Johnson, concluded that "As a rule, the only place a president gets real reactions from is the press." His staff supports his views and actions. When contrary views are reported, Reedy explained, "A president can always blame the press. It's either the damn liberal press or the damn conservative press or the damn northern press."[7]

President Nixon viewed coverage by the television press as the most important. As he told H.R. Haldeman, his chief of staff, "The only thing that matters is the TV." Nixon also believed intimidation of the television networks was the most effective approach to dealing with them.[8]

Herb Klein comments that the public most remembers the Nixon administration's "bare-fisted battles" with the media, but many of his own operations increased the scope of information available. He adds, "This is not to assert that the Nixon administration, like those which preceded and succeeded it, did not make a major effort to manage news and that it did not on far too many occasions take oppressive measures."[9]

At first Klein and Buchanan called reporters to stress favorable developments and straighten out errors. But in the eyes of Nixon and Haldeman they got poor results. The staff was then reorganized to do what was necessary to gain favorable publicity for the Nixon initiatives and accomplishments. Haldeman asked Jeb Magruder, one of his White House staff assistants, for a plan, and on October 17, 1969, Magruder wrote the now famous "The Shot-gun Versus the Rifle." The basic thrust was that attempts to handle complaints one at a time and person to person were getting nowhere—the shotgun—and that it was time to have a focused assault—the rifle. Magruder listed 21 requests from the President taken from the log of the previous 30 days asking for specific action against unfair news coverage. He wrote: "I would gather that there have been at least double or triple this many requests made through other parties to accomplish this same objective." He advanced a series of proposals which included "an official monitoring system through the FCC as soon as Dean Burch is officially on board as Chairman. If the monitoring system proves our point, we have then legitimate and legal rights to go to the networks, etc., and make official complaints from the FCC." Since the new Chairman of the FCC (Burch) would ask the networks for transcripts of their coverage, this would provide even greater impact. Burch was to coordinate the responses. The plan also contemplated the use of the Anti-Trust Division to make threats against the networks.[10]

The use of the FCC, the government broadcast licensing agency, to monitor broadcast news could certainly be expected to intimidate broadcast licensees. In the regulated broadcast industry, no broadcaster felt comfortable about an FCC inquiry and all were quick (and, for that matter, required) to cooperate with the agency in its general investigations and inquiries.

The administration's efforts to influence the television press in 1969 and 1970 were publicly challenged by leaders at both CBS and NBC. For example, Stanton addressed the annual national convention of the Radio and Television News Directors Association on September 24, 1969, and warned against a "deeply troubling trend toward government curbs on broadcast journalism." The next day, Nixon appointee Frank Shakespeare of the United States Information Agency, a former CBS executive, charged that many prominent journalists in broadcasting had a strong and visible liberal bias which he found disturbing.[11]

Television coverage of the Vietnam War was certainly a major problem for the Nixon administration. Newscasts showing American casualties constantly reminded the public of the human cost of the war, and reports on the peace negotiations showed they were making no progress. At the same time there was a major debate within the government itself about the advisability of the U.S. presence in Vietnam. Nixon saw news bias in the television news coverage of that debate. But Washington news producers remember it as an unusually demanding time of reporting on a significant dispute which continued for months and then years, with public statements by high government officials on both sides, many calling for withdrawal but many supporting the war.[12]

On taking office, one of President Nixon's primary objectives was to disengage from the Vietnam War "with honor." Some had urged that he just pull out and blame the Kennedy and Johnson administrations. But Nixon believed America could not cut and run. He sought a strategic withdrawal. His problem was that there had to be a credible threat of military action if peace negotiations were to get results. But the U.S. military threat seemed to have little credibility, even though President Johnson had committed 555,000 American troops and there were substantial South Vietnamese troops in the field.

There had been no declaration of war, and as a result, print and television news reporters were allowed to cover the fighting without the censorship customary in a declared war. The military facilitated that press coverage. It arranged for frequent flights to the front, where television cameras could record what was going on, including the fighting and the killing, which was then broadcast on the evening news. The military briefings from Vietnam lost their credibility as the military tried to come up with information to make conditions look hopeful, but the reporters could see for themselves, and then reported that

U.S. claims as to the enemy killed and the progress of the war were dubious. Anti-war demonstrations increased, and they were covered on television.

Nixon decided he would "go for broke," as he put it, and would attempt to end the war one way or the other, either by negotiated agreement or by an increased use of force. He set November 1, 1969, as the deadline for what would in effect be an ultimatum to North Vietnam. He also made a peaceful gesture. In the middle of September 1969, he announced the withdrawal of another 35,000 troops by December 15, which would mean a total of 60,000 withdrawn. "The time for meaningful negotiations has therefore arrived," he said.[13]

At the same time, he had to deal with the television coverage which, by reporting on the losses, the lack of the war's progress and domestic unrest, discouraged the American public and encouraged the North Vietnamese leaders. There was a need, in the view of the White House, to stop or reduce the critical press coverage quite apart from the desire for favorable coverage. Herb Klein was later to write that there were two matters that provoked great emotional intensity in Nixon during their association. One was his loss to Kennedy in the Nixon/Kennedy debate and the other was the war and his inability to end it.[14]

In the weeks before the November 1 deadline, Nixon wanted to orchestrate the maximum pressure on Hanoi. "But the only chance for my ultimatum to succeed was to convince the Communists that I could depend on some solid support at home if they decided to call my bluff. However, the chances I would actually have that support were becoming increasingly slim."[15] As Kissinger's autobiography notes, "The public was as ambivalent as the government planners: It wanted us to get out of Vietnam and yet it did not want defeat."[16]

The opposition calling for a unilateral cease-fire or a hastened withdrawal included Senate Majority Leader Mike Mansfield (D-Mont.), Senators Edmund Muskie (D-Me.), Edward Kennedy (D-Mass.), Charles Goodell (R-N.Y.), Charles Percy (R-Ill.), Mark Hatfield (R-Ore.), Frank Church (D-Id.) and Jacob Javits (R-N.Y.), as well as Cyrus Vance, Eugene McCarthy and others. Between September 24 and October 15, 1969, eleven anti-war resolutions were introduced in the Congress. Kissinger points out, "the opposition was vocal, sometimes violent; it comprised a large minority of the college-educated; it certainly dominated the media and made full use of them. . . . If we were to make progress in the negotiations, it was necessary to convince Hanoi that there were some irreducible conditions beyond which we would not retreat. . . . In the face of media and Congressional opposition, there never was any firm ground on which to stand."[17]

Some of the press, including mainstream publications like *Newsweek* and *Time* magazine, saw a "crisis of leadership. . . . On October 7, [they] even suggested the breakup of the Nixon administration was imminent. David Broder wrote in the *Washington Post* that 'it is becoming more obvious with every passing day that the men and the movement that broke Lyndon Johnson's authority in 1968 are out to break Richard Nixon in 1969. The likelihood is great that they will succeed again.' "[18]

The White House press corps complained about the infrequency of Nixon's press conferences. Even when he agreed to meet the media it was called the President's Conference, and every effort was made to control it. Nixon was not comfortable with it. He also could not control it.[19] Nixon concluded he would go over the heads of the press corps and address the nation directly to ask for their support for his policies. Nixon had Ron Ziegler announce on October 13 that the President would make an address about Vietnam to the nation on November 3.[20] There was some thought that the announcement, if made early, might temper the Moratorium demonstrations scheduled for October 15. It did not do so. On October 15, 250,000 protestors marched on Washington, 20,000 in the New York financial district, 30,000 on the New Haven green, 50,000 on the Washington monument grounds and 100,000 on the commons in Boston. Television covered them all.[21]

Nixon hoped his speech would solidify national support for an unpopular war. There was a great deal of speculation. Would Nixon announce a new policy? A pull-out? Or still more force? His cabinet was deeply split. Some in the administration were writing to Nixon that "escalation could lead to an uncontrollable domestic violence. The nation could be thrown into internal physical turmoil."[22] This was no idle concern. Klein says that during the period of the demonstrations, National Guard troops were secretly stationed in the corridors below ground running between the Treasury Building and the White House to be called out in the event the demonstrations could not be controlled by the police.[23]

Nixon worked on the speech alone in the Executive Building and at Camp David for many days. "Speculation about the speech reached fever pitch," Nixon wrote as the date approached.[24] He was counting on his ability to use television once again to reach the public for their support. It was critical that the television press not interfere with his message.

October 26, 1969

MEMORANDUM

TO: Bob Haldeman

FROM: The President

. . .

An especially effective group should be set up for the purpose of monitoring the three television networks and hitting them hard on the positive side of the speech and taking them on if they take a negative view. I want this handled in more than a routine fashion and a strike force is to be set up for each network.[25]

Haldeman notes of his meeting with Nixon on November 1:

Vital importance concentrate tomorrow nite
Z—Kl—everyone
Concentrate only on 3 nets.[26]

Haldeman wrote in his diary on Nixon's preparation:

"Nov. 2: . . . wants us to buy a full page ad in *NY Times* to run an editorial blasting them for what he expects their coverage & editorial to be. Also wants us ready to hit at all the TV networks for commentators' knocking the speech. . . ."[27]

"Nov. 3: The big day. . . . Did a great job on the air—content superb, delivery very good, with a few fluffs. Commentary after was mixed. Worst were Marvin Kalb & Bill Lawrence. Both seemed to be stunned—apparently really expected a major move. Then started a long night of phone calls. From 10:15 to 1:15 he was on & off at least 15–20 times. Started wanting to know what we were doing for all out counterattack (while nets were still commenting). . . . Then hit network mgmt for biased reports. . . . Then a plea—if only do one thing get 100 vicious dirty calls to *NY Times* & *Washington Post* re their editorials (even though no idea what they'll be)."[28]

Nixon wrote: "The message of my November 3 speech was that we were going to keep our commitment in Vietnam. We were going to continue fighting until the Communists agreed to negotiate a fair and honorable peace or until the South Vietnamese were able to defend themselves on their own—whichever came first."[29] As usual, the networks were provided copies of the speech in advance so they would have an opportunity to prepare their coverage, with the speech embargoed until it was actually given. Nixon had enlisted the help of Kissinger to make sure the press was briefed well in advance about its importance to the peace process.

Kissinger wrote that the speech "proved one of Nixon's strongest public performances. . . . It appealed to the 'great silent majority' of Americans to support their Commander-in-Chief. For the first time in a Presidential statement it spelled out clearly what the President meant when he said he had 'a plan to end the war'—namely the dual-track strategy of Vietnamization and negotiations."[30] Nixon referred in his speech to a letter he had received from Ho Chi Minh, the North Vietnamese leader, and said it offered nothing new toward peace. It was a significant observation about the attitude of the North Vietnamese leadership and their interest in a negotiated peace.[31]

Immediately following the broadcast, the networks provided "instant analysis." NBC correspondent Edwin Newman reported there was nothing new in the speech. Marvin Kalb of CBS went further. He said those who were not so willing to trust the President to get an honorable end to the war "will point out the absence of a new announcement on troop withdrawals or a definite timetable for total withdrawal of U.S. forces, and they may disagree with the President's judgment that the Ho Chi Minh letter was a flat rejection." Kalb said the letter contained some of the "softest, most accommodating language found in a Communist document concerning the war in Vietnam in recent years."[32] ABC correspondent Bill Lawrence also reported there was nothing new in the speech, and W. Averell Harriman was presented as a commentator.[33] Harriman was a leading Democratic figure, had negotiated with the North Vietnamese in Paris and expressed doubts about Nixon's approach. His appearance enraged Nixon and his staff.[34] But, particularly, the viewing public had no chance to reflect on what the President had said before being told by purportedly impartial newsmen that Nixon was wrong, and even not to be believed.

Nixon claimed he did not listen to the TV commentators, but the rest of the family did and "they were livid with anger. They said that the comment and analyses broadcast by the network news correspondents criticized both my words and my motives. Instead of presenting impartial summaries of what I had said and cross sections of political and public reaction, most of the reporters talked about the speech they thought I should have given."[35]

Dean Burch, by now the Chairman of the FCC, immediately called the heads of the three networks for transcripts of their commentators' remarks. This could be seen as a demand by a Nixon appointee for a government look at news content, to review it against some government agenda. That his request did not follow FCC agency procedures added to the force of the inquiry. Usually, the FCC staff asked in writing for material after receipt of a complaint. But this was a demand by the FCC Chairman. There was no doubt of its White House source. Klein and Ziegler told correspondents that, in the future, copies of instant analysis should be sent to the White House as well as to the FCC.[36] Inside the White House, Nixon asked for Burch's report on the networks.[37]

The print press saw the issue much as the broadcast press. The *New York Times* editorial on November 4 began, "President Nixon disappointed the nation's hope . . .". It reported, "The President resisted most of the critics' advice for a bold new initiative or announcement, such as a unilateral cease-fire or a public timetable for withdrawal." Other articles reported that "a common reaction among the doves . . . was that the President had chartered no new courses that might lead to an early end to the conflict. . . . Senator George Aiken of Vermont who had been calming his fellow doves 'acknowledged there was not anything new.' " John R. Coleman, the President of Haverford University, who had coordinated a letter to Mr. Nixon from presidents of 82 private colleges and universities a month before, urging a stepped-up timetable for withdrawal, said he was "heart sick." Mrs. Martin Luther King said Mr. Nixon was "trying to end the massive opposition to the war rather than seeking to end the war itself."[38]

But whatever the press criticism, the response of the public across the country was clear. It was a Nixon triumph. He wrote, "there were signs that the critics and the commentators were unrepresentative of public opinion. The White House switchboard had been lighted up from the minute I left the air. The calls continued for hours, and soon the first waves of telegrams began to arrive. . . . By morning the public reaction was confirmed. The White House mail room reported the biggest response ever to any presidential speech. More than 50,000 telegrams and 30,000 letters had poured in, and the percentage of critical messages among them was low. A Gallup telephone poll taken immediately after the speech showed 77 percent approval."[39]

In his diary, Haldeman wrote: "Nov. 5: Had lot of ideas on things to be done mainly in the area of hitting back at the nets for their biased coverage of the speech. . . . P. kept calling me in in between each event with more follow up on anti TV. Especially interested in Dean Burch project—having all nets turn in to him the transcripts of their Mon. nite coverage & analysis of P. speech. Really has them shook."[40]

Nixon wrote, "The outpouring of popular support had a direct impact on congressional opinion. By November 12, 300 members of the House of Representatives—119 Democrats and 181 Republicans—had co-sponsored a resolution of support for my Vietnam policies. Fifty-eight senators—21 Democrats and 37 Republicans—had signed letters expressing similar sentiments. . . . Now, for a time at least, the enemy could no longer count on dissent in America to give them the victory they could not win on the battlefield. I had the public support I needed to continue a policy of waging war in Vietnam and negotiating for peace in Paris until we could bring the war to an honorable and successful conclusion."[41] The feared impact of the television and print press criticism did not materialize. The public made its own judgment. But Nixon was under no illusions. "My speech had not proposed any new initiatives; its purpose had been to gain support for the course we were already following. I knew that under the constant pounding from the media and our critics in Congress people would soon be demanding that new actions be taken to produce programs and end the war."[42]

He then made the decision that was to create a particularly hostile atmosphere for the television press. With his public standing at an all-time high, Nixon concluded he would go after the television networks. A few days after the November 3 speech, Buchanan sent Nixon a memo urging a direct attack on the network commentators for their unfavorable responses and drafted a speech to be given by Vice President Agnew. Nixon agreed and personally rewrote it to sharpen and better marshall its arguments. He concluded his covering memo with the comment, "This really flicks the scab off, doesn't it?"[43]

In his memoirs, Nixon wrote of a loftier objective: "One result of the unexpected success of the November 3 speech was the decision to take on the TV network news organizations for their biased and distorted 'instant analysis' and coverage. Unless the practice were challenged, it would make it impossible for a President to appeal directly to the people, something I considered to be of the essence of democracy."[44]

Agnew was scheduled to speak to a meeting of Republicans in Des Moines, Iowa, on November 13. At the last minute, it was decided to have him deliver the speech during his appearance there.[45]

From Haldeman's diary: "Nov. 12: P. really pleased & highly amused by Agnew speech for tomorrow nite. Worked over some changes with Buchanan; couldn't contain his mirth as he thought about it. Will be a bomb shell & the repercussions may be enormous—but it says what people think."[46]

The networks learned of it only hours before it was to be given. Each concluded it was newsworthy. Beyond that, they did not want to appear to be denying the administration an opportunity to be heard, particularly when an attack was being made on the networks themselves. Stanton says, "I was out in Santa Monica at a trustees meeting when I got a call from either Dick Jencks or Dick Salant saying that this was coming up. They had just found out about it and they knew something about what was going to be in it. It was also going to come up right at the time of the evening news. There was no way we could cover it as a news item because we didn't have it yet. Had Agnew done that at a noontime speech we probably would not have covered it live. We would have taken excerpts for the evening news if we had been given a copy of it. To cover it live would mean preempting our nightly news in some markets and entertainment programming in others. If the speech turned out to be something that was not necessary, then we would have lost our regular news time and revenue and audience, but we had to make that decision and I would rather err on the side of too much than too little. There's just no substitute for disclosure. We laughed a little bit about Agnew, but we knew he was out there as a hatchet man and knew he wasn't doing that on his own."

In Des Moines, the public broadcast station was recording the Republican meeting and had an outgoing line in place. The networks quickly hooked into that and on November 13, 1969, Agnew's attack on the network news organizations was aired in full and live across the country. Nixon's memoirs reflect his own view of the speech: "For thirty minutes, Agnew tore into the unaccountable power in the hands of the 'unelected elite' of network newsmen. . . . A small group of men, numbering perhaps no more than a dozen anchormen, commentators, and executive producers, settle upon the film and commentary that is to reach the public. They decide what forty to fifty million Americans will learn of the day's events in the nation and in the world."[47]

Agnew's initial point was that President Nixon had delivered the most important address of his administration on the subject of Vietnam with the hope that he could "rally the American people to see the conflict through to a lasting and just peace in the Pacific. . . . [but then] his words and policies were subjected to instant analysis and querulous criticism. The audience of 70 million Americans gathered to hear the President of the United States was inherited by a small band of network commentators and self-appointed analysts, the majority of whom expressed in one way or another their hostility to what he had to say. . . .

"We do know that to a man these commentators and producers live and work in the geographical and intellectual confines of Washington, D.C., or New York City. The American people would rightly not tolerate this concentration of power in government. Is it not fair and relevant to question its concentration in the hands of a tiny, enclosed fraternity of privileged men elected by no one and enjoying a monopoly sanction that is licensed by a government? . . . The views of the majority of this fraternity do not—and I repeat, not represent the views of America. As for other American institutions, perhaps it is time that the networks were made more responsive to the views of the nation and more responsible to the people they serve." It was the phrase "made more responsive to the views of the nation" that was to strike the network chiefs as particularly ominous.[48]

Nixon wrote, "Within a few hours telegrams began arriving at the White House; the switchboards were tied up all night by people calling to express their relief that someone had finally spoken up, and within a few days thousands of letters began pouring in from all over the country. The networks purposely ignored the widespread public support Agnew's words received and tried to label the speech as an attempt at government 'repression.' The President of CBS, Frank Stanton, called it 'an unprecedented attempt by the Vice President of the United States to intimidate a news medium which depends for its existence upon government licenses.' The President of NBC, Julian Goodman, said that Agnew's 'attack on television news is an appeal to prejudice.' George McGovern reflected left-wing and liberal congressional reaction when he said, 'I feel that the speech was perhaps the most frightening single statement ever to come from a high government official in my public career.' "[49] Dean Burch said Agnew's remarks were "thoughtful, provocative and deserve careful consideration by the industry."[50]

Stanton says he was invited to have lunch with Agnew after the Des Moines speech. "It was just a recital on his part of much of what he had said. He was warning us on what the government might do if we didn't behave ourselves."

Operators of the affiliated stations publicly declared support for the network news divisions, but some quietly told reporters that there was a lot in what Agnew said. One Los Angeles–based network vice president told *Broadcasting* magazine: "Don't quote me because my opinion, of course, is drastically different from that of my home office in New York. But I'll tell you this—Agnew's blast was a long time coming. Why, these news guys, even in my own place, get away with murder."[51]

On November 14, the *New York Times* broke the story of the earlier Burch request for transcripts of the network correspondents' instant analysis. The *Times* article noted that there was wide agreement in broadcasting circles that Agnew's attack on television "would bring to a climax the years of argument over the visual medium's access to the news and its mode of presentation. Their common theme was that the Nixon administration and Congress were using TV as a target because the Federal licenses of stations come up for renewal every three years. . . . In their bitterness last night several minor TV executives likened Vice President Agnew's complaint to Gen. Charles de Gaulle's use of French television as purely a propaganda device."

Herb Klein added to the impact. He appeared on the CBS program *Face the Nation* three days after the Agnew speech and said, "All the news media needs to re-examine itself . . . if you fail [to do so] . . . you invite the government to come in. I would not like to see that happen." Some saw this as a threat—if you don't cooperate, we will make you cooperate. Reached by telephone later by the *New York Times*, Mr. Klein said that any industry failing to examine itself "opens the door for unscrupulous politicians to move in." He said, "the Nixon administration had no intention to do so and that his remarks were an observation, not a threat."[52]

On November 15, the network evening news coverage virtually ignored the fact that an estimated several hundred thousand Americans gathered in Washington for one of the largest anti-war demonstrations in the nation's history. There are of course a multiplicity of forces at work in arriving at news judgments, but certainly the government and even public attitudes toward the network news' coverage of the antiwar movement had turned more hostile. The networks' decision not to cover this protest as they had covered smaller demonstrations before suggests Nixon's White House was having an effect.

Dan Rather of CBS reported that Agnew's attack was causing concern among journalists. He said the President's staff had been telephoning television stations after Nixon's speeches to check on their treatment of his remarks and had asked that copies of any editorial comment be sent to the White House. At least 20 such calls were made to stations around the country after the President's November 3 address, most from Herb Klein's office. When CBS News correspondent Eric Sevareid commented on Agnew's speech about television coverage in a station interview in Phoenix, Arizona, the FCC telephoned the station and asked to hear a complete audiotape of Sevareid's remarks.[53]

The FCC took up the "instant analysis" issue but declined to act, in part because of earlier publicly stated policy positions. The FCC opinion letter of November 22 noted there had been complaints of news bias and distortion in network "instant analysis" and also complaints of possible government intimidation of the press. The FCC said its long-standing position was that its role was to see that a forum was open for the expression of all points of view, and its policy was not to interfere upon allegations of distortion, unless there was "extrinsic evidence" of bias outside the report itself. It was the FCC's judgment that government intervention to prove distortion based only on the material broadcast would likely constitute "a worse danger than the possible rigging itself." It did not speak to the question of intimidation.[54]

Senator Thomas Dodd (D-Conn.) joined in the debate to say that an inquiry into the power of the press might be in order. Senator Mike Mansfield of Montana, the Democratic majority leader, responded that he felt the press on the whole had done a fair job. Fred Friendly, Professor of Broadcast Journalism at Columbia University, pointed out that ABC's use of Harriman was hardly surprising. Senator Homer Capehart, an Indiana Republican, had critiqued Kennedy's Berlin crisis speech of 1961, and Republican Minority Leaders Everett Dirksen and Gerald Ford criticized Johnson's speeches often. "It was all part of the democratic process."[55] The attack on instant analysis calmed for the moment but was soon to appear again.

On December 16, Nixon announced he would withdraw 50,000

troops by April 15, which would bring the total to 110,000 since Nixon took office. The *New York Times* reported, "TV COMMENTS ON TALK ARE BRIEF AND FACTUAL. Television networks criticized for their 'instant analysis' of President's Nixon's speech on Vietnam in November, carried brief comments or none at all following his announcement today of additional troop withdrawals. Their statements were brief and much like the reports that followed the President's televised news conference Dec. 8. . . . For the most part, the network newsmen who appeared immediately after the President simply summarized Mr. Nixon's brief report on the war situation."[56] It appeared the television press was pulling back.

Agnew continued his part of the campaign and broadened it to include some of the print press. The *Washington Post* reported on February 22, 1970: "AGNEW REJECTS CALLS TO 'LOWER MY VOICE.' " Agnew vowed that he would not heed suggestions from critics because loyal-abiding Americans wanted someone to express their dissatisfaction with dissenters. Hubert Humphrey, in a speech to the Democratic Policy Council in Washington, charged that the Vice President's attacks were part of the Nixon administration's pattern of "executive arrogance, public relations gimmickry and blatant intimidation of the news media." Accusing Agnew of waging "media guerilla warfare," Humphrey said, "Nixon is condoning it. The public airways are repeatedly usurped by the President for partisan advantage, while lesser lights in the administration are dispatched to attack and intimidate the network news organizations."[57]

Nixon tried to keep his distance in public from Agnew's attacks. At his December 9, 1969, press conference, when asked about the Agnew speech and the subsequent speeches attacking the networks, Nixon said, "The Vice President does not clear his speeches with me," and added that Agnew had addressed the problem of unfair television news coverage in a "dignified and courageous way."[58]

The public was uncertain. According to an August survey done for *Time* magazine by a Louis Harris poll, "A third of those questioned distrusted television news." An ABC poll conducted shortly after the Agnew Des Moines speech showed 51 percent agreed with Agnew. The "Alfred I. duPont–Columbia University Survey of Broadcast Journalism" for 1969–1970 reported that "despite this weight in favor of Agnew [in the ABC poll], only one quarter felt that the news media had been unfair to the administration, while three-fifths felt they had not been unfair and should not ease up."[59]

Behind the scenes, there was still deeper hostility toward the television press. Early on Nixon had stressed to Haldeman that television "[is] all that matters."[60] In a *Life* magazine article about the retirement of Chet Huntley from NBC News, Huntley was quoted as critical of Nixon, saying, "The shallowness of the man overwhelms me."[61] Higby of the White House staff wrote Magruder about their subsequent attack on Huntley: "The point behind this whole thing is that we don't care about Huntley—he is going to leave already. What we are trying to do here is to tear down the institution."[62]

Charles W. Colson joined the White House staff in November 1969. As Special Counsel to the President, he became something of a Nixon favorite. Nixon's hobby was politics, and he liked to talk to Colson about it. Colson had been a Marine. He was tough and intensely loyal to Nixon. He would ultimately take over some of Klein's role, and he became Nixon's point man against the networks. He says that he reviewed with Nixon all his dealings with them.[63]

Leonard Garment, Counsel to the President, says that those familiar with Nixon's outbursts ignored his more extreme instructions, but Colson did not. White House Press Secretary Ronald Ziegler says, "I don't think that the fact that Colson went out and did what President Nixon said, and others stopped and waited, means much of anything except that if Colson had stopped and waited, something else would have taken place."[64] Colson was to write years later that "Vice President Agnew's verbal assault on the press rallied the silent majority but unfortunately solidified the antagonism of most journalists toward us. As the networks became merciless in their nightly barrages against the Vietnam War and Nixon policies, we in turn lost our capacity to be objective, seeing ourselves more and more the victim of a conspiracy by the press. Our attitude hardened newsmen's convictions that we were bent on destroying the free press. Thus the cycle continued."[65]

William Safire, who was part of the White House circle, saw a far greater presidential determination to intimidate the press. "Was there a conspiracy . . . on the part of the Nixon Administration to discredit and malign the press? Was this so-called 'anti-media' campaign encouraged, directed, and urged on by the President himself? Did this alleged campaign to defame and intimidate Nixon-hating newsmen succeed, isolating and weakening them politically? . . . [T]he answer to all these questions is, sadly, yes." Safire writes, "I must have heard Richard Nixon say, 'The press is the enemy' a dozen times."[66]

Chapter 8

Opposition Programming and *The Selling of the Pentagon*

In June 1970, Stanton proposed an opportunity for the political opposition to be heard and to provide a partial balance to what had become President Nixon's virtual domination of the airways. The Nixon reaction (headed by Charles W. Colson) was swift and effective, and the FCC was activated to stop it.

During the first eighteen months of their administrations, President Eisenhower had appeared on prime time network television three times; President Kennedy, four times; and President Johnson, seven times. By June 1970, Nixon had appeared on prime time network television fourteen times. This was in addition to appearances on regularly scheduled news events. Nixon had achieved dominance of prime time (or at least substantial exposure) which the opposing party could not begin to match.

Stanton announced that CBS would inaugurate a series of prime-time programs, *The Loyal Opposition*, during which the political party not in office would have a chance to air its views. Stanton said that the President, speaking as the chief executive, has an authority that has no counterpart and there is inherent newsworthiness in anything he says. But he said CBS records indicated "a very pronounced increase in the use of prime time by the [incumbent] President." Therefore, CBS would provide the principal opposition party free prime time on television "to present the views anyway it sees fit." He believed that the Democratic National Committee (DNC) was the appropriate organization to use the political party's time because it represented the party as a whole. He also indicated that the option remained open to cover third parties, depending upon the circumstances. The DNC chose its chairman, Larry O'Brien, as its spokesman.

Herb Klein announced White House opposition to the grant of time. To say the Chairman of the DNC has "equal basis for answering the President doesn't make sense anyway." Klein added that if O'Brien had a constructive program to offer, he could do so under the terms of the Fairness Doctrine. The Republicans proposed instead that time be sold to the parties. Stanton rejected this idea because the advantage would accrue to the party with the largest war chest and the result would not necessarily be the enlightenment of the public, which was the objective.[1]

On July 7, in free time provided by CBS, O'Brien appeared on the CBS network and responded to a number of Nixon's speeches on issues such as the Vietnam War, the economy, civil rights, and crime. The White House was infuriated. Klein said, "He just attacked the President." Under Colson's direction, the White House promptly had the Republican National Committee (RNC) file a complaint with the FCC demanding Equal Time or the equivalent under the Fairness Doctrine. But that would simply recreate the imbalance in access which the CBS offer was seeking to correct.

In the *Red Lion* case, the Supreme Court had held that broadcast programming and news could be regulated because the FCC's doctrines would provide "robust debate." On the face of it, the Stanton offer to provide free time to the opposition party to provide opposing views and debate fit regulatory and judicial objectives. It might have been applauded by a bipartisan agency, but that was not the FCC's reaction.

When the RNC filed its complaint with the FCC, it was appearing before a federal agency whose chairman and a majority of commissioners were Republicans, appointed by the President. Charles Colson says, "The President and I believed that Frank Stanton's 'Loyal Opposition' program was totally politically motivated, in poor taste, and biased in its presentation. I talked to Dean Burch about it. Dean's response was very professional. We did have a legitimate complaint."[2] The FCC decided that since the DNC had been given free time by the CBS network, the RNC had to be given an equal chance to respond to the DNC. CBS appealed.[3]

The White House pursued the question. Colson reported the FCC decision was an important win. He wrote Haldeman, "It is obvious that the other side is really being hurt as they begin to understand the FCC decisions. The Democratic National Committee is using every procedural move (and CBS is cooperating) to stay the decision. . . . I think it is time for us to generate again a PR campaign against the Democrats and CBS. . . . Obviously, CBS programs such as 'The Loyal Opposition' and other similar programs talked about by the other two networks would defeat the primary objective of the Nixon news domination campaign."[4]

In September 1970, Nixon sent Colson to meet with the network heads, Paley, Goodman and Goldenson, to stop the grant of any further prime time to the Democrats. Colson reported: "[W]ith their economic fortunes held on a tight tether by the Federal Communications Commission, the three men were unusually accommodating. The significance of my visit was not lost on them. We engineered a successful legal challenge to a 'loyal opposition' series giving free TV time to Democrats and believed we had tamed our foe."[5]

Colson also reported the networks were "apprehensive about us. . . . To my surprise CBS did not deny that the news had been slanted against us. Paley merely said that every administration has felt the same way and that we have been slower in coming to them to complain than our predecessors. He, however, ordered Stanton in my presence to review the analysis with me and if the news has not been balanced to see that the situation is immediately corrected. . . . In short, they are very much afraid of us and are trying hard to prove they are 'good guys.'

"Paley made the point that he was amazed at how many people agree with the Vice President's criticism of the networks. He also went out of his way to say how much he supports the President, and how popular the President is. . . . The only ornament on Goodman's desk was the Nixon Inaugural Medal. [Goodman says this was put there as a joke and clearly not his desk's customary ornament. Colson apparently missed Goodman's humor. The NBC Executive Vice President and chief of staff, David Adams, says Goodman was very firm in resisting Colson's threats.[6]] . . . Hagerty said in Goldenson's presence that ABC is 'with us.' This all adds up to the fact that they are damned nervous and scared and we should continue to take a very tough line, face to face, and in other ways."[7] When this report became public during the Senate Watergate hearings, all three networks voiced disagreement with it. Their recollection of the meetings was different.[8]

Colson later wrote Haldeman that he had worked out a plan with Chairman Burch, who had suggested a future filing be made when Burch had a 4–3 majority. A request for time to respond to the President would be turned down, and this would establish "that no one had the right to reply to the President."[9]

An appellate court ultimately reversed the FCC's decision granting reply time to the RNC for *The Loyal Opposition* with a condemnation sharply critical of the FCC's reasoning. It upheld Stanton's grant of time to the DNC. But Herb Klein says Colson's filing was successful, even though the courts ultimately reversed the FCC. He believes it perhaps "slowed down CBS in moving to grant other equal time opportunities to the Democrats." He also notes that Paley ultimately abandoned *The Loyal Opposition*.[10]

During 1970, the President continued to pressure the networks. For example, Haldeman's notes reflect Nixon's comments:

7/19	shdn't Agnew kick nets again
10/8	give CBS a rap re coverage after speech
10/9–11	Colson talked to Paley
	Paley agreed it was bad reporting & apologized—had already taken steps[11]

Colson wrote Haldeman on November 17, 1970, "Through Dean Burch we should keep heavy regulation pressures building. The networks are fully aware that we can influence the FCC in policy matters and this is a cause of great concern to them." He also noted that Julian Goodman had made three speeches "warning of the danger of government interference and political pressure on the networks."[12]

In the new year, 1971, Nixon held his own meetings with each of the networks. Colson wrote of the CBS meeting on March 9, presumably with an eye to Nixon's views. "(Fairness Doctrine problems were discussed and the President) made reference to the fact that any change in policies (on prime-time coverage) ought to be prospective and not retroactive—that if we lived on the outside with certain rules, those rules shouldn't be changed now because we happen to be on the inside (this was an obvious reference to Stanton and his attempt to start a loyal opposition series). The President looked directly at Stanton during this part of this meeting but Stanton said nothing. . . . (After discussions about Dean Burch and some broadcast issues) The President . . . told the CBS Executives that I was his 'expert' in this field and that I was a lawyer. Paley had earlier made reference to my meetings with him in New York. The significance of the President's reference was not at all lost on the CBS Executives. Stanton looked visibly taken aback by this comment and I am sure he fully understood its implication."[13]

"Within the White House everyone thought Bill Paley was a great friend," recalls Herb Klein. "He was seen as a lord of the industry who kept himself separate. There was no animosity centered on Paley, because everyone felt he wasn't controlling the direction of the news." While at one time NBC has been seen as the most critical, by 1971 Klein recalls "everyone in the White House felt CBS was against them. Their anger was aimed at Frank Stanton and Walter Cronkite and Dan Rather [then CBS's White House correspondent]. The general feeling was that CBS was the most anti-administration of the networks."[14] But all were targets. Nixon told Haldeman in his meeting on February 6, 1971, "Be sure to hit networks. Top level. Use our biggest guns."[15]

Klein respected Stanton. "From my standpoint, one of the most able broadcast . . . executives I have known is Dr. Frank Stanton. . . . Whenever Stanton perceived that CBS or the broadcast industry was under attack, he would leap into the battle with both fists flying, maneuvering with the skill one attaches only to a professional boxer. At that point friendship was placed apart and the battle would be waged impersonally according to what Stanton believed to be the right principles."[16]

When CBS News broadcast *The Selling of the Pentagon*, Vice President Agnew had attacked it, saying that the public "cannot rely on CBS documentaries for facts." Klein was also critical of it. "I thought it represented a biased attempt to slur the military public information program in Vietnam in 1971. CBS frequently took advantage of the services of the very information assistance program it was condemning. I looked at this as a double standard." As for the Staggers hearings, when critical Congressmen tried to subpoena outtakes, "I strongly opposed this as a violation of a newsman's right of editing and of reporting. I supported CBS because this was the TV equivalent of subpoenaing a reporter's notes. . . . I persuaded the President to side with the network president publicly as a matter of principle."[17] At Klein's urging, Nixon had not publicly supported the subpoena but it was his personal view that Stanton should be held in contempt.[18] Behind the scenes he supported the Staggers effort.

In March 1971, Colson had reported that Chairman Hébert would hold congressional hearings on *The Selling of the Pentagon* to investigate the issue of CBS "integrity." He wrote, "It seems to me that our side should use this as an opportunity to raise serious doubts in the public mind about network reporting. We are entirely on solid ground and therefore should not in any way be reluctant to press our case (through the Pentagon, of course)."[19]

On March 14, Nixon told Haldeman that CBS was very "negative"; he should get someone to work on it and Colson should "call Stanton." On March 30, Nixon told Haldeman to send a copy of the *Washington Post* editorial criticizing the CBS editing in *The Selling of the Pentagon* to "every newspaper and TV station and to all Congressmen and Senators, etc." Colson also had it circulated at the NAB Convention. On March 31, Nixon ordered Haldeman to get from J. Edgar Hoover, head of the FBI, a "rundown on top CBS people, Kalb, Salant, etc." Nixon told Haldeman to have some "good letters" on CBS from high-level people sent to *Barron's* magazine, which had been severely critical of CBS and *The Selling of the Pentagon.*[20]

Staggers had written to the FCC on March 9, asking what action it planned to take about *The Selling of the Pentagon*. He assumed that the FCC would find deception. On April 28 the FCC said it had no evidence of deliberate distortion and therefore no authority to intervene.[21] This refusal of the FCC to take action surprised virtually everyone. Staggers had expected a blast from the FCC. So did the White House. The Subcommittee staff thought the FCC opinion was "pathetic."[22]

The FCC noted that CBS presented an hour-long news special on April 18 for the stated purpose of affording an opportunity for contrasting viewpoints. "Lacking extrinsic evidence or documents that on their face reflect deliberate distortion, we believe that the government licensing agency cannot properly intervene." It said the broadcaster's editorial judgment may not be beyond criticism, but the FCC could not act as a censor and it believed its intervention would be a remedy far worse than the disease.

Since CBS had failed to address the questions raised by the technique of splicing together answers to various questions as a way of creating a new answer, the FCC urged broadcast journalists to ponder the questions raised. Because of its noncensorial policy, however, the FCC said it did not propose to question CBS further on this issue.

Staggers could not understand how the FCC could back away from a finding of distortion. He contemplated summoning Burch before the Subcommittee with the thought that the FCC could be made to see the light, but then decided against it.[23]

The FCC did ask CBS to submit more information on how it had fulfilled its obligation under the Fairness Doctrine to present all sides of a controversial issue. On May 17, CBS responded that it had presented contrasting views and listed the coverage it had provided. The FCC concluded that the network had afforded "reasonable opportunity for presentation of contrasting views" and said, "CBS has not failed to comply with the requirements of the Fairness Doctrine."[24]

The personal views of Chairman Burch were quite different from the FCC public decision. The FCC Broadcast Bureau had recommended investigating CBS for "deliberately" distorting the Henkin interview, using the editing itself as proof of an intent to deceive. Burch wanted to "lash the network," according to the *Wall Street Journal*, in a letter prepared but never sent because a majority of the seven-member commission wouldn't approve. Burch would have condemned CBS for refusing to admit "that editing techniques such as 'spliced' interviews might mislead viewers."

"What seems to be at work here, on the part of CBS," Burch wrote in his draft opinion, "is sheer hubris—overweening pride and even arrogance that simply will not allow of the possibility that error may have occurred, and that leads to the knee-jerk response of closing ranks against the critics, of 'we can refute all charges.' " The *Journal* reported that Burch also would have suggested "government intervention" if erring broadcasters didn't shape up. Although Burch disclaimed censorship intentions, the sharp tone he struck alarmed even some close allies, including Commissioner Robert Wells, who hesitated to approve even a softened second draft. Commissioner Thomas J. Houser, an Illinois Republican, had been appointed to fill an unexpired term which would end in a month. Since the three Democratic commissioners were united in opposition to Burch, he needed support from all three of his fellow Republicans to send his letter. But Houser asked for more time. "Mr. Burch fumed, in exasperation flinging his pack of cigarettes on the table. His intended letter, it was clear, couldn't command a majority. 'Houser put his renomination on the line right there,' one insider concluded."[25]

At the White House, Colson reported the FCC decision as a slam at CBS. Burch had kept Nixon informed and Colson wrote Haldeman on April 29, 1971, "You might enjoy reading the Commission's decision on the Selling of the Pentagon case. As Dean Burch indicated to the President, there was no basis to find 'deliberate distortion' as defined in the law. But the mere laying out of the facts, as he has done, clearly shows the deplorable editing techniques which CBS used. This should be considered as a serious black eye for them, although they will play it as if they were cleared." He wrote another White House staff member that the FCC gave CBS "a real rap on the knuckles by showing that they did indeed fudge in editing the tape. I don't know whether this has moved on the wires or not, but it is a good story and should be gotten out. If you get it out, be sure not to have it in any way traceable back to the White House, and be sure whoever writes the story really sticks it in to CBS as they deserve."[26]

The judgment of the news professionals was quite at odds with that of Chairman Burch, Chairman Staggers and Colson. For example, the CBS documentary, which had already received a Peabody Award, received an Emmy award on May 7 for "outstanding achievement in news documentary programming." Stanton said, "great pressure has been put on us in television news particularly us at CBS and this helps to ease that pressure."[27]

The Special Subcommittee then held an executive hearing to admit an affidavit from Colonel John A. MacNeil, who had given the lecture in Peoria, Illinois, favoring a military buildup in Southeast Asia. He stated he had no objection to any of the recordings or other material now in the possession of CBS being made available to the Subcommittee. On May 12, The Honorable Daniel Z. Henkin, Assistant Secretary of Defense (Public Affairs), made a formal statement to the Special Subcommittee. He insisted throughout that it was his deep personal conviction, and he added, one shared by Secretary of Defense Laird, as he had recently told the American Newspaper Publisher's Association, that "a strong, free country and a strong, free press go hand-in-hand." In an extraordinary statement for a witness called for the prosecution, Henkin insisted on the importance and value of television news coverage to the American people. And he did not support Staggers on the subpoena of outtakes. He said he believed that those who worked on the show operated under the full privileges of the First Amendment and he believed in the "sanctity" of the First Amendment "for all information media."

He positioned his criticism in these words: "I have never questioned the integrity of CBS News. . . . I was disappointed and concerned by the doctoring of words and the misrepresentations in this particular show. . . . The producer decided to edit and distort some of my words with a result that I was perhaps seen as having made an accusation. It was, in fact, the producer who made the accusation by his directing of my words." Attached to the Henkin statement was a comparison of the CBS interview as broadcast, with the original interview, together with comments previously supplied by Henkin in a letter to Honorable Edward Hébert dated March 4, 1971.[28]

Henkin's complete transcript of his interview with Mudd had been placed in the *Congressional Record*, but this was a two-edged proposition. It was said it was "documentation" of "distortion." But it also established, on the record, that the Subcommittee already had the outtakes it was subpoenaing.

On May 26, the Special Subcommittee met again in executive session. It voted to rescind its earlier subpoena, determining that CBS had satisfactorily responded to all but one requirement of its original summons, that is, the outtakes from the interviews that were broadcast. It issued a new subpoena calling for those outtakes and the personal appearance of Dr. Frank Stanton, President of CBS. The new subpoena made it clear that films related to interviews or events which had not been, even in part, in the actual broadcast were now excluded from the demand. The subpoena was not calling for reporters' notes or internal CBS memoranda. The Subcommittee thus improved its position for any court challenge, and Stanton noted at the time that he had lost the argument of an overly broad subpoena. The Subcommittee issued a press release pointing out that it could not be said to be seeking the private thoughts and impressions of a reporter. But significantly, Stanton had now been served with a subpoena to appear personally.[29]

Herb Klein commented upon the Subcommittee's new subpoena, "I believe this is wrong and an infringement on freedom of the press. It could lead to further subpoenas of a reporter's notes." He said he was "not in favor of further restrictions" on the communication media. "There has been no effort to intimidate the industry and there will be none." Klein went on to say that government officials, such as Vice President Agnew, have a right to criticize the news industry if they see a wrong, but the criticism should not be in the form of "coercion." Chairman Burch also opposed the subpoena.[30]

On June 2, Vice President Agnew was nonetheless to advance the attack in a speech to the National Advisory Board of the Mutual Broadcasting System. He objected to the cry of "intimidation," and he supported the Staggers Subcommittee effort. Agnew made light of charges that the administration was engaged in the "most formidable" challenge to a free press since colonial times. The President of Sigma Delta Chi, the journalism fraternity, said the media welcomed the administration's criticism, but not threats. The Vice President said, "Criticism of the media was neither new nor partisan. He said it was significant that it was a Democrat-controlled congressional Subcommittee of the House Commerce Committee that was investigating editing techniques used in the Columbia Broadcasting System's documentary, *The Selling of the Pentagon.*" Rather than respond constructively to charges of distortions or inadequacy, the media tended to yell "intimidation." And he particularly objected to the Emmy award given to CBS for *The Selling of the Pentagon.* "If the judges honestly thought that program merited an Emmy and didn't award it out of spite, then I am surprised."[31]

At the White House, Nixon was watching the Staggers proceeding. He had discussed proposed antitrust suits against the networks with Haldeman on April 21, saying they would "screw the networks good," but he decided they should not be brought up now because it "looks like a reaction to *Selling Pentagon*—[but] under no circumstances is it to be dropped."[32]

Beyond that, the administration saw how it could get at some of the print press through their broadcast properties. Some newspapers, such as the *Washington Post*, owned broadcast stations and in early 1970, an application was filed to deny renewal of the *Post*'s broadcast license for its Miami station, WPLG-TV, Channel 10. The challenge was filed by W. Sloan McCrea, a business acquaintance of Nixon and a partner of Bebe Rebozo, a Nixon confidant. WPLG-TV had an outstanding record in public affairs and news programming, and its performance was exactly what the Communications Act and the FCC sought. To most it was obvious that the challenge was an attempt to intimidate the *Post.* Ultimately the challenge was settled.[33]

Certainly, the risk to CBS and its licenses was significant. Stanton reported on it to the CBS shareholders meeting on April 21, 1971. He says he was "meticulous" in keeping Paley and the CBS Board of Directors advised. He remembers Paley as "nervous" about the risks, but several Board members were strong in their support of Stanton's stand. These included Robert Lovett, former Secretary of Defense and Deputy Secretary of State; Joseph Iglehart, an investment banker;

Millicent McIntosh, former President of Barnard College; and Henry Schacht, Chairman of Cummins Engines.

Klein says there were those in the White House who were determined to suppress critical news reports. "I played a moderating role. Had I not," he says, "things would have gotten very ugly."[34]

Nixon told Haldeman that the "press and TV don't change unless you hurt them. They are not honorable men—so you can't reason with them."[35] He "accused them, cursed them, tried to intimidate them."[36] There was no reflection on the place of the press in the American system. The government purpose in attacking *The Loyal Opposition* programming and the news documentary *The Selling of the Pentagon* was to restrict the flow of news to the public. But these events saw little public reaction. Nixon was to say in 1973 to White House Counsel John Dean, "One hell of a lot of people don't give one damn about this issue of the suppression of the press."[37]

Chapter 9

Is This Fight Really Necessary?

The CBS position on *The Selling of the Pentagon* was not the customary approach to a Washington investigation. Some lobbyists thought the smart thing would be for CBS to find a fig leaf, a convenient coverall to hide sins, real or imagined, and then provide the outtakes. To make matters more difficult, CBS refused to defend the specific cuts it had made. The point of resisting was, after all, to establish First Amendment protection for the broadcast press against a review of the edits made. The defense of individual edits would have inherently agreed that the Congress could review the cuts. This was exactly what Stanton opposed as being detrimental to the future liberty of television news.

Peter Davis, the producer, did not testify nor did he give interviews about how he did the editing. He wanted to speak on the subject, because he believed his edits were fair, but Dick Salant persuaded him that the company had to speak with one voice, and that had to be the voice asserting First Amendment rights. Salant told Davis the fight would be difficult and in the congressional investigation underway, the network was "teetering." Salant persuaded Davis to withdraw from lecturing on the subject, reimbursing him for the fee he had to return for the one talk he had agreed to give. He was not heard from throughout the investigation.[1]

Davis now explains he was originally asked to research a program about the use of taxpayer funds for public relations programs run by government agencies. After canvassing a number of agencies, he chose the Pentagon because it appeared to have the largest public relations program and was also the one doing the most important work in terms of forming national opinion on significant issues. He was known as a producer who was best at presenting material which created emotion in the viewer, not simply an intellectual reaction. He contacted Senator J. William Fulbright's assistants, Norville Jones and Walter Pincus, who had a great deal of material which Fulbright had collected for his book *The Pentagon Propaganda Machine.*[2] Davis conducted his investigation over many months—and when he finished, the senior executives in the unit, as well as Perry Wolff, the Executive Producer, Bill Leonard, the head of the CBS News documentary unit, and Dick Salant believed it was an important program and a public service.

Davis asked Roger Mudd to anchor the program. At first Mudd refused, but when the script was completed and Mudd saw it, he agreed to serve as the on-air correspondent.[3] Davis insists he had no antagonism toward the military. He was doing a documentary about Pentagon propaganda conducted primarily by Pentagon civilians, not the armed forces, and there was a factual basis for every point made. The television program was carefully reviewed by a number of experienced newspeople. The Executive Producer, Wolff, was one of the best in the business; his review of the program was exhaustive. It was closely reviewed by others, including Burton Benjamin, the Senior Executive Producer, and Bill Leonard. Leonard says the program was vetted more than any he had ever participated in.[4] It was reviewed for accuracy and then again to make sure that it was fair and responsible. It was also reviewed by the CBS News lawyers for libel and the rights to use film footage. CBS knew the program was going to be controversial, and it was reviewed by still other senior journalists at the network. Dick Salant also reviewed it.[5]

Twenty-five years later, the cuts which critics claimed distorted interviews on the program do not seem as significant as they did in the heat of the 1971 investigation or the feeling of the times about the war coverage and concern about the power of the networks. But lifting sentences from answers to some questions and positioning them as responses given to other questions certainly changed the apparent sequence of an interview and could distort the meaning. And an inference was drawn by some from the rearrangement that it reflected a subjective bias against the military and the Pentagon.

When editing of film (or tape) is smoothly done, there is usually no way the viewer can know that an interview has been edited, or how. The public believes that what they see is in fact what the person said, and said in the sequence and the manner presented on the air. That "you see it as it is" is television's appeal and its power. But this was not totally the case in *The Selling of the Pentagon.* News programs must usually be edited and condensed. In this instance, the edits complained of were primarily in the portrayals of Pentagon colonels urging the continuation of the Vietnam War and an interview about the use of public information.

At the beginning of the Vietnam War, the domino theory was one of the reasons given for American military intervention: If the United States did not fight in Vietnam, that country would be overrun by communist aggressors, and we would then have to fight at the next point, say, Laos, or Cambodia, as country after country in Southeast Asia toppled. There had been widespread questioning of this theory and by 1971 it was no longer a tenet of U.S. foreign policy. This was the background for one of the program's charges.

The program reported that the Pentagon had what was described as "the traveling colonels" touring the country advocating support for the Vietnam War and a U.S. military presence in Southeast Asia. The colonels' lectures had been approved by the Pentagon under Directive AR360-5 para. 9, which required that those speaking in an official capacity "must have their material cleared for accuracy, propriety and consistency with national policy." Pentagon public relations officials say the understanding was that the colonels could quote civilian expressions of policy and then point out their military implications, but they were not permitted to advocate policy positions. However, problems arose in question-and-answer periods after the lectures, when the colonels spoke their views spontaneously.

Marine Colonel John A. MacNeil argued at a public meeting that the United States should remain in Southeast Asia and that there would be a bloodbath should our forces withdraw. He quoted from Souvanna Phouma, the Prince of Laos, on the need to keep aggression from spreading by stopping it in Vietnam. He later used his own words to the same effect. The program did not show that in the same speech from which the Colonel took his quote, the Prince of Laos also issued a warning against widening the war into Cambodia and Laos. But the program made no point of this.

When the producer of the television documentary used that part of the Colonel's lecture that invoked the domino theory in the Colonel's own words and urged the continued presence of the United States in Southeast Asia, the reference to the foreign leader's statement was omitted. The segment did not show the Colonel using the foreign leader as a source.

Complaint was also made about "rearrangements" in the interview with Assistant Secretary Daniel Z. Henkin, a deputy in charge of Public Affairs. He was a man with considerable experience with the print press and had a good reputation among reporters. Davis says he turned to Henkin as the logical person to speak for the Defense Department on the issues in the program. He wanted to get the Department's views from a single source, and dealing with the press was Henkin's official job. He says the reason he compressed Henkin's answers to a series of questions into a few condensed answers was not only because of time limitations, but because he also thought that the condensed answers more fully and strongly presented the Pentagon's overall view. Davis thought Henkin did not seem particularly experienced in handling a television interview and tended to ramble, but did cover what he wanted to say with no difficulty.[6]

Mudd had interviewed Henkin at some length, and two edits were charged with distorting Henkin's statements. At that time, "staging" of news was a major issue in broadcasting. This was in part because "staging" had been discovered in prior broadcasts. It was thought to be particularly offensive because it was a deliberate distortion. What appeared to have happened on television had actually been set up by the broadcaster for the program. This was not revealed to the viewer. Usually the viewer would not know that the segment had been staged and, from a regulator's point of view, this called out for legislation or regulation.

In *The Selling of the Pentagon*, Defense Department "news" film showed South Vietnamese attacking from river craft and apparently advancing against North Vietnamese troops, when in fact there were no defending troops. The entire segment was staged. The purpose of the film was to create the illusion that South Vietnamese were participating in the fighting. There was never any denial of this staging by the Pentagon. When asked about staged filming, Mr. Henkin responded that the Army was trying its best to provide information but "there undoubtedly have been times when certain actions have been staged. I think this is true of all TV news coverage. . . . After all, this interview here is being staged, as one might say." Of course the two are not equivalent, and Roger Mudd was quick to say so. Davis kept Henkin's point but edited out "as one might say." While the compression was useful, it was seen as changing a passing comment about the arrangements for the interview into a depiction of Henkin arguing that the staging of troop landings was no different than the arrangements made for his interview. It made Henkin look argumentative, or even evasive. Davis points out that it could be said Henkin was doing his job as a good public servant, the kind of job that does require evasiveness at times when dealing with the press.[7]

In the Henkin interview, Mudd asked the purpose of the military displays at state fairs. Henkin replied that it was "informing the public about their armed forces." He went on to say it had an ancillary benefit of stimulating recruiting. Later in the interview, he said there was an obligation to respond to requests from Kiwanis or Rotary groups and others for speakers. He later said these speakers would inform the American public about "how we spend these funds, what we are doing abut such problems as drugs (and) the racial problem in the armed forces. . . . I think the American public has a valid right to ask us these questions." Still later he added, "Now there are those who contend this is propaganda. I don't—do not agree with this."

The producer edited the interview so that following Mudd's question about the purpose of the state fair military displays, he used the first sentence of Henkin's answer, that it informs the public about their armed forces, and then added from later in the interview Henkin's statement that the public had a right to learn how the military was dealing with drug and racial problems.

When Mudd asked in the interview if information about the drug and racial problems gets passed out by sergeants at state fairs, Henkin replied that he wouldn't "limit" that to sergeants at state fairs and said, "I thought we were discussing speeches." During the editing, had this last sentence been left in, it would have been clear what Henkin was saying and he would not have appeared to suggest that sergeants supplied such information at state fairs. But the producer dropped this second sentence and added a sentence from elsewhere about propaganda, so the answer to Mudd's question about information from sergeants at state fairs as it appeared in the program was: "No, I wouldn't limit that to sergeants standing next to any kind of exhibit. Now, there are those who contend that this is propaganda. I do not agree."

Henkin had not said in the interview itself that sergeants provided drug and race information at state fairs at all and it was not clear what was meant by "I wouldn't limit that to sergeants . . .". Thus, the editing of the interview could be said to have rearranged the answers and created an impression that Henkin was not credible, since he appeared to say sergeants were giving out drug and race information at state fairs, which obviously they were not. A member of the public who wrote to then Congressman Gerald Ford (R-Mich.) about the editing said, "It made Henkin look dishonest."[8]

Davis explains that his purpose was to present Henkin's answers relating to the theme of the program which dealt with public information. "I wanted his answers to stick to the point and the editing was to clarify, not distort." He says there was no intent to mislead and he knew his editing could be second-guessed, since Henkin made his own tape of the interview.

The public display of military equipment was not directly on the theme of public information. There had been questions about the value of the display of equipment at state fairs for recruiting, but no quarrel was made with Henkin's statement, "I think it serves the purpose of informing the public about their armed forces." This and the other first sentence of each of Henkin's answers to Mudd's questions were used and not deleted. But recruiting was not the point of the program.

After Mudd asked in the program whether sergeants at state fairs were used to provide information on budget, drug and racial problems, the segment carried Henkin's negative answer, and Davis says he gave it more force by adding Henkin's later statement that this was not propaganda. Immediately before this answer, the program showed Henkin saying he believed the Pentagon was properly informing the public about the military, including drug and racial issues. Taken together, there could be no doubt about Henkin's substantive position. Davis says it was only to move logically from point to point that sentences were moved from later in the interview to keep Henkin's answers directed to the information theme of the program.

As for deleting the statement "as one might say" after Henkin said, "After all, this interview here is being staged," Davis says Henkin turned his head away as he said it and Davis did not think the phrase added anything of substance. He says Henkin had asked that the interview be held in a studio rather than in his office. He had also asked to see the questions in advance. While Davis did not agree to this, he did provide a general idea of the areas to be covered. Two cameras were used to avoid the need for "reverse shots" so the interview could be filmed in sequence.

Davis believes the accusations of distortion were not substantive. "The editing was similar to what is done by any press editor and did not require any special effects but simply condensed material in fact presented by Henkin in a way that focused on the issue of public information." He says the charges did succeed in causing people to argue about editing techniques instead of the Pentagon's political agenda. He points out today that this agenda was pushed mostly by civilians who were frequently decades behind the policies of virtually all the presidential administrations in the later Cold War period. What could have been an occasion for public debate about the Pentagon's use of tax monies for military propaganda was aborted by attacks on press editing.

Davis insists there was condensation but not distortion. As for the substance, he says, "No charge was ever made, much less sustained, that editing changed anyone's true meaning. Neither Dan Henkin nor the Pentagon's traveling colonels, nor anyone else was ever shown saying or agreeing with anything he would not ordinarily say and agree with. Were the colonels shown opposing a war they fervently supported? Was Henkin depicted as being critical of or ashamed of a public relations effort he fully supported and justified? Of course not."[9]

But these statements were not offered by Davis at the hearings, whether fully an explanation or not, because Stanton's point was to establish that Congress should not review such editing judgment, whether or not the edits would be seen as reasonable by the government.

Quite apart from the tactical position of Stanton at the hearing to establish a point of principle, Stanton declines to defend the editing. Combining different answers to different questions is a practice one might argue should be disclosed to the public, even if done only for compression and certainly if a deception occurs. However, television cannot use the three dots used by the print press to indicate deletions, and one problem at the hearing was that there was no ready solution for this issue.

Even though the staff and the Subcommittee concluded there was distortion in Henkin's interview, it does not seem to rise to a level of wrongdoing that would prompt the outrage which members of the government expressed at the time. While few may have read the details of the staff report, it was said and accepted by many in Congress and elsewhere that CBS had seriously distorted the interview and misled the public. Such criticism of the program was certainly prompted by more than the claimed distortions. Underlying much of the controversy was the belief that the program was unpatriotic because it was seen as critical of the American military as well as the conduct of the war. Later, some critics were to point to *Hearts and Minds,* a feature film which Davis subsequently made, which was critical of the conduct of the Vietnam War by the military. The charge was then made that the earlier television program was influenced by the same view. Davis says they were separate projects.

The Defense Department ultimately did withdraw from circulation all the films that had been excerpted in the program.[10] But the exposures of Pentagon propaganda and improper use of taxpayer funds, both issues worth congressional review, were not addressed by Congress. Even a follow-up CBS program on the subject did not prompt congressional review of these substantive issues.

On April 18, 1971, CBS News broadcast a special report, *Perspective: The Selling of the Pentagon.* It added an overview and pointed out that the program was what news organizations should be doing to inform the public. The transcript reads in part:

> *Anchor George Herman*: Senator J. William Fulbright is Chairman of the Senate Foreign Relations Committee, and author of a book called *The Pentagon Propaganda Machine.* Arthur Sylvester was Assistant Secretary of Defense for Public Affairs in the Kennedy and Johnson administrations. . . . Adam Yarmolinsky was the Special Assistant to Defense Secretary Robert McNamara in the Kennedy and Johnson years. . . . S. L. A. Marshall is a retired Brigadier General. . . .
>
> *Sen. Fulbright*: The documentary, as well as [my] book, are not challenged as to their factual, substantive issues. It's an effort to inform the public . . . as to how the money is spent. . . .
>
> *Gen. Marshall*: . . . If anyone at this table thinks that it's easy for the Armed Forces to retain the affections of the people in a free society, he hasn't read very much of our history. . . .
>
> *Sen. Fulbright*: . . . They've been receiving somewhere around 50 percent of the total budget of our government now for many years. We've spent on military affairs close to . . . thirteen hundred billion dollars.
>
> *Mr. Sylvester*: . . . The demands of the Vietnamese war put absolutely new requirements upon the Defense Department to

handle 300 newsmen, provide them with backups, provide them with helicopters, provide them with everything you could think of. . . . Of course for military officers to speak on foreign affairs is forbidden and prohibited. The material that was used in that show of yours . . . passed the security review—so that there is no conflict between what the man is saying and the stated policy of the government. . . . Now what is not passed, and which you did not make clear, was maybe in the question and answer period, and this is the dangerous part of this—the officers then get off on their own. . . .

Herman: But if the military sees a need . . . for a bigger army, should they not be allowed to take it directly to the people, or should they only be allowed to take it to Congress?

Mr. Yarmolinsky: They should take it through the same channels that civil servants take their views to their politically-responsible masters who are appointed by the President, and then to the Congress, the White House and the Congress, just as our political process provides for all such questions to be raised.

Sen. Fulbright: . . . When Mr. Agnew criticized it and Mr. Hébert criticized it, it did not go to the substantive; it only went to the procedures of CBS. . . . I couldn't see one case where they challenged the actual, factual, substantive statements, either supported in the book or in the documentary. . . . I think the effect of the documentary was to bring the whole matter to the attention of the public in a way it cannot be done by the written word, because it is the major communication. I think it performed a great service.[11]

At the hearings on its editing, CBS relied on two major points: (1) subpoenas and investigations like the ones then underway had a chilling effect on news coverage, violating the First Amendment; and (2) the Henkin outtakes were already public, so no subpoena of CBS was needed for their production.

Virtually all journalists and press organizations see the protection of reporters' notes and outtakes as critical to the ability of news organizations to gather and report the news and to get at the truth. They say some people won't talk to them if they think their conversations will be disclosed, or they may somehow get into trouble should the government subpoena reporters' notes and broadcasters' outtakes. Reporters' sources dry up, and so does the flow of information. Also, reporters don't want their work critiqued by a government agency against a standard set by the government, often for political purposes, rather than by journalists.

As Stanton noted in his opening statement, "Professional associations representing every segment of journalism have joined in the protest." For example, the Chairman of the Freedom of Information Committee of Sigma Delta Chi had telegraphed Staggers, "protesting the Committee subpoena as representing government harassment." The NAB backed Stanton in a strong statement by its President, Vincent Wasilewski.[12]

CBS submitted to the Subcommittee a series of affidavits from CBS correspondents pointing out the great difficulty there would be for any press organization to cover the news if its outtakes had to be produced for government review of editorial judgments. Even the existence of the investigation was a deterrent to news coverage. Each of the correspondents made his own point:[13]

- Walter Cronkite, Managing Editor of the CBS Evening News, said that if the reporter and editor must be constantly looking over their shoulder for those who would have the product reflect the standards of those who are elected to public office on partisan platforms and who represent, properly, the special interests of their region, who by their political nature hold strong views on the issues of the day, then the coverage of the news cannot be done without "fear" or "favor," and that means it cannot be done at all. News coverage would cease to be an energetic seeker of the truth and a pallid conduit for that propaganda which is palatable to the majority of Congress or the administration of the moment.

  Any governmental panel that assumes the right to call a news organization to account must be presumed to be hostile. It scarcely would seek to investigate reporting with which it agreed. To place an electronic medium under the threat of such investigation is to place it permanently under the fear of accountability to unfriendly antagonists wielding the power of legal restraint.

  "If reporters, editors and producers must consider in their decision-making the possibility of being summoned before an investigative arm of the government to justify these [reporting and editing] decisions, I believe that independence and vigor in broadcast journalism will be inevitably sacrificed."

- Burton Benjamin, Senior Executive Producer for CBS News, said condensation was essential. He knew of no country in the world where government supervision and control had improved the vigor and integrity of the news.
- Marvin Kalb, Diplomatic Correspondent for CBS News, said outtakes were reporters' notebooks and reporters had to have discretion to edit.
- Bob Schieffer, CBS News Pentagon Correspondent, pointed out that often those being interviewed made mistakes or were awkward. To produce those for public consumption would serve no purpose and dry up interviews.
- Mike Wallace, CBS News Staff Correspondent, objected to what he saw would necessarily be the imposition of a government standard of truth.
- Daniel Schorr, CBS News Correspondent, said he would be inhibited if the government were to review his interviews, as would the person being interviewed. "Official inspection" would not lead to better news coverage for the public.
- Bill Small, News Director and Washington Bureau Manager of CBS News, pointed out that a review by Congressmen and non-journalists, whose motives would not be those of professional journalism, to examine raw material to see if the news presented could have favored one side or another would destroy the news process. The review of outtakes would not be the end, but would next include internal memoranda. Even the current investigation made those who would otherwise come to CBS News with reports unwilling to do so because CBS was in hot water with Congress, and who knows who their investigation would lead to.

The staff says they gave these affidavits from CBS no weight. They dismissed them as the usual "first amendment press rhetoric." In all events, they were looking at "rearrangement," not what it takes to cover the news. The Acting Chief Counsel, Daniel J. Manelli, says the Subcommittee's purpose was to expose the "physical rearrangement" which the viewer could not detect. These went beyond mere edits, changing audiotapes and video film as he understood it, and the Subcommittee's purpose was to stop it. He says the Subcommittee and staff were looking only at what was before them, the "rearrangement," and not how the news organizations worked.[14]

Reporters' concerns about subpoenas of their outtakes were not the subject of the inquiry. As in the investigation of the Chicago Convention coverage, if the government is looking only at what it thinks may be wrongdoing and ignores the reasons for news editing and whether the substantive information provided is accurate under the circumstances present, the result of government hearings will likely be condemnation. Ignoring the interest of the press will necessarily be chilling for the journalists and counterproductive for the flow of information, whatever the hearing and whatever the legislation or regulations adopted.

There can be no doubt that government subpoenas, congressional investigations and White House pressure can have a censoring effect. Columnist Tom Wicker noted Nixon's public disclaimer of support for the Staggers subpoena, but said it had to be looked at in light of the fact that it was the Nixon administration which sought to subpoena notes of reporters from the *New York Times* and news magazines. He said it was Vice President Agnew who maintained the critical pressure against the networks; it was a Nixon appointee, FCC Republican Chairman Burch, who interested himself conspicuously in network analysis of presidential speeches; and one reason for the House Commerce Committee's sweeping subpoena of material from *The Selling of the Pentagon* appears to have been administration pressure on ranking Republican committee members.[15]

On April 30, Attorney General John Mitchell, who had been conducting a program of subpoenaing the networks' notes and interview material for some time, publicly joined the Nixon administration's attack on the news media and criticized some of the press for "shocking contempt for truth and a cheap surrender to instinct."[16]

In the two years before July 1971, CBS and NBC were served with over 50 subpoenas by the government, primarily looking into civil disobedience. When a reporter refused to disclose his source for a story to a grand jury investigating the dissident Black Panthers, he was jailed. The Supreme Court upheld the lower court.[17] Government authorities were using journalists as an investigative arm of government. Certainly many sources of information about government abuse will not talk to reporters if they are perceived as agents of law enforcement.

The affiliates of both CBS and NBC were increasingly concerned about the Washington pressure. *Variety* reported that stations were "nervous" about attacks on TV journalism and influenced by the government's apparent attempt to widen the chasms between networks and the stations on news issues. At the May 1971 NBC affiliates meeting, NBC President Julian Goodman asked affiliates to recognize their community of interests. To gather support, "NBC's allies among the affiliates, including the officers of their organization, lobbied the delegates from the 200 stations all that morning and the evening before and by telephone in the weeks before that." The affiliates publicly stood with the network. Also at that meeting, a resolution was passed opposing subpoenas of reporters' notes and news film outtakes "reflecting the current concern after the administration's attack on the CBS News documentary *The Selling of the Pentagon.*"[18]

There were risks to CBS which were peculiar to the broadcast industry because of its station licenses. A primary tenet of the FCC and Congress had always been that a broadcast licensee must disclose fully to them any information required. Failure to do so reflected on the "character" of the licensee and was the one action for which there was no defense. A finding of dishonesty in dealing with the FCC could warrant the taking away of a license.[19] Certainly CBS would have had trouble renewing its broadcast licenses if the network was being charged with serious deception and was refusing to cooperate with—even defying—an investigation by Congress into that deception. If CBS were to go into contempt and fail in its judicial review, that would imperil its station licenses and its network as well. Misjudgments had led to the loss of broadcast licenses by others. The CBS business at that time was valued in the stock market at many billions of today's dollars. Certainly that value would be impaired if contempt of Congress were found and CBS defiance continued.

The consequence for an executive who refused to obey a lawful contempt order of Congress was a jail sentence. While CBS lawyers believed they had a reasonable chance of overturning a contempt citation by the House on constitutional grounds, no one could be sure what would happen. To enforce the subpoena, the House would refer the matter to the Department of Justice, and the Attorney General would then ask a federal court to place the person in jail for contempt until he purged himself by complying.

There was little legal authority to support a court's overturning an order of the Congress issued in the conduct of its legislative duties. A court order of prohibition would be a significant interference with the investigatory and legislative powers of a co-equal branch, the Congress. The Supreme Court had already ruled in several cases that the broadcast press could be treated differently than the print press under the Constitution. So freedom from congressional review and protection against the production of pertinent documents might well not be granted and the contempt would stand.

Beyond that, this was not "a good time" to take on such a free press issue. There was an overriding sense in government that the networks were simply too powerful. The popular epithet was "The three men in New York" who controlled access to the public. No one else had the authority to decide what was broadcast on national television. And, there was antagonism.

The FCC regulatory policy for many years had favored station ownership by members of the local community and management by local owners. Conglomerate corporations which had other economic interests not only were not local, it was thought that they could use their broadcasts to advance their other business interests. Thus, in any dispute about station ownership at that time, stations owned by CBS and NBC could be at some disadvantage under FCC policy. Although the networks were not regulated directly by the FCC, they could be reached through the stations they owned which were licensed. A mistake could become a matter of management irresponsibility, warranting a short-term license renewal or other sanctions on the network-owned stations. While no reputable, major licensee had lost its license up to that time, no broadcaster wanted to be the test case under the vague criteria for license renewals. The loss of license was not a fine; it put the broadcaster out of business. It would take only four votes from the seven commissioners appointed by the President to deny a broadcast license. Any significant wrongdoing or almost anything that could be called a character defect could give the FCC an opportunity to cast such a vote.

Another concern of network management was the possibility of additional legislation or regulations that would weaken the networks' economic base, their relations with affiliated stations or their audience reach. The FCC had already hurt the networks by adopting rules effectively barring them from broadcasting in certain time periods and from producing their own entertainment programming, requiring them to purchase Hollywood-produced programs. Even without legislation or regulation, the industry was sensitive to the "raised eyebrow" of the Congress or the FCC, which could achieve the government's objectives when broadcasters were unwilling to run the risk of governmental displeasure.[20]

Generally, the print press thought that broadcasters were unduly alarmed about the loss of their licenses; that they were "nervous nellies" and at the first sign of trouble with the government pulled back out of an unjustified fear that the government would take their licenses away. But much of the print press was not aware of what it was like to be a licensed and regulated press. Some of the print press held hard feelings about the broadcast press. It was a competitor, but of less merit. It had taken much of the public away from print and was threatening to take more. News anchors were paid large sums of money while even the best print reporters were paid relatively little and had nothing like the celebrity status of those who appeared on the network broadcasts every night before tens of millions of people. The working print press was not particularly sympathetic to network problems.

One print reporter did write at length about how the networks felt at this time of government pressure and intimidation. Robert Sherrill, the Washington correspondent for the *Nation*, wrote in the *New York Times* magazine section on May 16, 1971, about the confrontation over *The Selling of the Pentagon*. He said the program deserved the Peabody Award even though it was hardly a revolutionary story. He noted that even though most of the information about the Pentagon had appeared in newspapers and books, not many people had read this material. A great many watched television. "Some of Washington's most powerful pro-Pentagon politicians felt that their interests had for the first time been attacked in a truly significant and dangerous way. And it made them very angry."

Sherrill wrote that the networks felt they were under "a pestilential assault," although ABC might be exempted. "Julian Goodman, President of NBC and Frank Stanton, President of CBS agree that the 'heavy-handed' government attempts to 'influence' networks news is something new to their experience. They have pointed out that never before has there been an administration that publicly attempted to humiliate and whip the networks into line." As for why the networks didn't just shrug it off, David Adams, NBC's experienced and brilliant staff chief, went directly to the heart of the matter: "You haven't seen this sort of attack leveled at the *New York Times*, with this sort of drumfire . . . there haven't been daily and weekly attacks on the *Times*, and nobody has cut out the stories and pasted them up and said, 'Look what they're doing,' and invited Congressmen to come and look. Now, that's the difference. And the reason there is that difference is, we're a licensed press." Sherrill says no one yet has figured out how "to make licenses and freedom of the press compatible."

Sherrill described some of the problems the networks faced because of their documentaries, programs of importance to public knowledge. The CBS documentary *Hunger in America* "revealed that the United States Department of Agriculture was scuttling its own food-for-the-poor programs, with the encouragement of the Congressional farm committees." Sherrill wrote that producer Martin Carr said House agricultural leaders got the FBI to contact those "who had talked to or in any way assisted the producers of the show. . . . For more than a year he did nothing but answer inquiries, meet with lawyers and make trips to Washington to defend its production."

After *The Selling of the Pentagon* and by May 1971, Peter Davis had been required to prepare 70 pages of rebuttal. He said, "The Pentagon, now that we've told the truth about it, is telling lies about us, and they are telling them at a very rapid pace. . . . We have to answer each of these things." The cost of that was expected to exceed what the program cost to produce.

Similarly, Sherrill reported that either out of experienced insight or paranoia, the top network officials agreed that Klein's reading the Nixon message praising the local news at the NAB was divisive, setting the affiliates against the networks. He quotes Salant: "I think right now they've come to the realization that this is where they can really get us." He pointed to similar messages from such senators as William E. Brock (R-Tenn.), Roman L. Hruska (R-Neb.) and Clifford P. Hansen (R-Wyo.). "I think they [the administration] are saying to the affiliates, 'we know that you guys can shut off the network any time you want.' And indeed they can. It's against the law for us to require any affiliate to carry one of our broadcasts."

FCC Commissioner Nicholas Johnson said about the time of the Agnew speech in Des Moines in November 1969, "I received confidential personal reports that network management began taking a much more detailed interest in the attitudes and copy of its newsmen." According to reports at the time, an ABC commentator on the evening news, Frank Reynolds, was removed in response to demands from the White House; ABC denied it.

Sherrill's article concluded: "There is also a limit, some believe, to how much of a drubbing television newsmen and their bosses can take from the Government before they begin to give a little, to hold back the tough shots, to give even less depth to their coverage than is customary." While, "without exception," the top executives and news directors insist that this is not what has happened, Sherrill says, there are those who feel this could be a consequence. He wrote:

"NBC News President Reuven Frank: 'Every time you undertake something that is just not quite as bland as all the other things you do, you worry about, "will I be cited by the F.C.C.?" '

"NBC senior staff executive David Adams: 'If you are operating in the newsroom of a local broadcast station, and you are doing your job, and one day three lawyers from your company walk in with an F.C.C. inquiry about something you have treated, and you spend 18 hours going through your files, maybe next time you have an issue you want to treat you'll think, "Jesus Christ, do I have to go through all that?" and you may not do it the same way.'

"CBS News President Richard Salant: 'I have to worry about guys out in the field getting unhappy about being taken off the job to answer these things, and saying "Oh, to hell with it, I'll do stuff on ecology from here on out." '

"CBS President Frank Stanton: 'These things are bound to have an effect on your organization, no matter how much you try to protect your staff. After several experiences where they are pulled up short, where they have to testify, it's bound to have an erosive effect.' "[21]

Chapter 10

"You Are in Contempt"

On June 24, 1971, Frank Stanton was sworn in before the Special Subcommittee on Investigations of the Interstate and Foreign Commerce Committee of the House of Representatives. The Subcommittee had called its hearing to vote that he be held in contempt of Congress.[1]

This extraordinary proceeding was not called to investigate the substance of *The Selling of the Pentagon*, which had exposed massive Pentagon propaganda. Nor was it to reassert that foreign policy decisions are to be made by civilian authorities, not the military, and Pentagon propaganda on foreign policy was neither authorized nor acceptable.

When Chairman of the House Armed Services Committee Edward F. Hébert had asked his fellow Congressman, Commerce Committee Chairman Harley O. Staggers, to investigate the criticism of the Pentagon, Staggers set in motion an examination of what he called CBS News' deception of the viewing public. He had the support of the Democratic leadership of the House, including House Speaker Carl Albert and congressional Chairmen who effectively ran the Congress in those years, as well as a number of Democratic and Republican Congressmen who had their own complaints against the television networks and their news coverage. He also had the support of the Nixon White House.

As Stanton sat in the witness chair in the cavernous Hearing Room 2123 in the Rayburn House Office Building, waiting for the hearing to begin, he was well aware that this hearing could go badly. Congressional legislation could affect virtually all broadcast operations, either directly or indirectly. Congress had never hesitated to summon broadcast network executives before it to review network conduct. While Stanton had testified often on various network issues, this hearing promised to be different. Most observers expected that Stanton's continued refusal to provide the subpoenaed material would lead Congress to hold him in contempt. While congressional hearings often are directed to wrongdoing and even criminal conduct, a contempt proceeding is relatively rare. It deals with the defiance of Congress.

The five Subcommittee members, Chairman Staggers and Representatives William Springer (R-Ill.), James J. Pickle (D-Tex.), Leonard R. Blanton (D-Tenn.) and Richard G. Shoup (R-Mont.), sat high behind the elevated podium in the dark hearing room looking down on the witness seated in the well before them. Staff were behind them to advise on any issue that might arise. The Acting Chief Counsel of the Subcommittee also sat at the podium, since he would conduct much of the questioning.

Stanton was virtually on trial. He could sense the difference in the atmosphere of the large panelled room where so many others had been summoned to be grilled about their conduct. He had visited the members in their offices over the years and knew some of them, including Chairman Staggers, quite well. He had testified often. But this was different. This was a formal investigation of CBS and its President for failing to respond to the Congress as ordered. From his earlier talks with the members, Stanton knew that if he did not hand over the outtakes in this hearing, the Subcommittee would probably vote to hold him in contempt of Congress. He knew the members did not accept his position that broadcast news was protected by the First Amendment.

Stanton's friends in Congress had warned him of the hostile mood of the Congress, particularly toward CBS and some of its news programs. They also pointed out that the House of Representatives would, as an institutional matter, necessarily uphold its own investigatory powers, and if that meant holding him in contempt for his defiance of a chairman's subpoena, then even his friends would feel that was what they would have to do. For many years the Congress had never failed to uphold the subpoena of the chairman of one of its committees. John Dingell, the powerful Democrat from Michigan, pointed out that if Stanton could refuse to produce the material subpoenaed by the Subcommittee, the networks could deceive the public at will. Congress "will have completely lost control over how and by whom the airways are used."[2]

Stanton also knew that the White House was seeking to curtail what it saw as adverse news coverage and to destroy network credibility with the public. In addition, many individual Republican members believed the networks were anti-war, too liberal and unfair in their treatment of their party and their views. Efforts by some members of Congress to find a compromise had failed. Continued refusal to honor the Subcommittee's subpoena could only be viewed as contumacious. Staggers was adamant. He would establish the power of the Congress to investigate television news.

At the opening of the hearing, Stanton was advised he could have counsel present. Lloyd Cutler, Esq., sat at the witness table with him, but the Chairman made it clear that Cutler would not be allowed to address the Subcommittee.[3]

Staggers' position had been set out in his press release, which said that the issue was not the First Amendment, but the willful deception of the public. That was the issue for the government. As Staggers had said earlier, "One of the things we have discovered in the light of our previous investigations in this area is that once a distortion has been accomplished and incorporated into a final broadcast, it is virtually impossible to detect. This is why the original, uncut and unedited material must be examined."[4]

Editing to compress interviews is, of course, essential to publishing news. If denied to broadcasters, it would severely hamper, as a practical matter, their ability to cover the news. But if the editing results in distortion and deceives viewers, this could be a different question. Yet, First Amendment protection means reporters may make mistakes without investigation and sanction. If there is no such protection but rather, government investigation of claimed errors, the atmosphere will be one of deterrence. That was the issue for broadcasters.

At the beginning of the June 24 hearing, Staggers set out his justification for a contempt finding. But he had revealed additional concerns in an interview with the *Wall Street Journal*: " 'I would think we'll go all the way,' Rep. Staggers confides, dismissing network claims of government censorship and predicting that a special Subcommittee that he also heads will vote to take action against Mr. Stanton after hearing him testify next Thursday. . . . 'My impression is we were all voting to pursue this to the end. [And then to the point of concern to a number of political figures:] The (broadcasters) can ruin any man, any President, any institution and account to nobody,' Mr. Staggers complains, his dander up."[5]

There were other objectives. A number of the members of Congress and the Nixon White House now had an opportunity, as some put it, "to get CBS." And, exasperated at an inability to call the print press to account, Congress could reach a broadcaster, in this case a broadcaster who appeared to a number of members to be without a sense of restraint. The Acting Chief Counsel of the Subcommittee says that the immediate objective was to expose the editing distortion. Once what CBS had done was exposed, this would "embarrass" CBS and "humiliate them."[6]

As he faced the Subcommittee, Stanton was well aware of what it would take. "From the time I realized the seriousness or the roughness that I was facing in Washington, I said to my associates, 'I can't do this with my left hand behind my back. I've got to do this with all my skill and all the tools I've got.' I called on everybody to make suggestions about what we could do to fortify the position, because my neck was way out. I turned to everyone I could get to put strength behind our stand. And there were days when it looked pretty dark."

Stanton continued to try to talk to Springer, the ranking minority member, but Springer refused to see him. "I had lost Springer right at the outset. He was 180 degrees away from where he had been earlier in my relations. In my experience with him, way before this thing came up, he was a friend. He'd call me for favors. It was a pleasant relationship. If I was walking down the hall in his area, I could stick my head in and say hello and go on. And then the curtain came down and it was just a different relationship. I was down there on something else and stuck my head in during this period and his secretary said, 'I wouldn't try to see him,' or something like that, in a way that made me feel something had happened. I was no longer welcome after *The Selling of the Pentagon*. And I know we didn't have any fights. There wasn't anything of that kind that would have explained his behavior. My conclusion was that his eyes were on the other end of Pennsylvania Avenue and he got their message and that was that. Looking back on it, I can say I never had any trouble with the Committee prior to *The Selling of the Pentagon*. In the past there were things that the Committee was interested in and I didn't always agree with them, but I didn't have any tough problems with them. But boy, this crystallized it.

"In the Congress as a whole, I thought I didn't have much of a chance. If I had nine of the chairmen leaning my way it might be helpful. But a couple of interviews indicated to me that I couldn't get their vote against Staggers. Somebody at the White House staff had told me I was wasting my time if I thought I could get anybody to vote against Staggers. Also there was always the problem in the Congress that someone was sore at us for something we'd done. I remember one of many Senators like that. He said, 'I've got great respect for you and all that.' But apparently, Ed Murrow had invited him on a program about some treaty he supported and after he had made his case for what he wanted, Murrow had the other side come on, but he had not told the Senator that he was going to do that. The news people said that they had made it clear to him. But the whole problem arose because they hadn't gone out of their way to make sure that he understood what they were doing. And it was so foolish. I don't think he ever took his foot off CBS' neck from that time forward. He felt that he had been done in by CBS. And there were scores of stories like that. Congressmen would vote against CBS on this issue—not because of the issue but because of some personal grudge. I knew there were also a lot of people on the Hill who privately were saying, 'You know, the son of a bitch deserves it.' I knew we were in for a very rough time with Congress and they could really hurt us with legislation.

"Nixon was still a problem. I visited Ford to ask for his support and I knew Ford well and we liked each other. While Nixon didn't come out and say anything, we all knew he was calling the shots and Ford made that clear. The Nixon staff that I dealt with wasn't up to the quality of Nixon at all. If he had stayed around, I think he would have gotten rid of some of the weaker ones and brought stronger people close to him. I think if the office of the President had been used even more by Nixon to work on the press, there would have been a very definite negative impact on journalism."

Stanton says, "No one had to spell out the implications of a loss in Congress on this issue. I didn't necessarily think we were going to lose our licenses, but I would have hated to have to come out on that side. The time that I was really sweating the long-term potential dangers was between the time I got the subpoena and our first press release, because we threw down the gauntlet in the very first statement.

"There weren't very many people who encouraged me even in our own organization to think we were going to prevail. I know Ted Koop, who was in charge of our Washington office and covered relations on the Hill, was proud of the stand that we were taking. But he was saying to me privately, 'I don't think you're going to win and you'd better be prepared to decide what you're going to do.' One reason I treasured Ted Koop in the job he had, was he had come out of the news area, so that he wasn't as susceptible to the glamour of the White House and the Congress as some were. He had very good connections. But we saw that many of our good relations turned very nasty in the end. You could just feel the chill come down as you met people in their offices. They were listening out of kindness, but you didn't come away feeling like you had the vote. You asked friends on the Committee you hoped they would see our side. But their eyes glazed over. They were just having no part of me at all."

Stanton was sworn in as a witness. He read his carefully prepared statement. "Clearly, the compulsory production of evidence for a congressional investigation of this nature abridges the freedom of the press. The chilling effect of both the subpoena and the inquiry itself is plain beyond all question. If newsmen are told that their notes, films, and tapes will be subject to compulsory process so that the Government can determine whether the news has been satisfactorily edited, the scope, nature, and vigor of their newsgathering and reporting will inevitably be curtailed . . . this subcommittee's legislative purpose—to prevent distortion or to control editing practices in broadcast news reports and thereby engage in official surveillance of journalistic judgments—has no constitutional warrant and therefore no benefit that can be balanced against the chilling effect of this subpoena, let alone outweigh it." He respectfully declined, as President of CBS, to produce the materials covered by the subpoena.

Stanton went on to say that "We take this position as a matter of conscience, because of our obligation to uphold the rights guaranteed by the First Amendment. That Amendment embodies our national commitment to freedom of the press. It protects the rights of journalists, not to make them into a privileged class, but to safeguard the liberties of us all by preserving one of the most indispensable elements of responsible democratic government—the right to report freely on the conduct of those in authority."[7]

After questions to Stanton about his refusal to produce the program outtakes, Chairman Staggers said, "it is my duty to advise you that we are going to take under serious consideration your willful refusal today to honor our subpoena. In my opinion you are now in contempt."[8]

As was customary at that time in the conduct of such investigations, counsel for the Subcommittee, Daniel J. Manelli, Esq., questioned Stanton. He sought to explore the editing techniques used in the program. Stanton refused to be drawn into such a discussion, stating that CBS edited the program, accepted responsibility for what was broadcast and believed the program was fairly edited. He declined, however, to get into the details of what had been done. To discuss the edits would have been what CBS said should not be done (i.e., a government review of the edits and the CBS News judgment in making them). Still, in an effort to show CBS' awareness of the problem and willingness to respond to the need for fair editing, on the day before the hearing CBS had submitted to the Subcommittee new guidelines for editing which addressed the Subcommittee's concerns and which would in the future prevent the editing the Subcommittee was criticizing.

Manelli asked Stanton, "Do you think that there was anything in *The Selling of the Pentagon* which was likely to mislead a substantial number of people as to what they were seeing?" Stanton did not answer yes or no. He said CBS policies were constantly under review and if there was something that needed to be changed or explained to the public, "we do so." He added that CBS had been searching for a long time, both for radio and for television news, to find the equivalent, for example, of the three dots that the print press uses when an omission is made, but had not found such a device. He explained they had experimented with "jump cuts," that is, cutting from one scene to another with dissolves so that the "jump" is obvious, and an omission indicated. The editing would then be obvious, but this would lead to absurd appearances. Stanton had made demonstration tapes of different kinds of such cuts to show the staff how awkward and disruptive such identifying cuts would be.

Congressman Springer then questioned Stanton. Reading from his 1956 dictionary, which did not list television as journalism but only newspapers and writings, he argued that television news was not journalism and, further, was not covered by the First Amendment. He also quoted from the *Washington Post*'s initial criticism of the program, which said that television producers should go out of their way to preserve intact and in sequence the responses of those interviewed because to do otherwise would result in a material distortion. This was a cogent point, but he made no mention of the *Post*'s later statement that this was not an imperative in every case or its criticism of the subpoena.

Congressman Pickle said there was no way to deal with the controversy that had arisen without making the outtakes available and known to the public. He denied that their production could be seen as an effort to exert government control or to impose government standards of truth. It was to find the truth. "Now who else is going to pass judgment on these matters if it is not the Government . . . ?" Stanton answered, "Mr. Pickle, that is the whole point, that is why I am here, and that is the reason I refuse to comply with the subpoena."

At this moment in this intense interchange between Congressman Pickle and Stanton, Chairman Staggers interrupted. His staff says it was startling for the Chairman to do this, and they believe he did so out of concern for Stanton, his longtime friend. He knew Stanton was going to be held in contempt and he tried to give Stanton an out and to persuade him that defiance of the Subcommittee was the wrong course.[9] Others pointed out that Staggers was trying to get the outtakes without a First Amendment confrontation, but Pickle's line of questioning was leading to just that. In all events, in an extraordinarily solicitous gesture by a Chairman of a Committee, Staggers said in the hushed hearing room, "I think this has all gotten out of context. I think, Dr. Stanton, you and Mr. Cutler know why you are here, not to have anything to do with the First Amendment at all." He went on to say that Stanton had been "forced to come down here to defend your position because of others who forced it on you. I know of some of the arguments that have been had internally that have come to me . . . I would not hide behind the First Amendment because it has nothing to do with this, it does not have anything to do with your editing. You are here only because of the fact that you misplaced and misquoted and we want to find out if that is true. If it is not true, you ought to bring out the outtakes now."

Congressman Shoup then picked up the questioning to ask whether Stanton was defending the practice of portraying an interview falsely, and both Congressman Shoup and then Congressman Springer leaped in to say that false portrayals had nothing to do with the First Amendment and were not protected by it.

The Subcommittee pursued Stanton as to whether making up composite answers, taking material that reads on the same question from various places of an interview, was acceptable. Stanton said that it could be done if it was fair and objective reporting. One of the difficulties, in Stanton's view, was that legislation or a regulation requiring disclosure of such editing would be difficult to apply and almost impossible to administer.

Congressman Pickle, who had been interrupted earlier, reached for another sanction the networks feared. He threatened legislation to license the networks, in addition to FCC licensing of their owned stations.

Mr. Manelli said that if it was all right for individuals to make inquiries, and CBS and others agreed it was, why should it be wrong for the people to act through their elected representatives who could enforce their inquires with a subpoena? Stanton responded that the First Amendment is designed to protect the journalist from that kind of government surveillance.

Manelli still disagrees. He says that if you wanted to run a newspaper against the *Washington Post* you could organize one. The difficulty in broadcasting was that if you put up a transmitter, the incumbent broadcaster could call the FCC and say, "come down and tear down that transmitter," and that would be done. And that was the argument to the existing broadcasters—"you're in and everybody else is out." Manelli explains that this was important in Staggers' thinking. Broadcasters were in a protected enclave where they could use the airwaves and others could not. Therefore Congress had the right to ask these questions, particularly since broadcasters were public trustees and in a position different from the print press.[10]

Congressman Springer then pointed out that the Subcommittee had subpoenaed all the records of the preparation of *Project Nassau*, which contemplated an invasion in Haiti, and CBS produced them "without objection." This was an awkward point for Stanton. But there had been no program broadcast. He could only say that CBS had to look at each subpoena in turn and in the instant situation it was clear that the Subcommittee was seeking to review editorial judgments made about government misconduct.

Chairman Staggers insisted he did not blame Stanton personally, but the CBS organization. Stanton asked that he not be separated from his company and the News division he supported. He said CBS tried to hire the best professionals it could and it did review organizational changes when appropriate.

Speaking more and more rapidly and turning red with anger as the hearing room fell silent, Staggers, having urged Stanton to step aside from the defense of the CBS News division or at least from those who had participated in the program, said with great emotion:

> But Jesus picked 12 disciples and one sold him for thirteen pieces of silver, another denied him on the night that he was

crucified, and another doubted him when he came back. Now that is the kind of men we have today and that we had then.

Dr. Stanton: I think that is most unfair to refer to our news organization that way.

The Chairman: Being prophets and disciples of Christ?

Stanton: No; as being traitors.

The Chairman: I don't say they were traitors, I said Jesus had those men and he picked what he thought were the 12 most perfect men he could find.

Stanton: Then, sir, I misunderstood what you said.

The Chairman: I didn't call them traitors or anything like that; no, sir, I would not do that.

Mr. Pickle continued: "We are asking for facts and information. I know you want to give us the answer as well as we want the answer. If you don't give us the information, then we will have a confrontation." Staggers said, "I am going to ask that this matter be put in the record and say this, and I do it with hesitancy. I say that I was approached on the floor by a gentleman who said that he could not vote with me when it comes up for contempt charges. I said, 'That is all right with me,' but I said, 'Why?' He said, 'The TV station in my city has already told me that if I vote for contempt of Congress charges that I will not be elected to Congress next time, they would see to it.' He said, 'If you ever quote me I will have to disavow it because it was between him and me.' I am not going to mention his name but this occurred on the House floor.

"Now there are some editorials being written, some of them I think in broadcast magazines. I am not sure but I am certain that some of our staff would know, saying that I had canvassed every member of this committee and that I didn't have the votes to pass contempt charges. I say to you and to the public, I have only asked one man that is on the committee how he was going to vote because it was said to me that he had been approached and had promised that he would vote for the networks. I went to him because I wanted to know if this was true. His answer to me was, 'I don't believe what you are doing is right,' but he said, 'I will when the time comes to vote with you.' "

He again reached out to Stanton. "Now I want to say again to you that I hold you in the highest esteem and I have, as I say, for 20 years. I think you are a gentleman. I think that you have tried to do justice to your profession, but this has come to a serious point. I think this is a turning point one way or another as to which way America is going to go. I think you share with me some of the awesome power that your organization has and its influence, not only on the adults of America but the children of this land and its future.

"I think that you share with me, too, as an elected representative, that I and each one of these others has a duty that if we think that something has to be done, to do that job. I don't think you would dispute that. If we do it without malice, if we do it without trying to persecute, and to perhaps have legislation, that is all we are trying to do. That is what I want to assure you."

And then, despite Stanton's refusal, Staggers registered a surprising and incongruous personal note of gratitude. He said to Stanton:

> Again I say thanks a million for your cooperation. I think you have been very cooperative and I think you have been very fair in your answers, and I just say that I do want to ask before you go again, Dr. Stanton, to make the record clear I am directing you to comply with the subcommittee subpoena. What is your answer?
>
> *Dr. Stanton*: I respectfully decline.

The hearing ended.

Looking back on it, Manelli says the Committee was busy on many other things at the time and had it not been for the changes in the Henkin interview, there would never have been hearings. But, coming right after the Haiti events, the Committee thought it ought to address what it saw as irresponsibility. As one congressman said, "They still haven't got the message." While Manelli believed stopping "distortion" in news programs might not be susceptible to legislation, if what CBS was doing was disclosed so the public could see for itself what the "magic trick" was, this would be such an embarrassment to CBS that it would discourage that sort of thing in the future.

On June 29, the Special Investigations Subcommittee met in executive session. An 80-page memo of law had been prepared by the Committee staff. Years of legal authority supported the power of the Congress. The Supreme Court had said in *McGrain* v. *Daugherty* (273 U.S. 135, 161 [1927]) that congressional investigatory power flows, of necessity, from the power to legislate. Legislative investigatory power had also been upheld in cases involving the First Amendment. Congress had the power to regulate broadcasting, and the Supreme Court had upheld FCC authority to review "in general program format and the kinds of program broadcast by licensees." The Court had said in its *Red Lion* decision that differences in the "characteristics" of the news media justify differences in the First Amendment standards applied to them and upheld, even, regulation of broadcast news content. The Subcommittee staff memo argued that a viewer's unfamiliarity with the highly sophisticated techniques available to the television medium places him at a serious disadvantage when analyzing what he thinks he has seen, since "seeing is believing." The viewer reasonably expects that the visual recording of an event is a means of preserving that event as it occurred, and the viewer does not accord the same critical analysis to the visual reenactment of an event that it accords to the printed word.

The power to prevent deception in a news program had been asserted by the FCC in a decision dealing with question "rearrangement" in the broadcast of a panel interview with former White House Press Secretary Pierre Salinger and John P. Roche, Special Assistant to President Johnson. A question from the studio audience was asked after Roche had left the studio. It was later inserted into a portion of the broadcast during which Roche was ostensibly present and an impression was created that Roche could find no answer to the question. The FCC reprimanded the broadcaster, saying it had responsibility for exercising reasonable diligence to prevent the broadcast of false or misleading material. There was no appellate review of the FCC decision, but Manelli says this was considered an important legal precedent for the Subcommittee's action.[11]

The memo concluded that the right of Congress to legislate constraints upon those who communicate information to the public when their activities collide with the public interest was well established. Thus the government will not ignore charges of deception by technological means if the viewer may be misled. Manelli warns that digitalization will present even greater opportunity for deception which will require government oversight.[12]

The Wilmer Cutler law firm argued on behalf of CBS, in essence, that the Subcommittee investigation would inevitably restrain the presentation of controversial issue programming. Its legal memorandum pointed out that *Red Lion* held that the Fairness Doctrine does not violate the First Amendment, but it "does not authorize promulgation of an 'official government view dominating public broadcasting.' " It argued that it was apparent from some of the Subcommittee counsel's questions that the staff was pursuing questions of "prejudicial editing and selective inclusion," as was the case in its investigation of the Chicago Convention coverage. This was contrary to the Chairman's statement at the outset of the hearing that the Subcommittee had no interest in the question of "bias." The Subcommittee thus was enlarging the inquiry to determine bias by applying some governmental standard of truth.

It said that the inquest nature of the proceedings was demonstrated by the questions of Subcommittee counsel, which sought to confine or bind the witness to a position favorable to the Subcommittee's position. Thus counsel asked, "Do you think there was anything in [the program] which was likely to mislead a substantial number of people as to what they were seeing?" and, "do you believe that the program production practices were revealed so that the program as it appeared on the air was exactly as it appeared to be?" These questions sought to elicit an admission that the broadcast was distorted and biased, not factual. It appears that this is the *opinion* of the questioner and an attempt is repeatedly made to get Mr. Stanton to agree.

Mr. Pickle had said, "[Y]ou are saying that we are trying to set up Government censorship or Government control, that we are using Government standards of truth. Now who else is going to pass judgment on these matters if it is not the Government . . . ?" CBS counsel pointed out the obvious conclusion to such a rhetorical question was that a government standard would have to be used. Also, any sanction would inevitably involve the Committee in applying a presumed but government criteria of truth. Finally, in this case, the forced submission of outtakes and other internal materials for the Subcommittee's purpose would have a chilling effect on the news and this, under well-established First Amendment criteria, was unconstitutional.

At a meeting of the Subcommittee right before the vote was taken, one of the staff members urged the Subcommittee to decide the distortion and legislative questions and declare victory. He pointed out that the outtakes were publicly available, since Henkin had provided the full transcript of his interview to the Subcommittee and it was in the *Congressional Record.* The Subcommittee could therefore make the necessary evaluation of the issues before it. There was no need for the continuing confrontation with the press. The inquiry could also be said to have accomplished its purpose, since Stanton had issued new guidelines for news interviews which, in the future, would prevent what had happened on the program. CBS had taken the necessary corrective steps. While Stanton said these came about as a result of a continuing review, it was apparent that these new rules were drawn to meet the Subcommittee's criticisms.

This would give the Subcommittee an easy win. This kind of solution was often used in investigative proceedings and the outcome could be regarded as sensible and "fair." In the ordinary case, there would have been no compelling need to go further with the proceeding. On the other hand, it all came late in the process. Some of the staff and the Subcommittee felt that it was a little naive of Stanton and his lawyers to think that this last-minute offer of new guidelines would end the proceedings. No one knew what the CBS rules meant, how they would work in practice and whether or not they really would be followed. Congressman Pickle said, succinctly, CBS was saying that it hadn't done anything wrong and wouldn't do it again.[13]

Staggers rejected the suggestion out of hand. He wanted a vote to confirm his view of the power of Congress. He wanted a finding that there were distortions. He wanted to vindicate his investigation and his chairmanship in the eyes of his fellow chairmen and fellow Congressmen. John Dingell had cautioned the Chairman to be sure he had the votes before he issued the subpoena. He had said, "Do not draw your sword unless you are prepared to use it." But Staggers was fully confident that he had the support he needed. He was not about to leave open any question about the ability of Congress to investigate deception in television.

Following Staggers' leadership, the Subcommittee voted unanimously, 5–0, for the contempt citation.[14] The Subcommittee issued a press release on its June 29 meeting. It said CBS had engaged in "highly deceptive practices." Noting that the outtakes were the only real evidence that would lay the issue to rest, it had voted unanimously to recommend to the full House Commerce Committee that Stanton and CBS be cited for contempt for refusing to produce them.[15]

CBS issued a statement saying that it regretted the Subcommittee had seen fit to take this step. For months the Subcommittee had had access to the complete transcript (printed in the *Congressional Record*) of the specific interview which was the focus of most of the critical comments, and the compulsory demand for the outtakes, which raised grave constitutional issues, was basically unnecessary. "All this boils down to one simple and vital question: Is this country to continue to have a free press or is indirect censorship to be imposed upon it? The issue is as simple as that—and is crucial." Julian Goodman said, "The Subcommittee's action is a matter of grave concern to all who believe in a free press and a free society."[16]

The staff issued its report, which provided further basis for Staggers' motion for a contempt citation. It said distortion of speech and calculated deception in the context of a news documentary raised obvious questions as to the adequacy of existing laws and their administration by the FCC. The report addressed the fact that the Subcommittee already had the evidence of the Henkin interview in the transcript. It said it needed the outtakes of the program to see if the sequence of events had been inverted or spoken words rearranged; it had to see how the pictures, as well as the words, had been rearranged. Through analysis of such evidence it would be possible to determine the techniques, both sound and visual, which were used to conceal the manipulations from viewers. "Such information is essential if the committee is to consider appropriate legislation to deal with such techniques." Also, there could be information concealed in the outtakes which could be relevant.

As for the First Amendment, the Supreme Court had pointed out that calculated falsehood falls outside the exercise of the rights guaranteed by the First Amendment. The Subcommittee had sworn testimony and other evidence that the network appeared to have engaged in such calculated falsehood and some rather artful editing techniques. Thus, even if the First Amendment did apply to broadcasting, which the Subcommittee denied, it would not apply to investigation of calculated, deliberate falsehood.[17]

Following the Subcommittee vote on June 29, Staggers took the matter immediately to the full Commerce Committee which he chaired and on which Springer was the ranking Republican. The full Commerce Committee met in executive session on July 1. There were impassioned speeches on both sides, particularly by Congressman Lionel Van Deerlin (D-Calif.) opposing, and Congressman Springer favoring, contempt. The Committee voted 25–13 to move for a contempt vote by the full House, with 13 Democrats and 12 Republicans supporting the contempt motion.[18]

Staggers moved quickly to have the House take up the contempt vote. He believed the institutional authority of the Congress itself and its power to investigate had been defied. It was therefore an issue of "high principle," which under House rules could be brought up immediately for a vote. It did not require a three-day "lay over" ordinarily provided to give members a chance to read and review the matter.

On July 2, Representative Springer formally filed a motion with the House of Representatives to hold Stanton and CBS in contempt of Congress. Both he and Staggers were confident.

Chapter 11

Down to the Wire

The vote of the full Committee removed any doubt about the issue for those who hoped it all might just go away. From "Better him than me," station broadcasters began to see the risk to all of them, whatever their views about network news coverage. Anytime it wanted, Congress could call a hearing and compel production of outtakes, internal documents and film to investigate station newsrooms and their news directors' editorial judgment and then impose sanctions or legislate against what it did not like about particular kinds of broadcast news coverage or news practices. And this would be so even when the news content investigated by the government was a criticism of the government itself and, most important, even when it was true. Not just CBS and Frank Stanton, but the most important role the press can perform for a self-governing public was to be placed in jeopardy.

While counsel for CBS continued to think they had a chance to upset a contempt citation in the courts, Stanton says, "I was always very skittish about taking this thing all the way to the Supreme Court. I wanted to build a record over the years of responsible performance and hope that if it ever did get there that we would have had a body of experience behind us. You had to make this up as you went along. In all my contacts with the Congress I tried to persuade them of the wisdom of supporting the First Amendment and I tried to keep them away from the stuff about the war. Because the networks were perceived as having power, you couldn't come on very hard. You debated the merits. Either I was terribly naive or this was so ingrained in me that when the question was raised about the rights of the broadcaster in news, my decisions were just second nature. At the time of the Staggers subpoena, Dick Salant talked to me very seriously about the consequences of what I was doing. Dick was my closest friend, and obviously I took seriously his counsel. A lot of our affiliates thought my refusal was a foolish thing to do because they were worried about their licenses and their bottom line."

Stanton knew Nixon was hostile, but it was more than "hard ball," as Nixon was fond of saying. The President wrote to Haldeman on May 9, 1971, after attending one of the annual White House correspondents dinners (which have a tradition of jokes at the expense of congressional figures and the President, all in the supposed spirit of good fellowship), "Every one of the recipients was receiving an award for a vicious attack on the administration. . . . What I want everybody to realize is that as we approach the election we are in a fight to the death for the big prize. Ninety-five percent of the members of the Washington press corps are unalterably opposed to us because of their intellectual and philosophical background. Some of them will smirk and pander to us for the purpose of getting a story but we must remember that they are just waiting for the chance to stick the knife in deep and to twist it."[1] Later, on June 29, Nixon stressed to Haldeman that he should remember as a guideline for his handling of the press, "The press aren't interested in liking you. They're only interested in news or screwing me."[2]

When Nixon met with NBC executives on June 8, 1971, Colson wrote, "Julian Goodman [NBC's President] did address the question of attacks on the media and the networks. . . . He did make the point that the media credibility was challenged severely when there were loud public attacks, particularly by Government officials. The President answered by saying that, of course, people are always talking about the credibility of the Administration and therefore [it] is 'fair game' to talk about network credibility. He did not apologize for any of the attacks on the networks. . . . (Goodman said) that they, of course, tried very hard to be fair and objective in their reporting, that it was not really a question of not being objective; it was just how people perceived it. He said he wished the President would watch television and make his own judgments. [One NBC network executive present said the President mentioned that he had not attacked the media but some of his subordinates had. Goodman said, "But you do not gainsay them," and Nixon turned "beet red."][3]

"After Goodman explained his concerns over the attacks on the media the President, very quietly smiling and looking very calm, explained that he understood fully that most of the commentators and the reporters were biased, that their bias was quite obvious, but that this didn't bother him a bit; he understood it fully; he had come to accept it and live with it and so long as he had the opportunity to go directly to the American people from time to time, he didn't mind reporters being biased in their presentation of the news."[4]

Haldeman noted that Nixon had "whapped the NBC top management. . . . Colson was practically ecstatic over the effect that he thought it had on the NBC people."[5]

By this time, both the Congress and the White House felt CBS to be the worst of the three networks in terms of news coverage and behavior. Stanton saw this as only part of the challenge. He says, "I had not only to win friends outside of CBS but I had to make sure that the troops were behind me as far as the CBS affiliates were concerned. They had ties to their Congressmen and their Senators, the like of which no one else had. I couldn't call on them for help if they had doubts about the desirability of what I had done. In the end, there was no problem about the affiliates. I would be hard pressed to identify anybody who was dragging his feet when they came to see the critical nature of what I was doing. I talked to them from time to time on the closed-circuit about this. At 4:00 in the afternoon we had an island where we weren't furnishing program service and the lines were available to be used for sending other material to affiliates and I could use that. I spoke to them sometimes right from Washington.

"On the free press issue, there can be no giving up part of that freedom to a government committee. I turned to members of the print press. Some had editorialized in support of my position. But I think they were genuinely laid back. And many sort of hated our guts anyway. Some did speak up for us. There were people like John Cowles in Minneapolis, there was the publisher, Martin, in San Francisco who owned station KRON. There weren't many publishers who thought that there was any threat to them. But when you began as I did in a couple of instances to talk to them about the future application of electronics to the print media, they began to realize maybe this would be a way the FCC would get into their business. We sent out over 170 letters to journalism schools and faculty members asking for their support. Staggers made much of this as if we were doing something wrong. But we needed their help.

"A publisher held a luncheon for me in Cleveland, and invited leading citizens to it. If anyone gave me half an invitation, I was there to try to talk about the issue. I would like to think that things are judged on their merits. But I didn't want to take any chances on this because I knew we were in trouble, in the sense that the forces of the Congress and the White House were increasingly against us. I went out many times to meet with news editors on the print side because I had to make sure that they understood that while they thought they were protected, if we gave ground on this it could affect them because they were getting more and more into electronics themselves. Little did I know in 1971 what the computer or the information superhighway were going to mean and what the regulatory problems were going to be for print people as well as for broadcasters and cable.

"I would come home from a trip like that—a swing around the country—and I used to say, 'I just wished that I could bring this thing to closure.' Because fatigue begins to set in. My wife was very supportive. She was absolutely 100% and never, never even hinted at the idea that I ought to go down and say, 'is there some way we can write a plan that will bring honor to both of us?' Because it was impossible.

"Julian Goodman, head of NBC, was very supportive and made suggestions about people who might help. Goodman understood what was going on. He had been in news in Washington so he knew both the freedom of the press traditions and the Hill atmosphere. I don't recall anybody from ABC doing anything, but that doesn't mean that they were against us. And, some Congressmen who were on the sidelines in the sense that they were not members of the committees involved, were also helpful."

CBS retained several outside lobbyists in addition to its own Washington office, both because this was not the usual issue in-house executives were accustomed to handling and because the jeopardy to CBS had become very real indeed. Stanton says, "That is not the way I would like to see it work. But there was little doubt about the seriousness of our situation." Both the White House and many members of Congress were not available to CBS on this issue. They would not hear from CBS. Despite CBS lobbying and the calls by outside lobbyists CBS retained, by the time of the Committee vote there had not been much change in the views of many in Congress.

Congress had always believed that it was up to the Congress to represent the public in matters of broadcast press responsibility. That, and control, were at stake. Thus, John Dingell of Michigan described the issue as "control of how and by whom the airways are used."[6]

Then, on June 30, the Supreme Court upheld the right of the *New York Times* and the *Washington Post* to publish the classified *Pentagon Papers* and overturned prior restraints of their publication. This was a great victory for journalism and the print press. But it was to increase the concern of some members about the emerging power of television news and the need to hold it accountable if the print press was beyond reach.

During the *Pentagon Papers* cases, one legal issue was the possession of classified material by the *New York Times* and the *Washington Post.* Floyd Abrams of Cahill Gordon & Reindel, which had been retained by the *Times,* believed possession of such material in the circumstances and for the purpose of news reporting was defensible. The *Times* and the *Post* took that position. But were it held that such possession was a crime, this could have had an adverse impact on the newspapers and the broadcast licenses of the *Post.* Nixon and Attorney General Mitchell saw this as a possible pressure point on the *Post*. Parts of the *Pentagon Papers* were offered to the three networks but they turned them down and did not report on them until after the Supreme Court decision lifting the prior restraints against their publication.[7]

Congress could not understand the Supreme Court's permissiveness toward the press. This was particularly true of conservative members and Southern and Western members. Stanton recalls his concern at the timing of this decision. "The spirit of getting even with us for our news coverage over the years was very pervasive. The whole thing was then impacted by the *Pentagon Papers* decision. I knew that a lot of people I had met in Washington on the Hill in connection with the problems I had, were just as angry about the *Times* and the *Post.* I wished there had been some time for things to cool off before they voted on CBS. I really thought that some of my friends might desert me at that point because they were not happy at all about what the *Times* and the *Post* had done."

At the same time, many in the CBS News organization believed that if there were a contempt citation of CBS, this could lead to a ruling by the Supreme Court which would establish that the broadcast press was entitled to the same First Amendment protections as the print press. This would end the congressional and regulatory investigations of broadcast news content and establish the law of the land. A defeat of the contempt citation in Congress would not be as final. However, Stanton and Salant and CBS legal counsel did not have that same confidence that the Court would necessarily rule for CBS and also saw the risk of a Court adverse ruling as a further threat to television news freedom."[8]

By July 5, the House leadership saw it could be in for a significant First Amendment confrontation. *Television Digest* reported that a spokesman for House Speaker Carl Albert (D-Okla.) said Albert was "somewhat cool to the idea, but it's a matter of personal privilege so [Commerce Committee Chairman] Staggers (D-W.Va.) can bring it up any time he wants to." Staggers, who "lobbied other congressmen personally before the Committee vote, reportedly is determined—with strong backing from ranking Republican Springer (Ill.)—to bring the issue to the floor. . . . 'This confrontation should never have taken place,' Staggers told newsmen. . . . He maintained that Stanton, in April 8 letter, promised to deliver outtakes if Subcommittee would narrow scope of materials sought in original subpoena. . . . 'We did that, yet CBS refused again to provide outtakes from the *Pentagon*. . . . If they'd just simply come down and do what they promised to do, the case would end right there. . . . But they refuse to do even that.' "[9] This was a surprising assertion since at no time did CBS deviate from its opposition to the subpoena.

Concerned about the outcome and CBS licenses, Paley tried to find a way out of the confrontation. He approached House Speaker Carl Albert to find a compromise. Stanton says, "John Brademas, his Deputy, called me and said, 'What the hell is your boss doing down here?' Kidder Meade, the head of CBS corporate information, found out too, and he came in and said, 'Did you know that Mr. Paley went down to Washington yesterday or the day before to see Carl Albert about the stand we have taken and offered an olive branch to make peace somehow?' All Brademas knew was that Paley was on the calendar to come in, but Kidder had gotten more information about it. Paley never said a word about it to me and I never asked him. I didn't want anybody in a high position to think that Paley and I weren't side by side but it just cut me right to the bone. He never talked to me about it at all. But he didn't get to first base."

Stanton did try to approach the White House personally. He did not expect any help, but faced with the prospect of contempt proceedings for CBS, Stanton felt he should at least try to talk directly with the administration. Stanton says he met with Colson and Colson made his usual complaints about CBS' news coverage when Stanton talked of the Staggers hearing. Stanton said, as he had said before, he would look into the complaints and the meeting ended. He had gotten nowhere, as he expected.

Colson reported to Haldeman and Nixon about the meeting: "I said we'll try to get votes to keep you from going to jail for contempt of Congress. We're not asking that the news be pro-Nixon. . . . Stanton asked what we wanted and I told him 'Just fairness.' He was going up the wall. I never told him more than that. That was part of our warfare."[10]

It had become increasingly clear to the CBS affiliates, whatever their political views, just how serious the CBS situation was. Charles Crutchfield of Charlotte, North Carolina, had been a broadcaster since 1933 and had experience in radio and television. He had served on the CBS Affiliate Advisory Board for many years. He saw that Stanton and CBS could be held in contempt. If that were to happen and congressional review of news was accepted, it would "kill radio and television news."

Many affiliates had not liked the *Pentagon* program. Some did not clear it. Crutchfield even editorialized against it. He also thought it was broadcast at "a poor time," and believed, as did many, that it was not appropriate because of what was happening in the Vietnam War. Over the years, he had carried on a detailed correspondence with Salant about virtually all aspects of CBS News coverage.

On his own, without Stanton's knowledge, he called together a number of affiliates for a meeting to discuss what they could do to help keep the news free of government intimidation and control. Crutchfield told the group he believed it was essential for the affiliates to go back home and call their Representatives to protest the congressional contempt citation and to do all in their power to stop it. He said he believed the strongest measures had to be taken to save an executive of Stanton's standing and probity from being sent to jail. Paley owned the company and got credit for its success, but it was Stanton who had built it and gave it its integrity and preeminence.

But more importantly, he said, the affiliates would be fighting to prevent Congress from "killing television news." At the end of the meeting, the affiliates headed home on their rescue mission. CBS, Stanton and radio and television news were important to them.[11]

The affiliates knew their representatives well. Congressmen depended on their local stations for news coverage for election and reelection.

The feeling of the stations about the Staggers investigation and the threat to their news ran so high that some stations did not merely call their congressmen; a few said they would campaign against them. While this may seem an improper use of a television station's editorial position, affiliates believed that the CBS Television Network had no allies in Congress. And they were basically right. So, they acted the way the print press often does. They fought. At stake was the freedom of their stations' news.

As the print press had learned over the years, when government moves to control the news, only the press can save its own freedoms. Only the press can reach public opinion for support, and Congress is concerned about public opinion.

Chapter 12

"Dear Colleagues"

On July 13, after the Staggers Commerce Committee vote, a full constitutional debate would take place before the House of Representatives on government oversight or freedom for the American television press. Since most Americans got their news from the television press, the outcome would be of transcendent significance to the press and the country.

A number of congressmen had spoken out in the months since the Pentagon broadcast with objections to network news coverage. For many in the House, this was an opportunity to strike back at the networks in retaliation for real or imagined injuries. Chairman Hébert continued to voice his personal grievance. He spoke on the floor of the House on March 3: "As regards the false innuendos concerning me in the program, I answered extensively. . . . I never take lightly the charge of being the tool of anyone, the Pentagon included." On March 24, he said: "CBS widely advertised it would rebroadcast its documentary, *The Selling of the Pentagon*, although more accurately, it should be called *The Selling Out of the Pentagon*. It also announced that edited remarks of Vice President Agnew, Secretary of Defense Mel Laird, and myself would be televised after the documentary. . . . They sure did edit my remarks and now I have got them with the evidence in black and white.

"Obviously, CBS believes in the Goebbels method of propaganda—if a lie is told enough times, people will eventually begin to believe it. . . . CBS, in the Goebbels style, replies to the charges of inaccuracies with more inaccuracies, replies to the charges of misrepresentation with additional misrepresentation."[1]

On March 24, Congressman Henry R. Gonzalez (D-Tex.) again spoke about *Hunger in America*. He reported a CBS spokesman had said, " 'their documentaries were pretty good because they had good intentions.' Well, Hitler had good intentions and Herr Goebbels was a good propaganda minister because he clothed Hitler's good intentions with a lot of lies."[2]

Congressman William E. Minshall (R-Okla.) was to urge passage of his "truth in broadcasting" bill: "Within the last two decades the power of television has grown so significantly that a Roper poll, released in 1969, reveals that 59 percent of all Americans rely in large measure on television as a source of news, and that 29 percent of our citizens—one out of three—depend on TV as their only source of news. . . . Television networks today can make or break an individual, a cause, a political issue, even the moral fiber of a nation, simply by the manner in which they report the news. Such awesome power as this should be accompanied by a stern, yes, by a religious commitment to accuracy and truth. That full commitment is lacking.

"All of us in Washington know that when television reports a controversial event, our mail loads immediately reflect public reaction and the public generally follows where television has led them. We may know, and even document, that the facts were slanted or staged by the media, but it is difficult to overcome a viewer's conviction that 'seeing is believing.' And he saw it on television. It becomes gospel. Slanting news, rearranging questions and answers out of context, hoaxing the public with staged events, all of these practices are commonplace on television."[3]

Following the Commerce Committee vote, Stanton redoubled his efforts. He submitted the salient points directly to Carl Albert. He wrote he was fully aware of his duty to testify in response to a lawful congressional subpoena but said, "I also have a duty to uphold the First Amendment." The legal opinions of the Cutler firm included a quote from a decision in the Ninth Circuit Court of Appeals (*cert. then pending*) which reflected a growing awareness by that court of the problem posed by investigations of journalists: "It is not unreasonable to expect journalists everywhere to temper their reporting so as to reduce the probability that they will be required to submit to investigation . . . knowledge that their notes, films and tapes are subject to compulsory process will inevitably cause newsmen to curtail the scope of their news gathering activities."

A copy of Stanton's letter to Staggers was also enclosed, which pointed out that responsible journalists agreed it is appropriate to edit questions and answers in an interview; an answer to one question can be used in whole or in part in connection with another question with compression appropriate if the sense was not distorted. Those agreeing included Edward J. Murray, president-elect of the American Society of Newspaper Editors (formerly editor of the *Arizona Republic*); William Arthur, past president of Sigma Delta Chi and Chairman of the Executive Committee of The American Society of Magazine Editors; an editor of *Look* magazine; and others.

Carl Albert was also told that on June 24, Stanton had delivered a copy of the new CBS operating standards: if an answer to an interview question as it appeared in a broadcast was derived in part or in whole "from the answers to other questions," the broadcast would so indicate, either in lead-in narration, bridging narration lines during the interview or appropriate audio lines; if more than one excerpt from a statement was included, the order of their inclusion in the broadcast would be the same as the order of their inclusion in the original statement unless the broadcast specifically indicated otherwise; and transcripts of the entire interview would be made available to the interviewees after the broadcast, upon request. Thus CBS had gone beyond customary practice to meet the Subcommittee's objective.[4]

On July 8, Staggers sent a "Dear Colleague" letter to all of the House members. "Deception in broadcast news is like a cancer in today's society. . . . We have clear evidence of deceit—man's words electronically altered to change their very meaning." Staggers supported his contempt motion with something close to the hearts of all members: "The spread of calculated deception, paraded as truth, can devastate the earnest efforts of anyone of us seeking to represent our constituents."[5]

But a number of the full Committee had dissented, and they were concerned that Staggers would railroad the vote through the House. A "Dear Colleague" letter signed by the dissenting Republican and Democratic members—John E. Moss (D-Calif.), James T. Broyhill (R-N.C.), Lionel Van Deerlin (D-Calif.), Brock Adams (D-Wash.), Clarence T. Brown, Jr. (R-Ohio), Robert O. Tiernan (D-R.I.), Henry Helstocki (D-N.J.), Robert C. Eckhardt (D-Tex.), Richardson Preyer

(D-N.C.), James W. Symington (D-Mo.), William Roy (D-Kan.) and John Y. McCollister (R-Neb.)—was circulated. They pointed out that the Staggers citation was widely viewed as "an effort by government to crack down on a critique of government." They urged that the prestige of the House and validity of future congressional subpoenas not be put at issue behind the weakest possible case for such a test.[6]

On July 8, Congressman Broyhill circulated his own "Dear Colleague" letter. Such letters are not customary. They are highly effective because they are formal communications from one member to another and they also get attention. He saw a broader issue than the Staggers Committee's jurisdiction. The Broyhill letter made a point of agreeing with restrictions on illegal activities in commercial broadcasting and the Fairness Doctrine. But it said neither illegality nor the Fairness Doctrine was the issue: "News content is." Broyhill said the protection of the First Amendment "must be extended to the electronic media if they are to provide the same essential, and sometimes painful, function of keeping the public involved in and aware of the working of its society." He argued "decentralization" would be the path that best affords a cure "for what ails the broadcast industry," and he urged the networks to put their own house in order.[7]

On July 8, Ogden Reid (D-N.Y.) also circulated a "Dear Colleague" letter, pointing out that the Henkin transcripts were already in the *Congressional Record* and that CBS had presented the opposition critical of the program. He said television was entitled to the same protection as the print press.[8]

Opponents of the citation saw little or no chance of killing it on the floor. Congressman Van Deerlin said, "The Committee action is an absolutely outrageous intrusion into the freedom of the press." He predicted the court would rule in the network's favor, adding, "if CBS does lose, Dr. Stanton could become a hero to compare with [John] Peter Zenger." He says, after fighting unsuccessfully in the Committee and seeing the reaction, he had pretty well given up hope when he made his speech on the floor.[9]

The vote was delayed to July 13. Lobbying grew more intense. The majority of the Committee members planned to use the Pentagon papers decision to uphold the citation: "If newspapers can print stolen documents under the public's right to know concept, then the public has the same right to know what CBS did and did not use in *Selling of the Pentagon.*" Press reports noted, "the committee action is the first time the House ever has been asked to cite newsmen or news organizations for contempt and conviction calls for a maximum fine of $1,000 and a year in jail."[10]

Some congressional voices began to be heard in support of CBS. Jonathan B. Bingham (D-N.Y.) stated: "I have been concerned for some time about the level of expenditure and activity by the military in this area. . . . As the CBS documentary clearly demonstrates, much of it borders on pure military propaganda."

Congressman John E. Moss (D-Calif.) argued: "The real purpose of the Subcommittee was to review the editorial judgment exercised in the filming of the documentary *The Selling of the Pentagon*." The Subcommittee's counsel, Daniel Manelli, "repeatedly asked questions that did not elicit information but sought to confine or bind the witness to a position favorable to the Subcommittee's position. The interrogation became an inquisition."

Robert Tiernan (D-R.I.) felt a contempt citation would have an intimidating and chilling effect on all broadcast journalists and they were entitled to First Amendment protection. "Some of us lose sight of the public service which CBS rendered."

Congressman Clarence (Bud) Brown (R-Ohio) had originally criticized what he saw as an arrogant stand by Stanton. But he had given more thought to his vote. He came from a newspaper family and was torn between his strong disagreement with what he saw as the liberal network news, including their unfair coverage of Nixon and the war, and his belief that the government should not oversee the news. On July 8, he spoke on the floor. He said CBS was at least guilty of "sloppy or unprofessional journalism" or, at most, guilty of a "malicious attempt to mislead the public by misrepresenting public officials through unfair editing of actual interviews in order to propagandize." But if sufficient data were available for such conclusions by the Committee, one could then reject the subpoena citation on the theory that it was unnecessary. He chose, however, to strike at the fundamental point—that since the electronic media are now the method by which most people receive their news, this argues for the greater exercise of First Amendment freedoms by this medium rather than less.

Since untrammeled freedom can be tolerated in newspapers, certainly we can "risk the same freedom" in the electronic media. He thus spoke directly to the many who would supervise or censor television news because it is so powerful and because most people get their news from television. He pointed out that the First Amendment "is not limited to the truth." The amendment rather "guarantees the right to print and speak. The right of expression thus assured may be the truth to one and lies to another. It is up to the individual citizen to make the discrimination of which is which."

Finally, he made the point that with the proliferation of cable television and satellites, the monopoly exercised by the three major networks over spectrum broadcasting would soon become a thing of the past. The public would most benefit from the multiplicity of free voices from which to choose the truth. "To set a precedent now that could impair the rights and privileges of both the public and the free press, therefore, could have the greatest undesirable effects not just today in America, but into the future over the world."[11]

But observers at the time believed the odds were that Congress would uphold its own authority. Any member could see that if CBS escaped congressional oversight now, networks would feel free to distort other subjects as they saw fit, even the Congress itself.

Representative Brown's rough assessment at the time was that a maximum of 40% of the House would vote for the networks and their First Amendment position—no matter what. This group was comprised of some liberal Democrats, some who liked the networks' criticism of the war, some who did not like the idea of a contempt citation and the jailing of a prestigious executive like Stanton, and a number of conservatives who simply did not like the idea of government interference, even though they may have hated the networks and their news coverage.

He saw 40% voting against the networks—no matter what—because the networks had too much power, were too liberal, were engaged in program practices that were deceptive, were irresponsible or had made an attack on the military establishment, which was seditious during a war.

In his assessment, the lobbying was for 20% of the Congress, the critical swing vote. Although the Democrats controlled the House, potential splits on this issue meant they would need Republican support.[12]

Unexpected aid for Stanton then came from some members even though they believed television's news coverage was undermining the American struggle in Vietnam, as well as from others who believed television news was consistently ideologically biased against the Republicans.

Representative Broyhill (R-N.C.) believed two Committee Chairmen had abused their investigative powers for some time. He felt that both had punished and coerced those who appeared before them. One of them was Chairman Staggers. This time he was going to stop it. He was offended by the approach of Staggers and his Subcommittee. He likened it to the Staggers subpoena a year earlier of the mild and well-liked Rosel Hyde, then Chairman of the FCC, when Staggers coerced Hyde into producing privileged documents by subpoenaing him and FCC records on the day of Hyde's retirement. As Broyhill was to say of his success in getting some additional Republicans to oppose the citation, "It all started with Staggers' abuse of Hyde."

Broyhill believed deeply in the legislative process. He thought it essential that Congress undertake hearings on legislation only if there was a valid legislative purpose. Although he strongly disapproved of the television networks' news coverage, as a legislator he saw that the Subcommittee had failed to set out its legislative purpose properly. Originally the aim had been to investigate possible deception. Now it was saying it was investigating deception already found.

Broyhill went to the Democratic leadership and asked for 20 minutes (and ultimately more) to use on July 12 for opposition to the contempt citation, arguing that otherwise the opposition would never have a chance to be heard. Broyhill rounded up a number of Republicans who were either in favor of the contempt citation or on the fence about it. Gerald Ford gave him the use of a conference room near the floor of the House, and Broyhill sent these members in one at a time to meet with the conservative writer James Kilpatrick. Kilpatrick empathized with the Republicans about the bias of the network news. But he also pointed out that for government to investigate the news was to control news. He was worried about government control of news because he was worried about who controls the government.

For those to whom the First Amendment issue was not persuasive or the fear of government control of news not particularly alarming, Kilpatrick and Broyhill took a different tack. They argued that Staggers' subpoena of the outtakes was government intrusion into corporate decision-making. It was one thing for Congress to hold corporations accountable for what they did. It was something else, however, to subpoena their private files and to go into their internal workings. This was a telling argument for some Republicans.

Broyhill was able to turn around a number of Republican votes with the help of Kilpatrick and the lobbyists. As an experienced legislator, Broyhill knew that he had to create the impression of a growing movement against the citation. He rose to speak on the floor of the House on July 12 and submitted a good deal of material for the record. He then took supporting members, two or three at a time, onto the floor of the House to speak to the issue. Broyhill led the charge, objecting to the expansion of the scope of the original legislative justification as a matter of important legislative principle. Broyhill found no evidence that CBS was involved in a deliberate or malicious effort to publish a "calculated falsehood." He added that Staggers' statement now was far different from the Subcommittee's original statement of legislative purpose, which spoke of "practices which might result in misleading and deceiving the public."[13]

Others also spoke. For example, Congressman Brock Adams (D-Wash.) said that if the editing and producing of television news is to be reviewed by government, the press "will cease to be an energetic seeker of the truth but instead become a pallid conduit for that propaganda which is palatable to the majority of Congress or the administration of the moment." He argued that the First Amendment guarantee had as much validity now in terms of maintaining a free and open society as it had in the days of John Peter Zenger and Thomas Paine.[14]

Congressman John E. Moss (D-Calif.) said, "This is not a case of supporting and not supporting the Chairman. It is not a case of getting or not getting Dr. Frank Stanton." He said that if members "act on the basis of personal bias . . . then they will do a disservice to themselves and a disservice to this body."[15]

Congressman Robert Eckhardt (D-Tex.) felt that the Committee had become so "hot" on the scent of what is considered to be a basic evil that it was going beyond its original purpose. "You do not set up 'government standards' for news content." He felt an "inquiry had become an inquisition."[16]

The most startling development on July 12 was the unexpected appearance of Wilbur D. Mills (D-Ark.), the powerful Chairman of the Ways and Means Committee. He rose to address the House to say that he had "serious questions" about the contempt citation.

This was stunning. Wilbur Mills was an extremely important chairman. His remarks represented a major break in the line-up of Committee Chairmen backing Staggers. The House tradition at that time was that all chairmen supported each other. Why would he come out against his colleague? The statement by Mills was the result of several approaches. On the print side, the Association of American Publishers, of which CBS Publishing was a member, made one approach to him. James O. Powell, then Editorial Page Editor of the *Arkansas Gazette* in Mills' home state, was influential with Mills and also interceded on Stanton's behalf. Richard M. Schmidt, counsel to the American Society of Newspaper Editors, held Stanton in high regard for his leadership of the broadcast industry, particularly on First Amendment matters, and he also contacted Powell about the Staggers vote. Powell agreed it was "a threat to the free press and an infringement on the First Amendment rights of Stanton, CBS and all other news organizations." Stanton recalls that Julian Goodman of NBC as well as a local Arkansas station were helpful. Powell of the *Arkansas Gazette* reviewed the question with Mills. Powell called Schmidt to say, "Mills had made a commitment to vote against the contempt citation."[17]

Stanton says, "I went down to see Congressman Mills on the 12th. He said, 'why don't you let me talk with Lloyd Cutler' because he knew Lloyd, he didn't know me. I waited in the little ante room to Mills' office and a few minutes after that Mills came, I don't want to say racing out of his office, but he came out with a determined walk, and Lloyd said to me, 'he's going down to the House floor.' And what he said on the floor was, 'Not so fast, let's put this over.' And in putting it over, a lot of us had another opportunity to get in some more licks.

"Mills was the guy that really tripped it. I think he owed a lot to the guy in his hometown who called him and asked him to see me. I also think Mills was looking for national recognition. So this would get a network on his side. I don't have any question that Mills believed in what he was supporting, but these things helped. I didn't have time to think about that then, but on reflecting afterwards as to why he did it, I think that was it."

There were others who attributed Mills' decision to his belief at the time that he was presidential material and that were he to run for President it would be helpful if he had spoken up in favor of television press freedom in their hour of need. His constituents appeared to have no particular interest in the issue, one way or the other. But he was bright. What he said represented his view of what the House should do with this issue.

Mills' speech was seen as a signal that Staggers' effort was running into trouble. On the floor of the House, he said, "I have some serious questions in my own mind about the citation, with all due respect to my good friend from West Virginia, the Chairman of the Committee." He then made part of the *Record* the series of statements from the CBS journalists who described the chilling effect a subpoena of outtakes and government review would have on press coverage. Now the risk for the free press was being heard.[18]

Congressman Adams entered a list of newspapers and magazines across the country which editorialized against the subpoena.[19] The National Association of Broadcasters (NAB) was the broadcasters' trade association and had a lobbying arm of some significance. It was an association that should be concerned on an issue of the freedom of the broadcast press. It mobilized its legislation liaison activities group. The head of the NAB, Vincent Wasilewski, says a number of phone calls were made by local stations to their Representatives on Stanton's behalf and that the lobbying by radio stations was particularly effective.[20]

Thomas Powell, President of the Associated Press Broadcasters Association, urged Congress not to "establish the government as collateral overseer of every radio and television newsroom in the country." The Radio and Television News Directors Association and Sigma Delta Chi urged the House to reject the contempt citation. The American Civil Liberties Union opposed the citation. The International Radio and Television Society sent letters to 79 congressmen urging defeat of the citation. Other news organizations also supported Stanton.[21]

Stanton points out that all this shows how much effort and support it took by so many to mount an effective opposition to the government. Certainly no small or individual press organization could hope to do this. Indeed, although Stanton had great standing in Washington and the industry at the time, it was only with the heavy lobbying of a large number of individuals and organizations that he had any chance of successfully defying Congress on such a contempt vote.

Television Digest reported on July 12: "House Speaker Carl Albert (D-Okla.) over objections of Majority Leader Hale Boggs (D-La.) ordered assist whips to poll House Democrats, and result was surprising to many: 87 back citation, 67 were against it, about 100 are uncommitted (there are 255 House Democrats). Most Democrats backing House Commerce Chmn. Harley Staggers (D-W.Va.)—who has made fight against CBS a very personal thing—are southerners and congressional sources tell us that large majority of uncommitted voters are expected to back CBS. Unofficial surveys of House Republicans show they are backing Staggers by about 2–1. There are 179 Republicans in House. . . Several backers of citation—told us they see First Amendment questions but that they feel obligated to back play by a Committee chmn. . . . NAB marshalled its 50-man Future of Bcstg. Committee for personal contacts with all members of the House. . . . Lobbying was fierce last week. 'I was contacted by 12 broadcasters from my state last week,' one Congressman told us. 'That's usually high on any issue.' He's going to back Staggers, by the way, although he feels committee should never have voted contempt."[22]

Two days before the vote, the Democratic supporters continued to be confident and John Dingell, Democrat from Michigan and already a practical leader in the House appeared on *Face the Nation* on July 11, along with Congressman Robert C. Eckhardt, a Texas Republican and a member of the Committee, to be questioned by Mollenhoff of the *Des Moines Register and Tribune*, Nail of *Television Digest* and CBS News correspondent George Herman:

> *Representative John Dingell* (D-Mich.): I believe the entire House will vote to support the Committee because the Committee action, I think, is proper. . . .
>
> *Representative Robert Eckhardt* (R-Tex.): I don't know. I think that it may be very close, because I think the issue is a very close one. . . .
>
> *Representative Dingell*: The question is not . . . simply whether the Congress is going to get the information which it has sought as the basis for legislative action . . .
>
> *Representative Eckhardt*: There is no question of Congress' authority to look into the question of process, or the method by which publications or statements are made. But there is no authority in my opinion to set up a governmental standard of truth, and that I think is what this subcommittee slipped into in its total process . . .
>
> *Representative Dingell*: We want to know . . . whether our creature, the FCC, is properly carrying out its function in regulating the broadcast industry, as it should. Second of all, we want to find out whether there is basis for more legislation, so as to do as we did in the quiz show rigging, to enact legislation to prevent deceitful practices in broadcasting. Or whether it is necessary, let's say, for us to lean for example on the FCC to see to it that they do a more vigorous job, and whether or not it is necessary for us to perhaps go into the question and perhaps even network licensing. . . .[23]

In this news program, as in others, there had not been one word about the use of taxpayer funds for Pentagon propaganda.

Emmanuel Celler (D-N.Y.), Chairman of the Judiciary Committee and Dean of the House, sought a last-minute compromise. He believed that a vote on the House floor was not a good thing for either the House or the press. He also believed that Stanton would lose. He called Stanton to tell him that he had, contrary to all protocol of the House, as the Senior Chairman and for the first time in his life, left his own office to visit the office of another chairman. He told Stanton that he had tried to persuade Staggers to find some way to avoid the showdown on the House floor and to find an alternative solution. He asked Stanton if he would visit Staggers for that purpose.

Stanton says, "I had appeared before Emmanuel Celler's Judiciary Committee for a five-day hearing on network business arrangements, some years before. We started in those hearings in a very adversarial manner and at the end he gave me a tribute from the bench that made me feel very good. It made me recognize that you could have deep disagreements and still come out with respect for each other and it was that experience he alluded to. He said that he had come to know me and respected me.

"He was the Dean of the House and he said, 'I know this man,' meaning Staggers, 'and I know that it won't take much if you could just find some way to loosen him up a little bit because you're going to go down in defeat on the floor of the House.' It was all over as far as he was concerned. He would vote against the citation but there was more than a hint in his conversation that Staggers was not the kind of man who could change his mind and live with it. This was an emotional decision and it didn't make any difference whether it made sense or not, Staggers was going to stay with it.

"Then I got a direct call from Chairman Staggers directing me to be down there at 1:00, and not to tell anybody . . . just the two of us. And not to bring any lawyers. So I showed up and was ushered into his office and he was there alone.

"That was the strange part about it. You see him in the hallway and he was so friendly and yet on the stand he would stiffen up and at times was downright nasty. So he was one guy when I saw him alone; he was a different person when he was in front of his staff. But at this meeting in his office he greeted me very warmly and told me of his high respect for me and how long we've known each other and I wondered what was coming. Because it almost sounded as if he was prepared to say to me, 'I'm going to concede and we'll forget about the whole thing.' But he didn't.

"He said, would I produce just a little bit of the film? If I would produce just some of the outtakes for him to review, he would review them personally. He said he would never disclose the contents but would advise the members of the committee that the outtakes had been produced and that he had seen them and there was no need for further proceedings. And he said, 'That would end the matter.'

"I said I could not do that. I told him what the First Amendment meant. I said I wasn't going to move and he said, 'Don't you think we ought to pray about this?' With that he began to get out of his chair and get down behind his desk and he was obviously under tremendous emotional pressure. And, I got out of the chair on the other side and said, 'Mr. Chairman, we can't do this' or, 'I can't do this.'

"Just talking about it brings back the feelings that I had at the time. I could not believe the compromise that he was proposing. It's not unusual in Washington or a lot of other places. But also I couldn't believe his proposal that we should pray about it. When I told some of my colleagues about what happened, I could see that they didn't believe that I was reporting it right. Mr. Staggers was a very religious man, and I guess he thought that would be the thing that would work for him.

"He had cultivated his fellow chairmen assiduously. I was told this by a couple of chairman to whom I appealed for help on what I thought was going to be the final vote. And I was told that I was really expecting too much if I thought any of the major committee chairmen would turn their back on Staggers. He was a sweet, loyal, organization man and they owed it to him to go with him. Regardless of the merits."

This last attempt to avoid confrontation proved unsuccessful. When the hand of compromise, extended unilaterally by the Chair, was offered, it was rejected, confirming CBS' and Stanton's arrogance. From Staggers' point of view he had gone the extra mile. He had tried to compromise and Stanton had turned him down. The odds were that CBS would lose.[24]

Stanton says, "I got the clear impression that the hit and run was on at the White House. People I trusted had talked with people at the White House staff and earlier had come away with the distinct impression that they were cheering on the other side. With all the circulation among journalists in Washington about whether they really would throw me in the clink, some of it had gotten back to me and was disquieting, because I thought these journalists were a lot closer to the real attitude about things than maybe I could get."

Springer had been given a "green light" at the "highest level."[25] But then, inside the White House, some of the senior staff had second thoughts. They began to consider what would happen after the Staggers contempt vote passed in the House. In early July, John W. Dean, Counsel to the President, wrote to William H. Rehnquist, Assistant Attorney General, asking what the administration's role might be: "The House is expected to vote on whether to hold CBS President Frank Stanton in contempt. . . . In anticipation of this vote, I would appreciate your office preparing a memorandum detailing the legal authority upon which the House would be acting and setting forth the expected scenario of events and the various ways that the Executive Branch could become involved in the event that the House does vote to hold Stanton in contempt. Because House action on this matter is expected in the immediate future, I would like to receive your response as soon as possible."[26]

House Minority Leader Gerald Ford had not taken a public position up to that time, although Staggers and his staff believed they had Ford's support. One of Staggers' staff says he understood Ford had spoken directly to Staggers promising his support. Congressional observers say that would have been unlikely as a practical matter; Ford would have talked with Springer. But Ford was seen as generally supportive of the House traditions, its institutional prerogatives and its exercise of subpoena power in an investigation. The reports were that Ford had "promised several on his side, including Mr. Springer, that he would support the contempt citation." On July 12 he had written a response to the news director of a television station in Michigan, saying that he had not yet decided how to vote. He enclosed, however, the statement put out by Staggers about why the contempt citation was being sought. But he, too, was having further thoughts.[27]

The Republicans saw that if the contempt citation were passed, it would fall to a Republican Attorney General to enforce it. This meant that in 1972, an election year, the press would report that a Republican Attorney General was seeking to place a man of the stature of Frank Stanton in jail and perhaps seeking to destroy CBS by proceeding against its licenses. From a political point of view, this was not an attractive prospect. There would be constant press coverage of the event. And the Republicans would be bringing such a result upon themselves in aid of a Democratic Committee's subpoena.

Ford discussed the problem with the White House staff. Earlier Ford had also spoken to Attorney General John Mitchell about the substance of the issue. On the night before the vote, Ford, as the minority leader, also spoke to the Republican members of the committee, particularly Broyhill as well as Brown, and in addition, talked with the White House staff about his political concern.[28]

Some had speculated that Nixon could publicly disavow any intention of harming CBS and let a Democratic committee hold Stanton and CBS in contempt. The dawning awareness that a Republican Attorney General would wind up as the prosecutor of the press made any such indirect strategy unacceptable, whatever the administration's feeling about network bias.

At the last moment, Nixon, Ford and the White House staff agreed and they changed their position. On July 12, the Republican leadership decided to vote against the citation. Herb Klein says he talked with Nixon, urging the White House not to support the contempt vote, and he was with Nixon at San Clemente just before the vote.[29] Colson says he talked to Nixon and "The reason that we called him off was that we thought it was better not to have a confrontation with the media, particularly coming as it would have right on the heels of the Pentagon Papers case." Haldeman approved, saying, "Get something for it."[30] Colson adds, "Bill Springer did have a green light from the White House. The reversal came after I talked to both Bill Paley and Frank Stanton and came to the belief that we could gain more by saving them, so to speak, from a contempt citation; perhaps develop a more hospitable relationship with CBS; and at the same time, avoid giving the impression that the Republican party was trying to censure the media. I communicated to Gerald Ford the President's decision."[31]

Ford was later to explain that there were two basic issues: first there was the First Amendment argument. He thought a case could be made that Stanton and CBS had legitimately opposed the Committee's demand for outtakes. "There was no question that television and radio were covered by the First Amendment." As for the program, there was "probably deceitful editing of the interviews and material," but on balance it appeared Stanton's and CBS' First Amendment rights would have been violated if the material had to be produced for Committee review.

The second issue was political. Would a Republican White House under Nixon be placed in an awkward position if it carried out a decision of a Democratic-controlled Committee on this press issue?[32]

Representative Springer, who had supported Staggers throughout and would continue to do so, was bitter and angry at the turn of events. He said he had been informed at the "highest level" only a few weeks before that President Nixon had no objection to the contempt citation.[33] Springer tried but was unable to appeal the decision by Ford and the White House staff, since Nixon was in San Clemente and he could not reach him.

Many Republicans would vote for contempt anyway, because of their outrage about network news bias. Whatever his personal concerns about the television press, Ford carried out his responsibility to his party and, as he came to see it, to the Constitution which associates say he truly "revered." He was a respected member of the House and had helped many Republicans get elected. His sense of the right thing to do and his position as Minority Leader led him to campaign vigorously against the contempt citation of CBS on the floor of the House.

He confirms the great impact the CBS stations had on their home members and says this lobbying was probably the most influential. As Ford puts it, you can make the "high and persuasive argument on the First Amendment issue," but the constituent votes in the home district, in this case spoken for by the members' local television stations, were the most powerful consideration. After all, he says, "This is how a democratic system works."[34]

The Staggers Subcommittee staff was later to say that the Republicans worked all through the night on July 12 to get their members to block the vote. This does not seem to be the case, but Manelli understood that the White House decided its press relations were bad enough and it didn't want to pursue the subpoena. This was, according to a disappointed Manelli, "about on the par with the rest of the advice they were getting at that time." He says the Republicans "really got mobilized at the end."[35]

While Staggers still believed he had commitments from the Democratic leadership, most Democratic Committee chairmen, Democratic members and a number of Republican members, the Democrats were also having second thoughts. They were beginning to feel pressure from the press coverage and particularly from the affiliates' lobbying. On the night before the vote, Albert formally asked Staggers to drop the fight because it would be "embarrassing." Staggers refused. The Democratic leadership concluded that a decision on what should be done would be made the first thing on the morning of July 13.[36]

Albert, as Speaker of the House, would decide what would be voted on and when. Polls of the Democratic members may have shown that there was no overwhelming support for enforcement of the subpoena, but to withdraw the support that had already been promised to Staggers would be something unheard of in the Congress at the time. It also would mean that Stanton and CBS would have defied the Commerce Committee of the Congress with impunity.

Chapter 13

The Constitutional Debate: Historic Moment for the Press

Carl Albert and the Democratic leadership called an early meeting for the morning of July 13. They did not invite Staggers. They decided to back off the citation. At the same time they did not want the House to be voting against its own authority. Some suggested it would be appropriate to refer the matter to the Judiciary Committee. They finally concluded it would be less humiliating to Staggers to recommit the citation to the Commerce Committee.[1]

Albert apparently was unable to hold his party in line. He had no overriding personal interest in a contempt citation fight. One major reason was a final poll taken by the Democratic leadership showing that only 71 of the 225 Democratic members favored the citation, 93 wished to do nothing and 91 actually opposed it. Albert was also being cautioned by some liberal chairmen against taking an anti-press position in what could turn out to be a bad test case.

Staggers had been warned that lobbying and speeches had hurt his cause, but he believed he still had commitments from the Democratic chairmen and a large number of Democratic and Republican members. After all, some of the chairmen and members were largely responsible for his conducting the investigation. On learning of the strategy meeting, he rushed from the floor to Albert's office and arrived just as the group was breaking up. He was too late. He was told by a colleague that Albert had decided to defer the motion. Staggers was stunned. He had a strong belief in his case and he was incensed at what was, to him, a betrayal by his peers. He accused Albert of "conniving" to defeat him.[2] But he still had many commitments. He would continue to try for the contempt citation.[3]

A constitutional debate on the floor of the House is a rare and historic event. The galleries were packed. Speaker Albert was in the chair. Hale Boggs (D-La.), the majority leader, monitored the vote as John Dingell helped manage the Staggers forces on the floor. Gerald Ford, the minority leader, was circulating, speaking to the Republican members.

Stanton says, "On July 13, I wasn't down for the vote. I did not go and sit in the gallery. I wanted to, but I thought better of it and Ted Koop said, 'we'll cover for you.' He was on the phone and I had a wire open all the time to the gallery and Koop was telling me what was going on. It was high drama, you know. I went into it originally believing we were going to win and, of course, I had run right into a stone wall." Despite the decisions of the leadership, it was still possible that Staggers could prevail. A large Democratic vote could do it or a modest Democratic vote with a large Republican vote could do it. Over 460 votes would be cast on the issue.

Staggers believed the vote would be taken immediately as a matter of House privilege and was surprised and annoyed to hear that there would be an objection to this. On the way to the floor, he wrote out his argument that this was a matter of "high privilege." When the debate opened, Staggers rose to claim the privilege of the House since the question went to the authority of the House itself. If accepted, a vote could be taken immediately under the House rules. Staggers knew that the sooner the vote was taken, the better for his cause. He sensed his votes could slip away. Although some voiced opposition to the question being raised as a privileged matter, the Chairman ultimately ruled it was a report of "high privilege" and that under the inherent constitutional powers of the House, it would be accepted and the customary requirement for a three-day layover would not apply.

Staggers then submitted the report of the Commerce Committee calling for the contempt vote and offered the privileged resolution calling for the citation of Dr. Frank Stanton and the Columbia Broadcasting System for contempt of Congress.

The clerk read the report, which described the subpoena and

Stanton's refusal to produce the outtakes. Staggers had earlier said the Committee "came in to hold CBS in contempt and CBS held Congress in contempt." Now, on the floor of the House, he spoke first. He was angry. "Mr. Speaker, to me the question is a very simple one. This subcommittee issued a subpoena, a duly authorized subpoena, and it was duly served. The question is whether it was complied with. However, as you have heard and read, it was not complied with . . . those who were cited in the subpoena were in contempt of the Congress of the United States. That means all of this Congress, not just one person, one committee, but the whole Congress of the United States was defied when they said, 'We will not deliver the materials that were requested.' " He repeated the statements of his position made a number of times before and said, "I do not believe the first amendment is involved in this question in any way whatsoever. . . . When Dr. Stanton appeared before our committee and we asked him certain questions, he refused to answer those questions. If this House ever makes the decision that that is not in contempt of this Congress, then God save and help America."[4]

Emmanuel Celler (D-N.Y.), Chairman of the Judiciary Committee, responded, "The first amendment towers over these proceedings like a colossus and no esprit de corps and no tenderness of one Member for another should force us to topple over this monument to our liberties; that is, the first amendment.

"Does the first amendment apply to broadcasting and broadcasting journalism?

"The answer is 'Yes.'. . .

"There may be no distinction between the right of a press reporter and a broadcaster. Otherwise, the stream of news may be dried up. . . . Do I share the grave and well motivated concern of the Committee on Interstate and Foreign Commerce with the real danger of deceptive practices and abuse of the media in the exercise of their rights? Yes, but these are hardly new concerns. James Madison addressed himself to these evils of the press. He said: 'Some degree of abuse is inseparable from the proper use of everything; and in no instance is this more true than in that of the press.'

"The press and TV often are guilty of misrepresentation and error. Some of this is inevitable in free debate. But 'the media, even if guilty of misrepresentation, must be protected if freedom of expression are to have the breathing space that they need to survive.' "[5]

Over 50 members spoke during the debate.[6] There was little praise for broadcasters. For example, William Springer (R-Ill.) (citing past instances of CBS abuses, the quiz show scandals and *Project Nassau*, where outtakes were produced and reviewed): "In the case of *The Selling of the Pentagon* CBS did not show what it purported to show because they stated these were the questions and the answers as given when in fact they were not the questions and answers that were given at all. The committee believes that it is defending the right of the people to know when a deceit or fraud occurs. . . . The American viewing public bases its decision at the ballot box upon the information it obtains from its most prominent news source—the TV set. The raw naked power to manipulate by gross fabrication the input data is the power to manipulate, however well intentioned, the decisionmaking process of the American electorate."

James T. Broyhill (R-N.C.): "Mr. Speaker, no member of this House of Representatives has been more critical of the methods of the broadcast media than I have, but I say that today you should vote 'no.' . . . Why should we be called upon to take this drastic action today . . . after only very short debate and after very limited opportunity for members to study the full record?" He said the material necessary to evaluate the documentary was available to the Committee and if the Committee intends to legislate, "let them go ahead and legislate." If the Court overturned the House vote, CBS would be strengthened.

It was, of course, still possible that a strong Republican vote in support of Staggers could help save the citation. But Staggers received still another blow to what he had always understood would be a sure thing.

On the other side of the aisle, Minority Leader Gerald Ford was urging Republicans to vote against the citation. As he was circulating among the Republican members, Ford says he could sense a shift in the vote. "When you have been around as long as I have," he says, "you get a feel for how the vote is going and Staggers was losing momentum."[7]

There was some explicit recognition of the First Amendment:

Richard H. Poff (R-Va.) [a leading constitutional law expert]: "The collision here is between the privilege of the press to edit for journalistic purposes and the privilege of the Congress to investigate for legislative purposes." He would resolve the question in favor of the press.

Jack Edwards (R-Ala.): "We can insist that CBS give fairer treatment . . . [but] we must not trespass as a legislative body, as a branch of the Federal Government, on their constitutional right to use their own editorial judgment. . . . It would be ever so easy to vote 'yes' today. CBS has maligned the South, colored the news, handled the coverage of the war in a biased manner, played up the bad and played down the good—all of this and more. But I would not exchange all this, as bad as it may be, for the evil that would infect this nation from a controlled press."

Abner J. Mikva (D-Ill.) asserted, "The right of a free press is not conditioned on its being a fair press. The right of the government to regulate the traffic on the airwaves does not grant the government the right to impose an official standard of truth."

David R. Obey (D-Wis.) said that the basic question is just how you accomplish a determination to require those using the public airwaves "to conduct themselves in a responsible and sensitive manner." He urged greater diversity and concluded, "I do not have an abundance of confidence that those who control our broadcast media will always be able to guarantee fair and impartial use of the airways. . . . I have even less confidence in our ability as politicians to guarantee that same impartial use and so I urge you to vote the resolution down."

Congressman Clarence Brown (R-Ohio) said, "The search for truth is much easier in an environment of freedom because freedom permits the multiplicity of views where all shades of truth can be found. . . . We should face frankly what is the greatest danger in the freedom of the networks to broadcast their version of the news—and that is that the three major networks night after night command an audience of most of our population to the same view of truth as they see. But the question remains as to whether even that concentration of power over the dissemination of a version of truth should be subjected to a single power; namely the power of government."

Brown said further, "The potential for further proliferation of voices exists in the technology of cable television and satellites. . . . Congress would be much better advised to consider how it can hasten the day when there are more methods of transmission of views and more individual ownership of those methods. . . . The networks may, indeed, be at the height of their power today in influencing Americans and persuading them to the positions held by a small group of executives in a narrow geographical and philosophical fringe of our Nation. But the power of that challenge to our national diversity should not be responded to with an exercise of power by the House which would deny this or any other minority of its right to exercise its biased views simply because of what those views are."

John J. Howard (D-N.J.): "What this House is being asked today is to vote again on the John Peter Zenger trial which occurred in New York City in 1775 and which resulted in Mr. Zenger being found not guilty of seditious libel. . . . Today, we are faced with a new threat to freedom of the press. It is a subtle threat and if it is approved by the House, its value as a precedent-setting measure will lend enormous weight to the argument of those who would further limit freedom of the press."

John Dingell continued to push for votes. Many did support Staggers. For example:

Wayne L. Hayes (D-Ohio): Stanton told him, "We didn't make a deliberate lie to an answer, but we did combine some answers and tape parts of answers and use them with a question to which they were not the answer." Hayes said, "Now I think it is pretty fundamental as to whether we are going to allow the news media to contrive whatever they want by splicing, by cutting, by putting things together, by faking . . . there is no degree in fakery. . . . We are going to make a decision here this afternoon about whether to put these people under notice that 'You stick fairly close to the truth when you tape a show for broadcast later.' "

James G. O'Hara (D-Mich.): "CBS can certainly broadcast news and opinions as it sees fit, but I do not believe it can deny the U.S. Congress its right to inquire into the techniques employed or to examine the television tape recordings used in the broadcast."

F. Edward Hébert (D-La.): "They cry first amendment, . . . and they have had their chance to lie under the First Amendment. If it were not for the First Amendment, they could not have practiced the deceit that they have practiced. I am one of the victims of that deceit because I was shown in the *Selling of the Pentagon*. The film that was shown was obtained from my office under false pretenses." He said the public has a right to know and how will it know "if we do not make them show what they have under the table and up their sleeves."

Chet Holifield (D-Calif.): He said he had two unfortunate experiences involving television network bias. The first was a documentary for the CBS Morning Report which used an hour of his interview time on a program, *The Dangers of Radiation*, which he was assured would be balanced. When the program was aired, only two and a half minutes of his filmed answers were used, and the balance of the program hour was used for arguments against his position. He had a similar experience with an NBC news program about nuclear power.

Robert Sikes (D-Fla.) (quoting Mr. Staggers): "The spread of calculated deception paraded as truth can devastate the earnest efforts of any one of us seeking to represent our constituents."

James Wright, Jr. (D-Tex.): "Today the three television networks contain the most powerful group of men in the United States. They are not elected by the public. . . . The networks are not licensed the way local television stations are licensed. . . . By their selection and treatment of news, the three networks are in a historically unrivaled position to mold the minds and control the impressions of many millions of Americans."

Henry R. Gonzales (D-Tex.): "The issue is whether someone except CBS is to be the arbiter of truth. . . . [*Hunger in America*] contained outright errors—or lies—about San Antonio, and greatly distorted the actual situation in the city. Yet CBS never felt that it had to do so much as admit it could have been wrong."

Mr. Staggers concluded, "this issue has produced the greatest lobbying effort that has ever been made on the Congress of the United States. . . . If this Congress is going to be intimidated by one of the giant corporations of America, and give up to them, then our Nation will never be able to exist as a free nation. . . . They must not be permitted to intimidate this Congress on this issue. . . . Search your consciences . . . and then say . . . 'I am going to vote the way my people would want me to vote.' . . . by every indication we have received, by 6 to 1 the people have said that the contempt citation is right."[8]

The first test vote on recommitting, that is, to send the citation back to the Staggers Commerce Committee, was taken. The division was ayes 151, noes 147.[9] Staggers would lose. One staff member says, "Members had come up to Staggers during the debate and asked to be released from their commitment to him. They said, 'Since you are going to lose, do you mind if I don't vote with you?' He released them from their commitments. Before that, it was a much closer vote than the final vote." Another staff member says, "Once it looked like it wasn't going to go, then a lot of people asked to be released, so you got the final result."[10]

The question was taken to recommit to the Committee on Interstate and Foreign Commerce, and the division was yeas 226, nays 181, answered present 2, not voting 24.[11]

Not all of the Republican members agreed with Ford or the White House. A very large Republican vote was ultimately cast for the citation, as was a large Democratic vote. Had the Democrats held the line on a party leadership call, Staggers would have won. Or, had the Republicans voted as a bloc, he might have won. But once the leadership decided against the citation, there was little likelihood it could pass. But still, a large number of Democrats as well as Republicans, altogether a total of 181 (105 Democrats and 76 Republicans), voted for the citation.

Stanton issued a statement: "We are very pleased by the decisive House vote to recommit the proposed contempt citation to the Commerce Committee. As responsible journalists we shall continue to do our best to report on public events in a fair and objective manner." Staggers was bitter about his colleagues. One report noted, "He would have found some basis for reopening the whole thing if he thought he could be vindicated."[12] A staff member adds, "Staggers would take you by the hand and say a prayer and then as you were leaving he would then take you again by the hand. He could not understand how this could have happened to him."[13] For the first time since 1945, the House had failed to support one of its committee chairmen in a vote for his subpoena.

The House traditionally did business through commitments. The commitments made to Staggers by any number of members had been broken; he had been deserted by his own leadership and his fellow chairmen. Publicly and to his aides he claimed that the loss did not bother him, but it certainly had to. Congressman Van Deerlin says that since the House works by members' commitments, with the switch in votes, Staggers was entitled to be bitter.[14]

Had Staggers won, the impact on the television press would have been severe. The television press would be subject to continued second-guessing in congressional hearings called to review television news coverage for acceptability. It could not help but become weak, even submissive.

Some commentators said only a person of the stature of Stanton could have won. Neil McNeil, congressional correspondent for *Time* magazine, said that the political clout in Congress came from the affiliates around the country.[15]

Springer was reported as saying, "A lobbying campaign such as they had never seen before . . . reached the peak of its intensity on the eve of the vote. I must have personally talked to between 60 and 80 Republicans who ran to me and asked what the hell was going on. They all had been contacted, most of them several times, by TV and radio people. . . . I haven't seen anything like this in my 21 years."[16]

Ford's decision to oppose the citation was described later in the press as an "abrupt switch" decided by the White House.[17] Ford says he now does not recall whether he or the White House made the call, but he thought it would be bad public relations in an election year for the Republican administration to be backing such a move by a Democratic committee.[18]

Jack Anderson reported: "Usually affable House Commerce Committee Chairman Staggers (D-W.Va.) is still smarting from what he considers a personal insult from an old friend, Speaker Albert (D-Okla.)." But the real bitterness had to come from the fact that Staggers' fellow chairmen—his peers in the House—had not supported him. For a political figure who was a "member of the Club" and held his chairmanship in large part because of that, this defeat could not have been more cruel.[19] A staff member says Staggers kept a list of the members who voted against him that day.[20]

Stanton remembers, "I was Chairman of the U.S. Advisory Commission on Information and on the first Monday morning following the vote, the speaker on the calendar for that breakfast happened to be John Mitchell. I went out to meet John Mitchell and he smiled and said he didn't expect to see me. As we walked back to the room, he said, 'You know, we were all set to push you right through. We had everything lined up because we were going to make an example of you. We were told that we had the votes and we were absolutely dumbfounded when you pulled this one out.' "

Colson advised Haldeman on July 14, "I do not really believe they needed us. In any event, I am going to play it for all it's worth." Stanton met with Colson on July 15. He says he was apprehensive about the meeting because it might be misconstrued, but maintaining relations with the White House was important to CBS. He listened to Colson's complaints about CBS coverage, noted them and said he wanted to hear any pitches they wanted to make in the future so he would know about them. He made no commitments about news coverage. He says he thanked Colson for any help he had given because Colson said he had helped, but he says he did not think Colson had saved him from jail, as Colson claimed.

Colson reported on July 20 to Haldeman that he stressed this meeting had been initiated by CBS and there would not be the embarrassment that resulted when Ehrlichman visited Salant sometime before to ask for the removal of Dan Rather from the White House beat and Salant had gone public. He said he had told Stanton that all the administration wanted was "occasional fairness" and pressed hard on what he called "dishonest journalism." With material he had prepared, he compared the CBS coverage with that of the other two networks and argued Nixon had been treated badly by CBS in its coverage of the economy, Nixon's popularity in the polls and a list of subjects he wished corrected. Colson concluded, "I don't expect great things. Anything we gain will be a plus." He thought CBS had given them a little better treatment the last few nights but noted this was a typical pattern. "We got a rash of very good coverage for a few weeks," and then they fell back into their old ways. The report notes that the President was verbally briefed.[21]

Stanton made repeated efforts to see Chairman Staggers after the vote. Staggers would not meet him or take his phone calls. Stanton had written a personal letter to Staggers the day after the vote:

Dear Harley:

This note comes to you by hand because I want you to have it before you leave for home.

All through this whole matter that has preoccupied both of us for so many weeks, the most distressing thing for me personally was to find myself an adversary opposed to an old and greatly admired friend.

You would not have been the man I know you to be had you failed to take a position that seemed to you very important to the national interest. I know you recognized that, as spokesman for my associates, I was obliged to take an opposite view for the very same reason. The only thing that made me feel good about the confrontation was the knowledge that both of us were trying to do what we thought best for our country.

Have a good rest this weekend. I'd like to come down one of these days and have a visit with you.

Sincerely,

FRANK

14 July, 1971

Stanton says: "I never got a word back. I believe we saw each other at some event and he turned away. And I made the effort to come down and suggested to others that if he had some time I would like to come down and visit with him. Because this was not an evil man. In a sense, I felt sorry for him. But, he wouldn't respond and I was into that cold stare."

Staggers had said after the defeat he would not raise the contempt action again. He did authorize investigations into news practices on the West Coast.[22] His staff says a number of network and station cameramen came in secretly to report on staging. The investigation was expanded, and in May of 1972 another hearing was held on the news practices in television, covering all aspects of TV news gathering and broadcasting ranging from guidelines to staging. Testimony was taken primarily from cameramen. A staff report was published, but nothing came of it.[23] The feared legislation to license the networks was never enacted. The most telling comment was from Rep. Broyhill, who had helped save CBS despite his strong disagreement with their news coverage. He says, "I got even by voting for cable."[24]

One analysis showed that 55% of the Republicans voted against Staggers, with Broyhill taking the initiative and enlisting the help of Kilpatrick with 16 important Republican votes, all but one of whom voted to recommit. The Democratic leadership failed to close ranks behind Staggers, and the Albert and Ford positions made it easier for traditionalists to leave Staggers. Those voting against CBS included the big-city and industrial labor leaders as well as those with personal grievances.[25]

Stanton says, "I ended this whole experience feeling pretty good about Congress, because when the chips were down and they understood what the issue was and forget whatever they felt about the network and saw that this was central to the future, the guys came through and that gave me a very strong feeling. It's essential that you get to be heard in something like this. There are a lot of cynics around New York that think that Congress is just a rubber stamp. I came away from this experience thinking if you could do a reasonably good job of letting them know what's up, it'll come out on the right side. The trouble is that they are so busy that you can't get in. That's where the affiliates helped. I don't know if I would have been heard, although anybody in the network could have gotten some hearing.

"I don't know what might happen next time. We have to be concerned. Some public official may see an opportunity to make political hay out of a mistake by a news person and could lead the charge. Also, I don't know whether the *Pentagon* fight gave broadcasters, not second thoughts, but pause before they would take on the government again in an investigative report. Nobody wants to say that. Certainly a small station operator has got to say, 'who needs this?' and next time around, as they are quoted as saying, 'we'll do something on the ecology.'

"The desire for government regulation will affect the next media generations. No matter how much a broadcaster talks about his freedom, there's still plenty of room to be harassed by government leaders, whether it's on the local or the national level. You won't have a free press that embraces broadcasting with the same freedoms as print until the Supreme Court comes down and says so. I used to say to Dick Salant, you know, we'll fight, but let's be sure that we're so buttoned up that we're not going to be taken to court, because we just might lose.

"It's still too early to really know how all this is going to work, but the reconciliation of the tube and print will come sooner than we think, because of the introduction of online and other electronic services. The manipulation of the new computer and digital visual material is much more dangerous than anything done with splicing of audio or film. I don't even know how you would certify it, except with an interactive technique, as we now know it. If you said, this is happening in front of your very eyes and the viewer could say let me ask him a question, so I can see that he is live, then you could establish the certainty that what he was saying was taking place and, in time, build up credibility for that particular news organization. The fact that it could happen would tend to keep the program honest.

"And then you've got someone like Howard Stern who doesn't help you at all. At least we were fighting on a public issue. It's hard to ask citizens of the community to actively come to the defense of these freedoms when you do what he does. But you can't have any middle ground. In my opinion, you've got to slug it out and just hope that you prevail, because the government has got all the cards on their side and they usually don't really want a free press."

Chapter 14

The Public's Interest

Stanton's success meant Congress did not thereafter subpoena broadcast press outtakes to review news judgment. But there was little said by the government about the value of press freedom. Quite the contrary. The White House, Congress and the courts continued efforts to restrict the television press in pursuit of what they saw as appropriate government control.

At the White House, things continued as before. John Ehrlichman wrote the President in September 1971 that the Justice Department should go forward with the antitrust cases against the networks, which had been held up. A note, hand-written by Nixon, said "vitally important to plan the P.R. aspects. Get Coulson [*sic*] in on this phase of it."[1] Government antitrust action against a licensed industry has greater risks than for business generally. Conviction on any count would carry civil penalties but, for broadcasters, it could be a demerit against license renewal and grounds for the loss of broadcast licenses.

In October 1971, Colson wrote to Haldeman, "We have been putting some very intense pressure on CBS through their affiliate board. I just obtained a copy of a memo from Salant to one of his assistants which would indicate that perhaps the pressures are doing some good . . . it's clear that continuous pressure does at least penetrate the news organizations to some extent."[2]

In December 1971, Klein visited each of the network heads with a friendly warning that if their news coverage did not change, antitrust suits would be brought against them. He says he had seen a draft of the complaint and says the data were about 20 years old. Its use was "suspicious." The FCC had already blocked the networks from broadcasting in the early evening and had limited their production of prime time programs. Klein says he could see how the networks would conclude that the suits brought now on the same subject were in retaliation for their news coverage.[3]

The networks did not change their news coverage to meet the administration's views, and in April 1972 the Nixon Justice Department did bring antitrust suits against them. The court initially dismissed the cases because of defense charges of political purpose and the Justice Department's refusal to produce documents on that issue. But the court did so "without prejudice" and later, under the Ford administration, the Justice Department, once committed to the course, refiled the suits. They were ultimately settled by consent decrees. When the suits were brought, the *New York Times* said in its editorial of April 18, 1972: "There are elements in the background of the present Federal action against the broadcasters which engender doubt whether its origins may not lie as much in politics as in zeal for law enforcement. . . . A regulated medium of communications, subject to periodic license review, is particularly vulnerable to hints of governmental harassment. When those hints come as frequently as they have from this administration, the danger that they will exert a chilling effect on freedom to comment and to criticize—especially in a national election year—is incontestable."

The *Washington Post* later learned of other White House efforts directed against the press, including "an April, 1972, break-in at the Georgetown home of Dan Rather, the CBS television news reporter. Rather had been accused earlier that year of bias in his reporting by John D. Ehrlichman, then President Nixon's top domestic aide. . . . Acting FBI Director William D. Ruckelshaus, in a statement later confirmed by a White House spokesman, said . . . that 13 government officials and four reporters had their telephones tapped between May, 1969, and February, 1971. The White House spokesman later said that Mr. Nixon had personally authorized the wiretaps." Nixon was also to use the FBI to investigate CBS correspondents Marvin Kalb and Daniel Schorr and the IRS to audit Kalb's tax returns.[4]

Certainly of importance to the administration was the *Washington*

Post exposé of the Republican-supported break-in at Democratic headquarters at the Watergate complex. At the White House, the *Post* was seen as the problem and the need was to keep the story contained, at least until after the election.

In June 1972, the networks had reported the Watergate break-in, accepting the White House characterization of it as a "3rd rate burglary attempt" and its statement that Nixon was not involved. For months, the *Washington Post* had reported there was more to the story, but it remained "inside the beltway" and not a "national story." The networks did not follow up, and some have put this down to fear of Nixon.

Daniel Schorr writes that then, in October 1972, "Knowing nothing of the [CBS] empire under siege, we in our little news province, proceeded to steer CBS into greater danger. At this of all times we decided that Watergate needed more attention on television."[5] CBS decided to devote two unusually long segments to the story on Walter Cronkite's *CBS Evening News*. The first, which took up two-thirds of the program, aired on Friday, October 27, 1972. It reported on charges being made of a "high level campaign of political sabotage and espionage apparently unparalleled in American history." Stanton saw it on the 6:30 edition. He suggested Paley watch the 7:00 edition because he knew there would be objection from the White House. Paley called him later that evening to say he thought it was too long.

Colson had earlier learned of the report and called Stanton and argued that such a report would be unfair. When Stanton did not agree, Colson finally said the question was not whether the report was unfair. It should not be broadcast at all. Stanton replied that CBS News would cover the story. Colson called Paley after the broadcast. Sally Bedell Smith writes, "Colson was more exercised than usual in his call to Paley on October 28 [about the report]—only days away from the 1972 presidential election. CBS had reason to be especially sensitive. The previous April, Nixon's Justice Department had filed an antitrust suit against the networks and the FCC was debating whether to force each of the networks to sell its complement of five local television stations. . . . 'Colson talked to me for a long time,' Paley recalled. 'He was pretty vicious.'

"The following Monday, Paley convened a meeting with Stanton, Richard Salant, and other top CBS executives. Paley never mentioned the Colson call, but he was extremely agitated. He insisted that the segment had been too long and had violated CBS standards by mingling fact and opinion. . . . Paley said his longtime second-in-command agreed with him completely. Stanton, in fact, disagreed. 'I didn't share Bill's concern over the Watergate piece,' said Stanton. . . . Although Paley did not explicitly refer to the second part, Salant knew the chairman well enough to decipher his message: shorten the segment, or even better, kill it.

"Back at the CBS News offices, Salant postponed the second segment for a day and worked with the evening news producers to shorten it. 'They knew I had been on the carpet with Paley,' said Salant. 'They knew I was troubled when I said, I hope I feel this way because I am fair and honest.' "[6] The segment ran seven minutes instead of the planned fourteen, and in the view of some had become a superficial summary minus the detail that could have given it muscle.[7]

Months later Salant deduced that the White House had been involved in the censorship effort after a speech by Colson, which used much the same attack Paley had recited. After the election, Henry Cashen, assistant to Colson, said to Schorr, "We didn't stop your goddamn Watergate spectacular, but we sure cut you down a bit, didn't we?"[8]

At an Oval Office meeting on September 15, 1972, White House transcripts reflect a conversation between Nixon and John Dean, his counsel, in which Dean brought up the *Washington Post* investigation of the break-in:

> *President*: The main thing is the *Post* is going to have damnable, damnable problems out of this one. They have a television station . . . and they're going to have to get it renewed.
>
> *Haldeman*: They've got a radio station, too.
>
> *President*: Does that come up, too? The point is, when does it come up?
>
> *Dean*: I don't know. But the practice of non-licensees filing on top of licensees has certainly gotten more . . . active in . . . this area.
>
> *President*: And it's going to be God damn active here.

On October 27, 1972, Colson asked for the dates when the licenses owned by the *Washington Post* came up for renewal. A challenge was ultimately filed against the *Post* station in Jacksonville, Florida.[9]

The 1972 Nixon reelection campaign was highly successful. Nixon had written that modern presidents "must try to master the art of manipulating the media," and some believed his campaign was a "virtually flawless case study of media manipulation." In the opinion of some, "the press generally gave the president a free ride."[10] William Safire writes that it was obvious to White House insiders that their anti-press activities forced the networks to tone down criticism of presidential speeches.[11]

After the election, CBS sought to maintain relations with the White House. Stanton recalls receiving a threat from Colson about CBS licenses and its business. Colson later denied making such a threat.[12] Public disclosure is usually the best defense the press has against the use of government threats against it. And while network executives did go public about their general concerns over the use of government power against them, they spoke little about the threats made in private meetings and telephone calls. Daniel Schorr points out that had government intimidation of the magnitude used against the television press been used against any other regulated industry, it would certainly have been thought newsworthy and reported by CBS, among others. He says that the networks did not do so because of "the fear of escalating the cold war into open hostilities against an enemy who seemed to control the weapons of massive retaliation."[13]

There was also the issue of news integrity. Stanton says he made the decision not to publicize the threats both to insulate the CBS reporters and to maintain the integrity of CBS News coverage of the White House. Disclosure of the threats could affect the news staff and affect their public credibility. He also did not believe he should use the CBS News organization to defend its own interests when its professional obligation was to cover the White House as an impartial news organization. Moreover, if the network used its facilities to attack the administration, the affiliated stations would be involved and this could bring down government sanction on them and jeopardize their licenses for decisions they did not control and might not agree with. It was something the network, in good conscience, could not do.

The same judgment was reached at NBC by its President, Julian Goodman. The head of NBC News at the time, Reuven Frank, says that Stanton made the right decision, and the administration threats should have been kept from the news reporters if they were to do their job in an impartial manner.[14]

After the election, official threats were made against the network affiliates in an effort to bring network news into line with Nixon-approved views. Dr. Clay Whitehead, who had been appointed Director of the White House Office of Telecommunications Policy said to the news association Sigma Delta Chi in December 1972: "Station managers and network officials who fail to act to correct imbalance or consistent bias from the networks—or who acquiesce by silence—can only be considered willing participants to be held fully accountable . . . at license renewal time."[15] Nicholas Johnson, an FCC commissioner, said that what the words appeared to mean was that "individual stations will be expected to correct their real or imagined bias on anti-administration news and comment." Senator Sam Ervin saw it as a "a thinly veiled attempt to create government censorship over broadcast journalism."[16]

Even before Whitehead's speech, some CBS Network affiliates had put up slides stating that what the viewer was seeing was CBS NEWS NETWORK ANALYSIS or stating "THIS DOES NOT REPRESENT THE VIEWS OF THIS STATION." *Sticks and Bones*, a prizewinning play which opposed the Vietnam War, was cancelled by CBS when 80 of the 184 CBS affiliates said they would refuse to carry it. When Whitehead was asked what he thought of the network's folding to its affiliates, Whitehead said, "This is a good example of how the process ought to work."[17]

On June 6, 1973, after Stanton retired, Paley announced that CBS would no longer provide instant analysis after the President's speeches on television. The following week, Nixon's speech about his peace plans for Vietnam was carried by the three networks. The other networks offered post-speech commentary but CBS did not and returned to its entertainment programming, *Sonny and Cher*. The *New York Times* reported there was speculation, since Paley was unavailable for comment, that the decision "represented, at least in part, a response to pressure from CBS-affiliated stations."[18] One CBS newsman, who asked that his name not be used, said, "Analysis is one of the things we've always done better than the other networks. When the going got tough on this matter after Agnew's blast, C.B.S. didn't buckle, but now it has—on the executive level." Some thought it had knuckled under to the White House.[19] Stanton says, "Paley's friends called him and said, 'you shouldn't do this.' He really didn't stand up to protect the opportunity for news coverage. And it's too bad." Paley's decision to end instant analysis was seen as "catastrophic" by CBS newsmen.

Congress continued its oversight. In the face of massive lobbying, it had not supported the Staggers contempt citation. But it took no action to stop the White House threats against the licensed broadcast industry and its new coverage. It made no effort to change its licensing system. When Bill Paley dropped instant analysis from CBS, Senator John Pastore, who as Chairman of the Senate Subcommittee on Communications had been instrumental in seeing that regulation of the broadcast press was maintained, issued a statement calling Paley's action "a mistake." He said the "networks should not be intimidated by the government."[20] But such an exhortation would not likely offset a White House move to put a station license at risk.

In 1973, the Chairman of the House Subcommittee on Communications, Torbert MacDonald (D-Mass.), condemned the Nixon intimidation. After referring to the White House actions against the networks and the censorship plan announced by Whitehead, he said, "there's nothing the Executive Branch can do to or for you. Your job is to see to it that the news is reported accurately and fairly, by professional journalists, period. And to the newsmen themselves, I say keep on calling it as you see it. . . . And I, for one, will fight for your right to report them."[21] But he did not fight for such a right.

In the early 1970s, the FCC, under Chairman Richard Wiley, had sought to limit its Fairness Doctrine as burdensome to the flow of information. Wiley said that there was no scarcity of radio in the big cities (scarcity had been the technological basis for the Supreme Court's approval of the Fairness Doctrine), and consideration should be given to releasing these thousands of radio stations from the Doctrine: "It may be that the marketplace would be able to handle the situation in the absence of governmental regulation." Senator John Pastore, Chairman of the Senate Subcommittee on Communications, stopped him.[22]

Finally, in 1985, under Chairman Mark Fowler, the FCC issued an exhaustive report showing the Doctrine clearly chilled speech and, under successor Chairman Dennis Patrick, the FCC refused to enforce portions of the Doctrine.[23] Congress objected to this but was unable to take action. Its efforts to enact the Doctrine into law were vetoed by President Reagan, and a veto was threatened by President Bush.[24]

Requirements for certain amounts of public affairs programming may have served the public, but content regulation did not. Smaller stations feared fairness complaints, the cost of their defense and their threat to license renewals. Well-financed special interests used the FCC to silence opposition. For example, groups which opposed nuclear power threatened stations which ran pro-nuclear views with Fairness complaints. The FCC found two-thirds of the threatened stations refused to provide time for pro-nuclear views because of concerns about FCC proceedings. This was an all-too-common occurrence. The FCC found over 60 reported instances of this kind of inhibition. The Doctrine did not encourage debate, much less robust debate.

Bill Monroe, the Washington editor of NBC's *Today* show, explained: "We . . . know there are stations that don't do investigative reporting. There are stations that confine their documentaries to safe subjects. There are stations that do outspoken editorials, but are scared to endorse candidates. My opinion is that much of this kind of caution, probably most of it, is due to a deep feeling that boldness equals trouble with government, blandness equals peace."[25]

In its review of programming the FCC even counted lines of transcript and timed segments with stop watches to measure statements on various sides on what it thought were the controversial issues addressed and the "twists" in the various arguments. It could require more or different programming for "fairness." It was government-approved, but it was not news coverage.[26]

In upholding the constitutionality of broadcast press regulation in *Red Lion*, the Supreme Court used the First Amendment prohibition against laws abridging press freedom as authority for abridging that freedom where there was electronic scarcity. It also accepted the doctrine of the FCC that a central government agency with members appointed by the President would see that the press provided fair news coverage and robust debate better than the press would on its own.

In light of what has happened since then, it is increasingly obvious that the Court's approach was unfortunately uninformed and its technology premise now seriously out of date. Fred Friendly's book, *The Good Guys, the Bad Guys and the First Amendment*, tells of his investigation of the *Red Lion* case. He reports that, at the time, there was a campaign by one political party to silence voices of the other. Political speech stands at the highest level of speech protected by the First Amendment because it is the most important to the public. Yet this speech was suppressed.[27]

Friendly reports that the Kennedy campaign believed it was unfairly attacked by right-wing conservatives and used FCC Fairness Doctrine proceedings or the threat of them to force them off the air. The DNC then set up a front organization to harass stations which criticized the Johnson administration. It reported that its 1,035 letters threatening stations were successful in "inhibiting the political activity of these right-wing broadcasts," particularly because the stations were small and had little revenues.

The events leading up to *Red Lion* apparently prompted attention from this organization. When Cook criticized Rev. Hargis in a magazine, Harris then criticized Cook over the air in time he bought on the Red Lion station. Cook asked for free broadcast time to reply to Hargis. The station refused that request, offering to sell Cook time. The Democratic front group volunteered information to Cook about filing a complaint with the FCC. The FCC held that the station's refusal violated its rules, and the Supreme Court upheld the FCC. It held the FCC's Fairness Doctrine and right of reply rules constitutional because of spectrum scarcity and its view that the FCC rules would promote the broadcast of contrasting views and robust debate. The Court and lawyers did not know of the campaign to use those same rules to drive particular political views off the air.[28]

In all events, the decision was a significant departure from traditional First Amendment holdings protecting speech and the print press. No rational case can be made that there is electronic scarcity now in the presence of the great abundance of electronic channels and delivery systems, and since that decision, the FCC has found that its Fairness Doctrine, in fact, chills speech and press. Still, the Court has not set aside *Red Lion*. Its reasoning remains a threat for future electronic systems, and the case continues to be cited as authority for electronic speech and press regulation.

For some who do not like or fear the imperfections of a news process of great reach, it was and is tempting to turn to an imagined, impartial central government agency to make the news "fairer" or more "responsible." Some commentators still see regulation by a government agency as a desirable way of providing "access" and "good" news programming.[29] But, as the FCC found, the experience of broadcasting shows that government regulation necessarily restricts the flow of information, news and opinion to the public. This is made particularly acute when news organizations are part of a government-licensed industry.[30]

Judge David Bazelon of the federal appellate court in Washington, D.C., wrote: "To argue that a more effective press requires a more regulated press flies in the face of what history has taught us about the values and purposes of protecting the individual's freedom of speech."[31] If belief in speech and press regulation is part of the judicial approach to the electronic media, *Red Lion* will continue to undermine First

Amendment protection for the news media. As the print press moves onto the Information Superhighway, its electronic delivery of news and information may also be subject to the apprehensions reflected in the *Red Lion* decision and subsequent cable decisions.

Jack Fuller, the president and publisher of the *Chicago Tribune*, recently warned of what he calls the government's "temptation to regulate" the press and its opportunity to do so in the new electronic Information Age. It is not only that *Red Lion* is a precedent. He points out that "the media represents a locus of countervailing power against government, thus they offer government an attractive regulatory target." The other way government officials seek to control the media is to "exercise the power of the state directly upon them. For a number of reasons, the danger of this is increasing." He concludes that in the constant conflict between the press and the government, the balance has tilted further and further toward the government side, "especially in the regulation of the electronic media. No matter how much you hear about deregulation, do not expect government officials to give up this power without a fight . . . already new reasons are being incubated."[32]

Cable does not use "scarce spectrum." But the Supreme Court recently held in the *Denver* case that cable could not have full First Amendment protection for its content because, it said, cable was "pervasive." In determining the constitutionality of the Cable Television Consumer Protection and Competition Act of 1992, which restricts indecency on cable, only Justice Kennedy, joined by Justice Ginsburg, used historical First Amendment criteria to protect free speech.

Several Justices explicitly moved away from traditional speech guarantees, and Justices Breyer and Souter effectively ruled that censorship regulation is appropriate for an evolving technology, with Justice Souter saying, "the judicial obligation is, 'First, do no harm.' " Justice Kennedy noted that if there was concern about technology's direction, the Court should begin "by allowing speech, not suppressing it." Certainly, "giving the government the benefit of the doubt when it restricts speech, is an unusual approach to the First Amendment, to put it mildly." It could be said that the view of a plurality of the Court appears to be that government restraint on press and speech has become acceptable for the electronic mass media. As the *New York Times* observed on July 1, 1996, the Court's approach cannot help but create "nervousness for publishers of news."[33]

Since the provisions at issue in the *Denver* case were for the protection of children, recognition of the government's interest was given particular weight. But adults are usually not limited to material acceptable for children, and "indecency" has long been considered protected speech, unlike "obscenity." Moreover, cable is not available "free" over the air. A viewer must subscribe and must pay for the programming, like print material. Among other things, the Court's opinion denies the adult viewer the ability to select such programming when regulations prohibit.

On April 1, 1997, in another decision, the Supreme Court held (5–4) that cable systems "must carry" local broadcast station signals. As the *New York Times* reported, the regulations were upheld as affecting industry structure and were "content neutral," that is, not directed to program content. In all events, the Court said they did not violate the First Amendment.[34]

The Internet holds great promise for the flow of information in the Information Age. In 1996, government steps were taken to restrict its content through the creation of the Communications Decency Act (C.D.A.), which made it a federal crime to display indecent material online in a way available to minors. "Indecency" is often the wedge used to assert control over content. Criminal prosecution or its possibility can make users timid. A special three-judge court held the C.D.A. unconstitutional. It said that the Internet was the most participatory form of speech yet developed, and concluded that the very chaos of the medium was its greatest potential and greatest protection from government regulation.

The technological scope of the Internet may in all events make effective legal control difficult. But, significantly, this same court explicitly accepted and reiterated the *Red Lion* decision that radio and television cannot have full First Amendment protection because they use scarce spectrum.

On June 26, 1997, the Supreme Court agreed with the special three-judge court and declared the C.D.A. unconstitutional. In a 7–2 decision, Justice Stevens held that the Internet was not constitutionally subject to the vague censoring of the C.D.A. The fault in the statute was that, "In order to deny minors access to potentially harmful speech, the C.D.A. effectively suppresses a large amount of speech that adults have a right to receive and to address to one another." Moreover, under the broad statute, a parent communicating, for example, to their child about birth control could be subject to criminal prosecution.

In fact, the courts would have difficulty in overseeing Internet communications since it already has over 60 million users of material from worldwide sources with vast, diverse and privately interconnected networks of communication. While the Court recognizes the government's interest in protecting children, it repeats earlier statements that the government may not reduce the adult population to "only what is fit for children."

Thus, the Court provides broad First Amendment protection to Internet communications. Whether narrower statutory prohibitions could be sustained is not entirely clear. Internet sources promptly announced that they would now increase efforts to regulate the Internet privately to prevent access by minors to unacceptable material through technological and empowerment techniques, enlisting the aid of parents, schools and libraries to oversee children's use of the Internet.

The Court still does not depart from its rationale for government control of broadcasting and cable. As the *New York Times* reported, the protection given to the Internet is similar to that for books and newspapers. "That stands in contrast to the more limited First Amendment rights accorded to speech on cable and television, where the court has tolerated a wide array of government regulation." Justice Stephens supported the Court's continuing approval of such regulation on the grounds that there are "special justifications" for regulating broadcasting; for example, a "history" of extensive government regulation, frequency scarcity at its inception and its "invasive" nature. On the Internet, computer users must search for material, and in the case of indecent material they "seldom encounter it accidentally." Thus, the Court's threat to speech and press in its *Red Lion* and *Denver* decisions continues at a time when the Court looks to freedom of speech and press in the Information Age.[35]

The Court substitutes "pervasiveness," "intrusiveness" and "invasiveness" for the now-obsolete rationale of "scarcity" so that broadcast and cable programming remains subject to government oversight and regulation, and the public's primary source of news remains at risk of government interference and future censorship. What does the Court fear from broadcast and cable news services? It seems to have no willingness to provide "bright line" protection for these known and established sources of information about government and government abuse.

For many years, the Supreme Court was noted for its courage in upholding First Amendment protections. In an earlier Supreme Court decision, Justice Black said, "the press was protected so that it could bare the secrets of the government and inform the people. Only a free and unrestrained press can effectively expose deception in government."[36] Justice Brandeis warned that "Experience should teach us to be most on our guard to protect liberty when the government purposes are beneficent."[37] Judge Learned Hand had a large view of freedom of speech and press for our nation's future. He said, "Right conclusions are more likely to be gathered out of a multitude of tongues, than through any kind of authoritative selection. To many this is, and always will be, folly; but we have staked upon it our all."[38] But today the Court turns inward to impose constraints on a new service, like cable, based not on our traditions of freedom but on failed policies for regulated broadcasting.

Whether print, broadcasting, cable, satellite, telephone or Internet, the real question is: Is it news? If it is, then it should have full First Amendment standing. That is the teaching of the First Amendment and the need of a free people.

The effort should be to put news beyond the reach of government. The consolidation of media organizations in recent years makes this issue no less significant. As such companies approach Washington to advance their economic interests, which are increasingly dependent upon government grant and good will, trimming the news to avoid offending the government may well seem prudent, if not irresistible.

In January 1995, the Chairman of the House Commerce Committee, Thomas A. Bliley (R-Va.), held a two-day meeting on how the new Information Superhighway should be organized and who should get what. Over 40 CEOs of cable, telephone, satellite, broadcasting, print, computer and other media companies attended a meeting closed to the public and press. At the final dinner, Newt Gingrich, the speaker of the House, "lit into the media." No one rose to object or defend the obligations of the press as in years past. When asked how the news could be made more "fair," the Speaker said corporate owners were responsible for keeping their reporters in line.[39]

International communications magnate Rupert Murdoch was reportedly quick to drop British Broadcasting Corp. news from his satellite television service in Northern Asia because of Chinese complaints about the BBC. Apparently, specific complaints were made about a program on Chairman Mao broadcast in Europe.[40] Gerald M. Levin, head of Time Warner, Inc., has said the distrust of the press will only be encouraged if owners have no history and regard for the importance of the integrity of journalism.[41]

Joan Konner, Dean of the Columbia University Graduate School of Journalism, voiced concern about news being managed "for the last nickel." She asks, "What owner or manager in the communications media today is publicly articulating the themes of higher standards and high ideals?"[42] The *New York Times* noted in an editorial on November 17, 1995, "Perhaps the biggest change in recent years was increased business pressures on news rooms." Since corporate executives "set the amount of financial risk" they are willing to take, "the decline of the First Amendment traditions are part of the changing values in the news business."

Rather than resisting the government, if large organizations accommodate the government to advance their economic interests, then intimidation may not even be necessary. Acceptance of "reasonable rules" for the "responsible" use of the highway or for "access" to the highway will simply be part of the bargain, explicit or implicit, that new media owners will make.

Thomas W. Hazlett, formerly Chief Economist of the FCC and a teacher of economics and finance at the University of California–Davis, wrote in the *Wall Street Journal* on May 6, 1966: "As one FCC official recently told me, the broadcasters are 'tripping all over themselves to give up their First Amendment rights.' It is unseemly when politicians pander to the electorate; it is positively dangerous to our democratic health when the press panders to the politicians."

Stanton points out that once government regulation is in place, resistance is hazardous and costly. Referring to his own experience with *The Selling of the Pentagon*, he says, "If you were a station operator in Yakima, Washington, and you ran into this kind of a problem with the Congress, you would be bankrupt in no time because this is a costly thing to do. With a small newspaper, the print press is so well organized or has become organized over the years that some of the larger papers would probably have come in to help. I don't know whether broadcasting at that time was that mature. In fact, I don't even think it's that mature today. I don't just see how an independent operator could have had the muscle and the deep pockets to really do it."

The time has come for *Red Lion* and its doctrine of press regulation to be abandoned. The Court should withdraw it as authority for the regulation of electronic news. Pressure could still be exerted on broadcast licensees, and this has its own dangers. But full First Amendment standing for all electronic news would strengthen support of news freedom and the willingness to protect it.

Chapter 15

On a Personal Note: Stanton's Departure

Stanton had announced his intention to retire on his sixty-fifth birthday, which was the rule he imposed on other executives and to which he held himself. There were awkward tensions with Paley during his last year. Stanton believes his stand on *The Selling of the Pentagon* put a severe strain on his relationship with Paley.

"While Paley didn't say, 'don't you think we ought to find some graceful way to concede,' I had the impression that if somebody had given him an olive branch he would have taken it. He would have said, 'let's call it quits and get the hell out of this mess.' And of course he did try to make a deal with Carl Albert to get out of it. But that didn't work. He couldn't get anywhere with the White House either.

"When we got the vote in Congress that afternoon on the contempt issue, obviously the *Times* was on my tail for a statement and I made a statement. About fifteen or twenty minutes after that Bill came into my office and he said, 'Has anybody called you from the press about this?' And I said yes, the *Times* had been on, and he said, 'What did you say?' And I told him what I had said. Well, he thought that was an exaggeration. I said it was a vindication but he didn't like it. I think there was a lot of jealousy. And I don't know, perhaps there was a guilt feeling on his part that he hadn't asserted himself enough in this direction. There are other reasons why, but I can trace the difficulties of the last couple of years of our association and its tensions back to this particular issue of *The Selling of the Pentagon* very clearly.

"In many ways, I think if CBS had lost, he could have said, 'See, I told you so.' He was not out in front for the company on that issue. He didn't have the stomach for it and that hurt him. It also embarrassed him in front of his friends, who asked why I was and he wasn't. It certainly hurt our relationship." Disputes were created by Paley in the final days before Stanton left. Stanton says, "The thing I had to do was not to let anybody know. I had to keep a stiff upper lip because I thought CBS would be hurt.

"Paley called a meeting after I retired in which he said he didn't want to be bothered by this Loyal Opposition stuff. Maybe it was something Frank thought was good but it was a nuisance as far as he was concerned. At another meeting after I retired, in front of some of the senior people, Paley said he still thought it was a mistake that we had resisted the Congress in *The Selling of the Pentagon.*" Stanton says, "When he said I made a mistake in taking the stand as I did on *The Selling of the Pentagon* this documented to the group the cleavage that existed at the top of the company on important policy points. I don't know what would have happened—I really don't know—if the two men who came up to serve the Staggers subpoena had gone in his door instead of mine. He wasn't named in the subpoena—I was—but if they had looked in the table of organization and seen the CEO they might very well have served it on him. It would have been a different story because I think he would have said, 'let's just somehow find a way.' He would have called me and said, 'see if you can't settle this thing.'

"There's no question about what Klauber [the operating chief of CBS News at its beginning] would have done. It just was second nature to him. It wasn't as much second nature to me because I hadn't been a newspaperman. But it's the sense of what's right and wrong that you get when you're doing a job. I remember Dick Salant calling me after Paley's statement about *The Selling of the Pentagon.* Dick was about ten years behind me in age and Dick was in shock that Paley had said to the group that he thought it was a mistake to have defended *The Selling of the Pentagon.* Dick just thought that the whole ground had been shot out from under him. I don't think that Paley interfered as I was developing my case against Staggers. He really had left it to me to decide and act on. But I would have kept away from everybody a private division between us on that. If I had known it, I would have done everything I could do to persuade him I was right and that we couldn't show any sign of a divided leadership on this thing.

"The immediate threat was always the Congress because they could do something easily, such as destructive legislation and certainly quickly act to make a contempt finding as they almost did in the *Pentagon* investigation. Nixon represented a more general threat and a constant threat, but it would have been harder for him to strike at us directly. If Paley had any Nixon connection, he never talked to me about it. I don't think he ever trusted Nixon. He wasn't alone in that, but I think he sensed there was difficulty."

Stanton became Chairman of the American Red Cross on leaving CBS and served on many corporate and public boards. It was not until some years later that Paley sought Stanton out once again for advice. He also sought to resume their relationship. "Some years after I retired, Bill called me one day and he said Nixon wanted to have dinner with me. Paley put together a dinner for Nixon with himself, Jock Whitney's associate, Walter Thayer and me. Half way through the dinner, Nixon wanted to know what the feeling was on something and turned to me and asked me what my assessment was. And I told him and from that point on in the dinner it was as though just the two of us were there. I kept trying to push it away. And then he recalled some of the heated periods we'd gone through and was very jocular and very friendly.

"He spoke at length to me in part, I think, because we had been through the wars together. Among other things, he referred to the Staggers vote and said he was on my side, had not put any blocks in my way and was not unhappy at the way it came out. I didn't believe all of that and thought he was being, shall we say, overly polite. It was as if he were trying to make amends. He did say he hadn't changed his mind about some of the people who worked for CBS, but it seemed he wanted to be closer to people in the mainstream."

Bill Leonard was in charge of the CBS documentary unit at the time of *The Selling of the Pentagon*. He witnessed 40 years of broadcasting, winning, among other awards, a George Foster Peabody Award for Lifetime Achievement. He was president of the leading television press organization for many years. He writes of Stanton: "For decade after decade he stood firm, a reasoned voice of leadership in the cause of equal rights for broadcast news under the First Amendment, rights still not fully achieved." He also writes of the need for the strength of the publisher and the publisher's support: "The worth of any news organization is limited by the support it receives from its managers—financial and moral. Year after year, Frank Stanton gave us both."[1]

Afterword

Stanton's stand in 1971 was a challenge to government to give the electronic press room to do its job. But it was also a challenge to future leaders of the press. Will they protect news coverage from government oversight and interference? Will they risk corporate and personal interests to establish and maintain freedom for the electronic flow of information and news to the public?

If the government is permitted to oversee editorial news judgment on the new Information Superhighway, then we can expect, as history has repeatedly shown, that the government will try to control or restrict the news to serve its own agenda. Government arrangements to provide "access," "fairness," "equal time," or "responsibility" all sound useful but all eventually become instruments used to distort news coverage.

There will be those who believe that government should bring responsibility to the news, or at least the kind of responsibility the group advancing the regulatory scheme believes in. But a government agency will reflect the allegiance and agenda of its members at the time. If the concept of government involvement in news coverage is accepted, there will neither be an independent press nor the necessary flow of information to the public, particularly about the government itself.

As Stanton says, "I keep telling my former colleagues that press freedom is something that they are going to have to work awfully hard to maintain. There will be greater challenges to their credibility because of the temptation to dub in a picture or to dub in sound which can be done so skillfully that we will not know that it has happened. Even changing the direction of the sunlight can be effected so that the shadows are different. That can all be done now with clever manipulation, not in the control room, but in the editing room.

"The viewer said, 'I saw it. Khrushchev took his shoe off and hit the desk. I saw it.' That could be faked now. Even the explanation of the technology that created the picture causes a problem. I don't think many have the technical knowledge to understand how it takes place.

"Ultimately you have to hope that the integrity of the news people will be such that they won't indulge in that." Beyond that, he says, "It's one thing to bring the First Amendment into the picture but there is a common decency that has to be applied to what you do."

Stanton, with his years of experience, says, "Many haven't seen how people in government really don't want the press getting in the way of publishing something that may be awkward or embarrassing. A lot of people don't understand what a free press really means. They would subscribe to it until it stepped on their toes and then they say, 'You shouldn't be allowed to do that.' That part of our society that supports a free press is diminished when their own ox is being gored. It takes a big person to step back and say, 'You know, the free press is an important thing and I've got to take my lumps.'

"It often seemed to me that congressmen were saying things that didn't support a free press. If they had implemented what they were saying, they'd have come smack into the area of the First Amendment.

"I know I shocked some of the affiliates at one meeting when I said something about the price we had to pay to maintain the freedom of the press and not just for us. At the beginning of the discussion they were not very supportive. But they came to see what I was saying was true."

Notes

CHAPTER 1

1. U.S. Congress, House, Special Subcommittee on Investigations of the Committee on Interstate and Foreign Commerce, *Hearings on Subpoenaed Material re Certain TV News Documentary Programs*, 92d Cong., 1st Sess., April 20, May 12 and June 24, 1971, Series No. 92-16, pp. 2–3 (hereafter cited as "Subcommittee Hearings"); U.S. Congress, House, Report of the Committee on Interstate and Foreign Commerce, *Proceedings Against Frank Stanton and Columbia Broadcasting System, Inc.*, 92d Cong., 1st Sess., 1971, H. Doc. No. 9203491, pp. 138–39 (hereafter cited as "Committee Report").

2. Interviews were conducted with Dr. Frank Stanton during the period August 1994–1997 in New York, N.Y. Quotations from those interviews appear throughout the text. The interviews have also been used as source material and identified in the text when appropriate.

3. Erwin G. Krasnow, Lawrence D. Longley and Herbert A. Terry, *The Politics of Broadcast Regulation*, 3d ed. (New York: St. Martin's Press, 1982), pp. 15–25.

4. Stanton interviews, New York, N.Y..

5. *Television Digest*, April 12, 1971, p. 2.

6. "The Selling of the Pentagon," press release, April 8, 1971, CBS Library, 524 West 57th Street, 8th Floor, New York, N.Y.; Committee Report, pp. 142, 149–56.

7. Committee Report, p. 187.

CHAPTER 2

1. "The Selling of the Pentagon" may be screened at the Museum of Radio and Television, 25 West 52nd Street, New York, N.Y. The text is set out in Subcommittee Hearings, pp. 234–45.

2. Walter Cronkite of CBS was one of them.

3. *New York Times*, February 24, 1971.

4. *New York Times*, March 1, 1971.

5. Peter Davis, telephone interview by author, April 4, 1995; letter to author dated February 12, 1997.

6. Subcommittee Hearings (Transcript), pp. 245–46.

7. *Barron's*, March 1971.

8. *Washington Post*, March 21, March 30 and April 9, 1971; *New York Times*, April 6, 1971.

9. *Broadcasting*, March 22, 1971, p. 37; *New York Times*, March 19 and March 25, 1971.

10. Stanton interview; CBS Broadcast Group, letter to Stanton, March 24, 1995.

11. Subcommittee Hearings, pp. 245–49. Assistant Secretary Daniel Z. Henkin was repeatedly asked to appear on CBS to present his views, but he declined to do so.

12. Cong. Rec. (CBS Staff analysis), 91st Cong., 2nd Sess., E. 13493–99, 13697–700; Davis, telephone interview and letter to author. Davis states it would have been foolish to try to mislead the Chairman, and he was not misled.

13. *New York Times*, March 25, 1971.

14. *Washington Post*, March 24,1971.

15. *New York Times*, April 6, 1971.

CHAPTER 3

1. *Broadcasting*, July 5, 1971.

2. Subcommittee Hearings, pp. 10–12; Subcommittee Staff interviews by author: Daniel J. Manelli, Esq. (Acting Chief Counsel), Washington, D.C., August 17 and December 8, 1994; Michael F. Barrett, Jr., Esq. (Attorney), Washington, D.C., March 8, 1994; Mark J. Raabe, Esq. (Attorney), Washington, D.C., March 1994; Marguerite Furfarie (Administrative Assistant to Rep. Harley O. Staggers), Washington, D.C., March 1994.

3. House, Report of the Committee on Interstate and Foreign Commerce, Proceeding Against Rosel H. Hyde, Chairman, Federal Communications Commission, 91st Cong., 1st Sess., 1969, House Report (Committee Print).

4. Robert Hynes, Minority Counsel, House Committee on Rules, interview by author, Washington, D.C., May 31, 1994.

5. Charles W. Colson, letter to author, May 11, 1995.

6. Congressman Clarence Brown (R.-Ohio.), interview by author, Washington, D.C., Fall 1994; Congressman James Broyhill (R.-N.C.), telephone interview by author, April 4, 1995.

7. Subcommittee Hearings, pp. 6–13.

8. Manelli interviews.

9. Subcommittee Hearings, pp. 12–13, 151–89; Howard Monderer, Esq. (NBC Washington Counsel), interview by author, Washington, D.C., December 1994.

10. Subcommittee Hearings, pp. 13–30.

11. *New York Times*, March 30, 1971.

12. *New York Times*, April 10, 1971.

13. *Washington Post*, April 11, 1971.

14. *New York Times*, April 19, 1971; *New York Times*, April 18, 1971.

15. *New York Times*, April 19, 1971; Herbert G. Klein, interview by author, San Diego, Calif., September 9, 1995.

16. *New York Times*, April 10, 1971.

17. *New York Times*, April 19, 1971.

18. *New York Times*, April 18, 1971.

19. *New York Times*, April 13, 1971.

CHAPTER 4

1. Sally Bedell Smith, *In All His Glory: The Life of William S. Paley* (New York: Simon & Schuster, 1990), pp. 391, 399.

2. Stanton interviews.

3. Smith, *In All His Glory*, p. 449.

4. Ibid., p. 369.

5. Fred W. Friendly, *Due to Circumstances Beyond Our Control . . .* (New York: Vintage Books, 1968), pp. 243–54.

6. Irwin Segelstein, CBS Programming Vice President and subsequently NBC Vice Chairman, interview by author, New York, N.Y., November 1994.

7. Reuven Frank, *Out of Thin Air: The Brief Wonderful Life of Network News* (New York: Simon & Schuster, 1991), pp. 110, 127.

8. Ibid., pp. 222, 223, 229.

9. Gordon Manning, Vice President and Director of News, CBS News, interview by author, New York, N.Y., September 21, 1995. Stanton was widely known for nurturing CBS News and setting high standards for it. Hugh Carter Donahue, *The Battle to Control Broadcast News: Who Owns the First Amendment?* (Cambridge, Mass: The MIT Press, 1989), p. 120.

CHAPTER 5

1. Lucas A. Powe, Jr., *American Broadcasting and the First Amendment* (Berkeley: University of California Press, 1987), pp. 156–59.

2. Klein interview; Klein, *Making It Perfectly Clear* (New York: Doubleday & Company, Inc., 1980), p. 102.

3. Ibid., pp. 105–6.

4. Ibid., p. 105; Klein interview.

5. Ibid., p. 106; Richard Nixon, *Six Crises* (New York: Doubleday & Company, Inc., 1962), pp. 422–23.

6. Klein, *Making It Perfectly Clear*, p. 104.

7. Richard A. Wiley, telephone interview by author, February 28, 1997; *Aspen Institute Program on Communications, etc.*, 55 FCC 2d 697, 35 RR2d 49 (1975), *aff'd on appeal sub nom*, *Chisolm* v. *FCC*, 538 F2d 349, 36 RR2d 1437 (D.C. Cir. 1976), *cert. denied*, 429 U.S. 880 (1976); Henry Geller, 95 FCC 2d 1236, 54 RR2d 1246 (1983), *aff'd sub nom*, *League of Women Voters* v. *FCC*, No. 83-2194 (D.C. Cir., March 8, 1984).

8. Walter Cronkite, *A Reporter's Life* (New York: Alfred A. Knopf, 1996), pp. 185–86.

9. Klein, *Making It Perfectly Clear*, pp. 208–9; *Broadcasting*, April 26, 1971, p. 37.

10. Frank, *Out of Thin Air*, p. 325.

11. Powe, *American Broadcasting and the First Amendment*, pp. 140, 153.

12. Ibid., p. 140.

13. Ibid.

14. Klein, *Making It Perfectly Clear*, pp. 208, 209.

15. Manelli interviews; Barrett and Raabe interviews.

CHAPTER 6

1. Communications Act of 1934, as amended; *Red Lion Broadcasting Co.* v. *FCC*, 395 U.S. 367 (1969).

2. House, Special Subcommittee on Investigations of the Committee on Interstate and Foreign Commerce, Staff Report, "Television Coverage of the Democratic National Convention in Chicago, Illinois 1968," 91st Cong., 1st Sess., 1968 (Committee Print, 1969), pp. 10, 14, 21.

3. Ibid., pp. 1–2.

4. Ibid., pp. 10–11, 14.

5. Ibid., p. 24.

6. Ibid., p. 25.

7. Ibid., pp. 20–21, 27–28; Manelli interviews.

8. Ibid., pp. 4, 23–24. The memorandum from Stanton had instructed the CBS staff to "obey all police instructions instantly and without question." Stanton memo to Staff, "Chicago Convention," CBS Library, New York, N.Y.

9. Subcommittee Report on Convention Coverage, pp. 27–29. Presumably, if a complaint were made the government would have to decide if the label was required and review the news content and editing process. Since compression is often necessary, this would affect most news coverage.

10. Frank, *Out of Thin Air*, pp. 267–85.

11. Ibid., p. 284; Daniel Walker, *Rights in Conflict* (New York: Bantam Books, 1968).

12. In re Complaints Concerning Network Coverage of the Democratic National Convention, 15 RR2d 791 (1969); 16 FCC2d 650.

13. Frank, *Out of Thin Air*, p. 284.

14. Subcommittee Hearings, p. 10.

15. House, Special Subcommittee on Investigations of the Committee on Interstate and Foreign Commerce, "Report on Deceptive Programming Practices, Staging of Marihuana Broadcast—'Pot Party at a University,' " 91st Cong., 1st Sess., 1969, House Report No. 91-108.

16. Ibid., p. 20.

17. In the Matter of Inquiry Into WBBM-TV's Broadcast on November 1 and 2, 1967 of a Report on a Marihuana Party, WBBM-TV, 16 RR2d 207 (1969); 18 FCC2d 124.

18. Subcommittee Report on Marihuana Broadcast, p. 23.

19. Ibid., p. 23.

20. House, Subcommittee on Department of Agriculture and Related Agencies Appropriations of the Committee on Appropriations, Columbia Broadcasting System Television Program on "Hunger in America," 90th Cong., 1st Sess., 53 (1969). The FCC decision appears at In re Complaints Covering CBS Program, "Hunger in America," 20 FCC2d 143 (1969); Donahue, *The Battle to Control Broadcast News*, pp. 124–25.

21. House, Special Subcommittee on Investigations of the Committee on Interstate and Foreign Commerce, "Report on Network News Documentary Practices—CBS 'Project Nassau,' " 91st Cong., 2nd Sess., 1970, House Report No. 91-7319.

22. Nick Zapple, Professional member of the Staff, Subcommittee on Communications of the Senate Interstate and Foreign Commerce Committee, interview by author, Washington, D.C., April 26, 1995.

23. Timothy B. Dyk and Ralph E. Goldberg, "The First Amendment and Congressional Investigations of Broadcast Programming," *The Journal of Law and Politics* (University of Virginia) 3:4 (Spring 1987): 633. While the House Committees said they were conducting hearings into news coverage under their oversight powers, they did not call government agency officials. "The only apparent purpose of many of the hearings was to provide a forum for exposure and criticism of broadcast editorial practices that were already the subject of FCC or other regulation or that were beyond the power of Congress to reach."

CHAPTER 7

1. Joseph C. Spear, *Presidents and the Press* (Cambridge, Mass.: The MIT Press, 1984), pp. 49–50.

2. Ibid., pp. 53–56.
3. Ibid., pp. 57–63.
4. Richard Nixon, *The Memoirs of Richard Nixon* (New York: Grossett & Dunlap, 1978), pp. 354–55.
5. Ibid., pp. 67–69, 75–78, 122.
6. Gordon Manning, interview by author, New York, N.Y., November 1995; Spear, *Presidents and the Press*, pp. 34–35.
7. Ronald Kessler, *Inside the White House* (New York: Simon & Schuster, 1995), p. 27.
8. Nixon Presidential Materials Project, White House Special Files (hereafter WHSF), Staff Member and Office Files, H.R. Haldeman Notes, April 24, 1971, Folders April–June '71. Also, "just do what we want for the news on TV" (6/30/71); "must realize importance of TV" (8/9/71) (Folder August '71); "putting all we've done together, will hit Stanton" (8/18/71) (Folder August '71), National Archives at College Park, Md.; Spear, *Presidents and the Press*, p. 128.
9. Klein, *Making It Perfectly Clear*, p. 182.
10. Spear, *Presidents and the Press*, p. 113.
11. Ibid.; see also *New York Times*, November 14 and November 25, 1969.
12. Robert Mulholland, NBC News (Washington) producer, interview by author, Naples, Fla., December 1995.
13. Nixon, *The Memoirs of Richard Nixon*, pp. 391–95, 397–400.
14. Klein interview.
15. Nixon, *The Memoirs of Richard Nixon*, p. 398.
16. Henry Kissinger, *White House Years* (Boston: Little, Brown and Company, 1979), p. 286.
17. Ibid., pp. 292–93.
18. Nixon, *The Memoirs of Richard Nixon*, pp. 400–401.
19. Spear, *Presidents and the Press*, pp. 81–83.
20. Nixon, *The Memoirs of Richard Nixon*, p. 401.
21. Ibid., p. 402.
22. Walter Isaacson, *Kissinger: A Biography* (New York: Simon & Schuster, 1992), p. 247.
23. Klein interview.
24. Nixon, *The Memoirs of Richard Nixon*, p. 408.
25. Nixon Presidential Materials Project, White House Special Files (hereafter WHSF), President's Personal Files, Memoranda from the President, 1969–1974, Folder RN Memo 1968 to Memo December 1969, National Archives, College Park, Md.
26. WHSF, H.R. Haldeman Notes, Folder (July–December '69 Part I).
27. Nixon Presidential Materials Project, Donated Material, Handwritten Journals and Diaries of Harry Robbins Haldeman [hereafter Haldeman Journal], Vol. III, November 1, 1969, National Archives, College Park, Md.
28. Ibid., November 3.

29. Nixon, *The Memoirs of Richard Nixon*, pp. 409–10.

30. Kissinger, *White House Years*, p. 306.

31. *New York Times*, November 4, 1969.

32. Ibid.

33. Ibid.

34. Spear, *Presidents and the Press*, p. 114. Harriman (CBS Transcript) said it would be "presumptuous" to give "a complete analysis of a very carefully thought-out speech," adding, "No one wishes him well any more than I do." But he then indicated where he thought Nixon's approach might be flawed; Frank, *Out of Thin Air*, p. 296.

35. Nixon, *The Memoirs of Richard Nixon*, p. 410. David Eisenhower watched the speech with the President and said Nixon commented on the Ho Chi Minh letter, "Kalb could be right"; Daniel Schorr, *Clearing the Air* (Boston: Houghton Mifflin Company, 1977), p. 38n.; Marvin Kalb, *The Nixon Memo* (Chicago: University of Chicago Press, 1994).

36. Powe, *American Broadcasting and the First Amendment*, p. 126.

37. WHSF, H.R. Haldeman Notes, Folder (July–December '69 Part I), November 5, 1969.

38. *New York Times*, November 4, 1969; *Wall Street Journal*, November 4, 1969.

39. Nixon, *The Memoirs of Richard Nixon*, p. 410.

40. Haldeman Journal, November 5.

41. Nixon, *The Memoirs of Richard Nixon*, pp. 410, 411.

42. Ibid., p. 411.

43. William Safire, *Before the Fall: An Inside View of the Pre-Watergate White House* (New York: Doubleday & Company, Inc., 1975), p. 352.

44. Nixon, *The Memoirs of Richard Nixon*, p. 411.

45. Klein, *Making It Perfectly Clear*, pp. 170–72.

46. Haldeman Journal, November 12.

47. Nixon, *The Memoirs of Richard Nixon*, p. 411.

48. *New York Times*, November 14, 1969. The leading network correspondents originally were from North Carolina, Montana, Louisiana, South Dakota, Iowa, Oklahoma, and Texas.

49. Nixon, *The Memoirs of Richard Nixon*, p. 412.

50. Spear, *Presidents and the Press*, pp. 114, 116, 146.

51. Frank, *Out of Thin Air*, pp. 296–97.

52. *New York Times*, November 16, 1969; Klein, *Making It Perfectly Clear*, pp. 172–73. Klein writes that the entire "Agnew-press fracas . . . brought the opposite result of what any of us wanted: a major series of attacks and counterattacks which in the end were damaging both to the news media and to the presidency" (p. 175).

53. Spear, *Presidents and the Press*, pp. 116–17; Dan Rather, "CBS Evening News with Walter Cronkite," November 18, 1969.

54. FCC Opinion Letter on Instant Analysis, November 22, 1969; "Con-

cerning Fairness Doctrine Re Network's coverage of President's Vietnam Address," FCC 69-1288, November 20, 1969, 20 RR2d 1223.

55. *Washington Post*, March 25, 1969.

56. *New York Times*, December 16, 1969.

57. *Washington Post*, March 25, 1970.

58. Spear, *Presidents and the Press*, pp. 116, 120.

59. Ibid., p. 120.

60. WHSF, H.R. Haldeman Notes, Folder (June 1969), June 12, 1969.

61. Huntley called the White House and denied he said this. WHSF, H.R. Haldeman Notes, Folder (July 1970), July 16, 1970.

62. Spear, *Presidents and the Press*, p. 144.

63. Klein, *Making It Perfectly Clear*, pp. 289, 293–94. Colson understood he was to ride herd on the networks. See also Schorr, *Clearing the Air*, p. 41. Colson writes in *Born Again* (Old Tappan, N.J.: Chosen Books, 1976) of his excitement at becoming part of the President's staff at the age of 38 and working for the "single most important man in the world" (p. 33). While Klein writes that he underestimated Colson, it appears that Klein's sense of values and press, which differed from Colson's, left him long after the events with his reputation as a moderate in press matters largely intact.

64. Leonard Garment, Esq., Counsel to the President, telephone interview by author, July 18, 1997; Deborah Strober and Gerard Strober, *Nixon: An Oral History of His Presidency* (New York: HarperCollins, 1994), p. 279. Garment says that those familiar with Nixon often overlooked his emotional statements. He adds that studies of Nixon should not ignore his accomplishments in foreign policy, including the opening to China and the detente with Russia, his efforts to effect a strategic withdrawal from Vietnam, and his domestic programs, including legislation in the fields of health and civil rights and reform of the relations between government and the American Indian. As for the impeachment proceedings, these have already been fully reported. Nixon expressed his own view at the end, "I handed them the sword and they stabbed me and twisted it." Garment interview.

Certainly, when it came to the press, Nixon saw enemies. Press coverage may have been unforgiving, but he could not deal skillfully with it and he responded with distrust and outrage. Kissinger writes of the underlying emotion at the time of the Vietnam withdrawal efforts. Nixon believed that "what he really faced was not a policy difference but the same liberal conspiracy that had sought to destroy him ever since the Alger Hiss case. Here were all the old enemies in the press and in the Establishment, uniting once again; they would even accept if not urge the military defeat of their country to carry out the vendetta of a generation." Kissinger, *White House Years*, pp. 298–99. Garment sees the division as resulting from an alignment of gut emotional dislike and ideological differences. Garment interview.

65. Colson, *Born Again*, pp. 41–42.

66. Safire, *Before the Fall*, pp. 175–76, 341.

CHAPTER 8

1. Powe, *American Broadcasting and the First Amendment*, pp. 148–51.

2. Charles W. Colson, letter to author, May 11, 1995; Colson, *Born Again*, p. 41.

3. Powe, *American Broadcasting and the First Amendment*, pp. 148–49.

4. WHSF, Charles W. Colson Files, Chrono Folder, August 1970.

5. Colson, *Born Again*, p. 41.

6. David C. Adams, NBC Executive Vice President, interview by author, Purchase, N.Y., January 5, 1994.

7. WHSF, Charles W. Colson Files, Chrono Folder, September 1970.

8. Ibid. Colson's reports were obviously written with a view to impressing Haldeman and Nixon with his success. The networks' disagreement with the style and substance of Colson's report was outspoken when the report was made public. Hagerty of ABC was particularly critical; Spear, *Presidents and the Press*, p. 316n. 129.

9. WHSF, Press and Media No. 1, Part 2, Colson memo to H.R. Haldeman, August 15, 1970.

10. *In re Committee for the Fair Broadcasting of Controversial Issues* v. *CBS, Inc.*, 25 FCC2d 283 (1970), *In re Republican National Committee* v. *CBS, Inc.*, 25 FCC2d 739 (1970), *reversed sub nom*, *CBS* v. *FCC*, 454 F2d 1018 (D.C. Cir. 1971); Klein, *Making It Perfectly Clear*, p. 291; Klein interview.

11. WHSF, H.R. Haldeman Notes, Folder (July–October 1970).

12. WHSF, Charles W. Colson files, Chrono Folder, November 1970.

13. WHSF, Charles W. Colson files, Chrono Folder, March 1971. Nixon met with ABC on January 28, 1971 and with NBC on June 8, 1971.

14. Klein interview.

15. WHSF, H.R. Haldeman Notes, Folder (January–March 1971).

16. Klein, *Making It Perfectly Clear*, p. 209.

17. See Chapter 2; Klein, *Making It Perfectly Clear*, p. 210; Klein interview.

18. Colson, letter to author, March 11, 1995.

19. WHSF, Charles W. Colson Files, Chrono Folder, March 1971.

20. WHSF, H.R. Haldeman Notes, Folder (March–April 1970). Colson, who arranged for the critical *Washington Post* editorial to be circulated at the NAB Convention, reported, "This little campaign seems to be having its pay off." WHSF, Charles W. Colson Files, Chrono Folder (March 1971), March 30, 1971.

21. "Hon. Harley O. Staggers," 30 FCC2d 150; 21 RR2d 912 (1971).

22. *Television Digest*, May 3, 1971; *Wall Street Journal*, June 18, 1971.

23. *Television Digest*, June 18, 1971.

24. *Television Digest*, May 3, 1971.

25. *Wall Street Journal*, June 18, 1971.

26. WHSF, Charles W. Colson Files, Chrono Folder, April 1971.

27. *New York Times*, May 8, 1971.

28. Subcommittee Hearings, pp. 31–36, 36–75. Col. MacNeil sued CBS and the *Washington Post* station for damage to his reputation and Staggers dropped him from the witness list because of his personal interest. At a panel discussion at the Woodrow Wilson International Center for Scholars on "Media and the Government," Marvin Kalb of CBS said, "to take a technological problem and then suddenly to impart to the entire industry a desire to mislead and manipulate reality, I think, is grossly unfair." Assistant Secretary Henkin said, "Let me just say that to the best of my knowledge in my service at the Pentagon, . . . I know we have not made any such allegations" (Salant Memo to Dr. Stanton, July 1, 1971, "Selling of the Pentagon," CBS Library, New York, N.Y.). Henkin's Deputy, Jerry Freidheim, says that Secretary of Defense Melvin Laird saw a need to restore the credibility of the military and the Pentagon after the Johnson administration, and information was not to be manipulated. Accordingly, Henkin did not support the subpoena because its use was not a good thing for the press or the country. Jerry Freidheim, former Pentagon spokesman and Deputy Assistant Secretary of the Army, telephone interview by author, March 17, 1997.

29. Subcommittee Hearings, pp. 32–63, 76–78.

30. *New York Times*, May 27, 1971; Klein said, " 'I think the subpoena is representative of a danger to a free press. It is my feeling that while there's been a healthy debate between some of the Executive Branch & the media, that too often the media has overlooked where its real danger point is, and that is with the Congress which has the opportunity to subpoena . . . or it has the opportunity also of passing legislation which could be highly restrictive. . . . I believe that in going beyond what was broadcast and asking to get, in effect, notes of the program, that they infringe on the ability of broadcasters or print media to develop a story.' . . . Asked if there is difference between print & broadcast journalism, Klein said: 'Licensed journalists . . . sounds like a fair & fancy thing to many of the public, but what you are really saying is that you are restricted journalists, and there is no way to make a better journalists because he is licensed or unlicensed.' " *Television Digest*, April 26, 1971, p. 3. *Television Digest* also reported that FCC Chairman Dean Burch said that Congress has no right to subpoena outtakes or reporters' notes, that First Amendment is "definitely involved."

31. *New York Times*, June 2, 1971.

32. WHSF, H.R. Haldeman Notes, Chrono File, April 30, 1971 (April–June 1971, May 20–June 30, Part II).

33. Spear, *Presidents and the Press*, p. 133.

34. Klein interview.

35. WHSF, H.R. Haldeman Notes, Chrono File (April–June 1971, May 20–June 30, Part II).

36. Spear, *Presidents and the Press*, p. 40.

37. Ibid.

CHAPTER 9

1. Davis, telephone interview and letter to author, February 12, 1997.

2. Ibid.

3. Roger Mudd, interview by author, Princeton, N.J., Fall 1995.

4. William Leonard, interview by author, Washington, D.C., March 15, 1995.

5. Davis, telephone interview and letter to author. After reviewing the program, Leonard wrote Salant, "I should say that I think it is going to be one of our great broadcasts and is a superb job of investigative reporting which is a real public service." Leonard, memo to Salant, December 17, 1970, Salant Files, Salant Reading Room, New Canaan Library, New Canaan, Conn.

6. Davis, interview and letter to author.

7. Ibid.

8. Correspondence, "The Selling of the Pentagon," Gerald R. Ford Library and Museum, 1000 Beale Avenue, Ann Arbor, Mich.

9. Davis, interview and letter to author. Davis wrote an extensive explanation of the edits and a defense against the Pentagon charges in an exhaustive memo to Salant, March 12, 1971, Salant Files, Salant Reading Room, New Canaan Library, New Canaan, Conn.

10. Davis interview.

11. "Perspective, The Selling of the Pentagon," CBS Library, New York, N.Y.

12. Committee Hearings, p. 74; *Television Digest*, April 12, 1971, p. 2; *New York Times*, April 10, 1971.

13. Cong. Rec., 92d Cong., 1st Sess., H. 6577–80.

14. Manelli interviews; Barrett and Raabe interviews.

15. *Washington Post*, May 3, 1969.

16. *Washington Post*, May 19, 1969.

17. *New York Times Magazine*, Section 6, May 16, 1971.

18. Frank, *Out of Thin Air*, p. 328.

19. Krasnow, Longley, and Terry, *The Politics of Broadcast Regulation*, pp. 87–114, 206–10.

20. Ibid. Broadcasting history clearly shows congressional and executive investigations have a chilling impact. See also Dyk and Goldberg, "The First Amendment and Congressional Investigations of Broadcast Programming," pp. 632–40.

21. *New York Times Magazine*, Section 6, May 16, 1971.

CHAPTER 10

1. Subcommittee Hearings, pp. 65–70.

2. Committee Report, p. 187.

3. Subcommittee Hearings, p. 70.

4. Ibid., p. 11.

5. *Wall Street Journal*, June 18, 1971; Staggers press release, "The Selling of the Pentagon," CBS Library, New York, N.Y.

6. Manelli interviews. Manelli says Staggers believed in congressional supremacy and refused to be crossed by someone regulated.

7. Subcommittee Hearings, pp. 71–75.

8. Ibid., p. 79 (a transcript of the full proceeding appears at pp. 71–150).

9. Manelli interviews.

10. Ibid.

11. *Metromedia*, 14 FCC2d 194 (1968); Manelli interviews; Committee Staff Memorandum, Committee Hearings, pp. 267–348. Some of the legal memoranda and opinions of CBS Counsel, Wilmer, Cutler & Pickering, appear at Committee Report, pp. 149–83 and Supplements appear at Committee Hearings, pp. 361–66 and in the Cong. Rec., July 12, 1971, H. 6585–95. A complete set of what was published is at the firm's Washington, D.C., offices, and Lloyd Cutler, Esq., was gracious to share them with the author.

12. Manelli interviews.

13. Ibid. Barrett says CBS could have been withholding materials because if it were caught lying, that could have been taken into account by the FCC; Barrett interview.

14. Committee Report, p. 10.

15. Manelli interviews; Subcommittee press release, *New York Times*, June 30, 1971.

16. Ibid.; *New York Times*, June 25 and June 29, 1971.

17. Committee Report, pp. 12–111.

18. Committee Report, p. 11; Manelli interviews.

CHAPTER 11

1. WHSF, H.R. Haldeman Notes, Chrono Folder (May–June 1971).

2. Ibid., June 29, 1971.

3. David C. Adams interview, Purchase, N.Y., January 5, 1994. The omission is consistent with the view of some commentators that Colson's reports must be carefully assessed since he was apparently writing to please Nixon and Haldeman. See also William E. Porter, *Assault on the Media: The Nixon Years* (Ann Arbor: University of Michigan Press, 1976), pp. 70, 73.

4. WHSF, President's Files, Chrono Folder, June 1971.

5. H.R. Haldeman Journal, June 8, 1971.

6. Committee Report, p. 187.

7. Spear, *Presidents and the Press*, p. 131.

8. William Leonard, CBS News Executive, interview by author, Washington, D.C., March 15, 1995; *New York Times*, April 10, 1971.

9. *Television Digest*, July 5, 1971, pp. 3–4.

10. WHSF, Charles W. Colson Files, Chrono Folder, July 1971.
11. Charles Crutchfield, telephone interview by author, May 1995.

CHAPTER 12

1. Cong. Record, 92d Cong., 1st Sess., March 3, 1971, H. 4993–95.
2. Ibid., March 24, 1971, H. 5875.
3. Ibid.
4. Stanton, letter to House Speaker Carl Albert, July 7, 1971, "The Selling of the Pentagon," CBS Library, New York, N.Y. The new guidelines were burdensome but thought necessary. The Ninth Circuit's observation about the burden on the press cited by CBS counsel was later rejected by the Supreme Court which held that the grand jury's need for reporters' information outweighed the "uncertain burden on news gathering." *New York Times*, June 30, 1972.
5. Staggers, letter to colleagues, July 8, 1971, CBS Library, New York, N.Y.
6. Dissenting Members' Letter to Colleagues, July 8, 1971, Cong. Rec. H. 6572.
7. Broyhill, letter to colleagues, July 8, 1971, CBS Library, New York, N.Y.
8. Reid, letter to colleagues, July 8, 1971, Cong. Rec. H. 6572.
9. *Television Digest*, July 5, 1971, p. 4; Congressman Lionel Van Deerlin (D-Calif.), interview by author, San Diego, Calif., September 8, 1995. *Broadcasting* had reported on July 5, "Straws in the wind all point to House vote solidly in favor of contempt citation. . . ." *Broadcasting*, July 5, 1971, p. 7.
10. *Television Digest*, July 5, 1971.
11. Cong. Rec., 92d Cong., 1st Sess., July 8, 1971, Extension of Remarks, E. 7501–8, E. 7476, E. 7513.
12. Congressman Brown, interview by author, Washington, D.C., Fall 1994.
13. Congressman Broyhill, telephone interview by author, April 1995; Cong. Rec., 92d Cong., 1st Sess., July 12, 1971, H. 6563–71.
14. Cong. Rec., 92d Cong., 1st Sess., July 12, 1971, H. 6571–75.
15. Ibid., H. 6575.
16. Ibid., H. 6581.
17. Richard M. Schmidt, Esq., interview by author, Washington, D.C., March 30, 1995.
18. Cong. Rec., July 12, 1971, H. 6577–80.
19. Ibid., H. 6595.
20. Vincent Wasilewski, telephone interview by author, Spring 1995. The NAB had already adopted a resolution supporting Stanton; *New York Times*, 26 June 1971.
21. *Television Digest*, July 12, 1971, p. 4. Tom Wicker said if such broad-

cast news investigations could be pursued, "the airwaves would quickly become a propaganda medium." *Washington Post* (In the Nation), July 13, 1971.

22. *Television Digest*, July 12, 1971, p. 4.

23. "Face the Nation" transcript, July 11, 1971, pp. 200–215.

24. William Leonard, *In the Storm of the Eye: A Lifetime at CBS* (New York: G.P. Putnam & Sons, 1987), p. 166.

25. Colson, letter to author.

26. WHSF, John W. Dean III, Corresp. File, July 1971.

27. Manelli interviews; *New York Times*, July 18, 1971; Correspondence, "The Selling of the Pentagon," Gerald R. Ford Library and Museum.

28. President Gerald Ford, telephone interview by author, November 15, 1994; Congressman Broyhill and Congressman Brown interviews.

29. Ford, telephone interview; Klein interview.

30. Schorr, *Clearing the Air*, p. 48.

31. Colson, letter to author.

32. Ford, telephone interview; Gerald Ford, letter to constituents, July 1971, Gerald R. Ford Library and Museum.

33. *Washington Post* (Evans and Novak), July 14, 1971.

34. David Hartman, Counselor to President Gerald Ford, interview by author, Washington, D.C., May 31, 1994; Ford, telephone interview.

35. Manelli interviews.

36. *Television Digest*, July 19, 1971, p. 2.

CHAPTER 13

1. *Television Digest*, July 19, 1971, p. 2.

2. Ibid.

3. Manelli interviews. Staggers had no doubt that "as a member of Congress he had the right to demand the networks' obedience and the clout to enforce it." Porter, *Assault on the Media*, p. 125.

4. Cong. Rec., 92d Cong., 1st Sess., July 13, 1971, H. 6639–43.

5. Ibid., H. 6643–45.

6. Ibid., H. 6640–70.

7. Ford, telephone interview.

8. Counsel Manelli and a lawyer from Wilmer Cutler & Pickering, who were watching, say it was an extraordinary experience. Manelli says he could see how a debate on such an issue could decide the question as the force of the speeches affected those in the House. Manelli also observes that very little was said about the Vietnam War. Manelli interviews; Wilmer Cutler counsel interview, Washington, D.C., Fall 1994. Congressman Brown notes there was an undercurrent of antagonism against the "Eastern" establishment whose views were not shared by many elsewhere in the United States. Brown interview, Fall 1994.

9. Cong. Rec., 92d Cong., 1st Sess., July 13, 1971, H. 6669.

10. Manelli and Raabe interviews.

11. Cong. Rec., 92d Cong., 1st Sess., July 13, 1971, H. 6669–70.

12. *New York Times*, July 14, 1971.

13. *Television Digest*, July 19, 1971, p. 1.

14. Van Deerlin interview. Van Deerlin says Staggers never forgave Albert. Van Deerlin, telephone interview by author, April 1, 1997. Mark Raabe says he represented the Committee and advanced its interests as a lawyer, but he now believes the country, as well as the press, were better served by a vote against the contempt citation. Raabe interview.

15. Interview with Neil McNeil by Robert Conley, "All Things Considered," National Public Radio, July 22, 1971.

16. *Television Digest*, July 19, 1971, p. 1.

17. *New York Times*, July 14, 1971.

18. Ford, telephone interview.

19. *Washington Post*, July 18, 1971. One frustrated anti-CBS Republican said, "when the going got rough, Jerry finked. He ran, and so did Carl, and so did Boggs. Oh hell, they ran like rats around here. We would have won if it hadn't been for such tough lobbing." *New York Times*, July 14, 1971. Some broadcasters saw the fight as an example of how difficult it is to defy the government. Avoiding controversy might still be prudent. Peter Davis says no serious television documentary has since been done on the abuses of a government agency, such as the FBI, the Department of Justice or the CIA. Davis, telephone interview by author. Julian Goodman, President of NBC, warned that 44% had voted on "emotional and legal" grounds against CBS which was symptomatic of the friction between some politicians and the electronic media. *New York Times*, July 27, 1971.

20. Barrett and Raabe interviews.

21. WHSF, Charles W. Colson Files, Memo, July 20, 1971, Chrono Folder, July 1971; Colson had also advised Haldeman on July 14 that Paley had called with "profuse" thanks. Chrono Folder, July 1971. *Broadcasting* reported that Chairman Mills' statement on the floor of the House persuaded the House leadership to "dump Harley Staggers." *Broadcasting*, July 19, 1971.

22. *Variety*, August 6, 1971.

23. House, Special Investigations Subcommittee of the Committee on Interstate and Foreign Commerce, "Inquiry into Alleged Rigging of Television News Programs," 92d Cong., 2d Sess., No. 92–96 (1972).

24. Broyhill interview.

25. Report on congressional vote on "The Selling of the Pentagon," CBS Library, New York, N.Y.

CHAPTER 14

1. WHSF, Presidential Office Files, Ehrlichman Memo, September 11, 1971, Folder (September 1971).

2. WHSF, Charles W. Colson Files, Chrono Folder, October 1971.

3. Klein interview; Klein, *Making It Perfectly Clear*, pp. 214–15, 218–19, 221.

4. *Washington Post*, June 23, 1973.

5. Schorr, *Clearing the Air*, p. 53.

6. Smith, *In All His Glory*, pp. 476–78.

7. Ibid., p. 478.

8. Schorr, *Clearing the Air*, p. 34.

9. Spear, *Presidents and the Press*, p. 133; WHSF, Charles W. Colson Files, Chrono Folder, October 1972.

10. Spear, *Presidents and the Press*, pp. 85, 187. A journalism study concluded, "In the opinion of many political observers the press generally gave the president a free ride during his run for reelection." The press did not dare embarrass or anger the White House and this, "coupled with the shrewd manipulation of the media by Nixon officials, has moved the American news system closer to becoming a propaganda arm of the administration in power." Ben H. Bagdikian, "The Fruits of Aggression," *Columbia Journalism Review* 11:5 (January–February 1973): 9–20.

11. Safire, *Before the Fall*, pp. 175–76. Powe notes in *American Broadcasting and the First Amendment*, "Richard Nixon's full-scale attack on the broadcast establishment succeeded in toning down opposition to his policies. . . . Nixon was aberrational only in his intensity . . . the party controlling the White House has often fared well in broadcasting decisions that involved politics. . . . The willingness of the Commission to use every power of censorship at its disposal is notable." He asks, "[H]ow do we explain severing from the First Amendment protection the very source of news for most Americans? Furthermore, if broadcast dominance of our viewing habits is drawing to a close, how do we intend to treat our new technologies? To what extent does the past govern? What can be learned from it? (p. 194).

12. Stanton swore in an affidavit dated April 25, 1974, filed in *U.S.A.* v. *CBS, Inc., et al.*, No. 72-820-RJK United States District Court, Central District of California [The antitrust case against the networks], that in early November 1972, "Mr. Colson called me on the telephone and . . . said, in substance, "We'll bring you to your knees in Wall Street and on Madison Avenue." This call has been described as including a threat to take away CBS licenses. On May 26, 1974, Colson said on the CBS program *60 Minutes* that "I think it's fair to say that I never had a conversation like that with Frank Stanton." Spear, *President and the Press*, p. 150n. 152. Schorr writes that Colson described an administration plan to Stanton which included loss of station licenses and licensing the networks, and Stanton wrote this down. Schorr, *Clearing the Air*, pp. 57–58; Klein, *Making It Perfectly Clear*, pp. 212–13.

13. Schorr, *Clearing the Air*, pp. 52–53.

14. Frank interview, New York, N.Y., Winter 1997.

15. Powe, *American Broadcasting and the First Amendment*, pp. 134–37; Spear, *Presidents and the Press*, pp. 150–52; Porter, *Assault on the Media*, p. 173.

16. Spear, *Presidents and the Press*, p. 152.

17. Ibid., p. 174.

18. *New York Times*, June 7, 1973.

19. Porter, *Assault on the Media*, p. 205; Spear, *Presidents and the Press*, p. 174; Congressman Van Deerlin, who was a staunch congressional defender of press freedoms, decried what he saw as a "surrender" to the Nixon administration. Cong. Rec., June 1, 1973, H. 1850.

20. Schorr, *Clearing the Air*, p. 62.

21. House, Cong. Record, 93d Cong., 1st Sess., November 15, 1973, E. 7357–59.

22. Richard A. Wiley, telephone interview by author, Washington, D.C., March 4, 1997.

23. "Fairness Doctrine," 58 RR2d 1137 (1985); 102 FCC 2d 143; *Syracuse Peace Council*, 63 RR2d 541 (1987), 2 FCC Rec. 5043, *affirmed on recon.*, 64 RR2d 1073 (1988), 3 FCC Rec. 2035. *Syracuse Peace Council* v. *FCC*, 867 F.2d 654 (D.C. Cir. 1989), *cert. denied*, 493, U.S. 1019 (1990). Personal attack and equal time regulations continue. The lower court in *Syracuse* did not reach the constitutional question, and *Red Lion* remains a legal precedent. Some still support it, arguing that broadcasters can abuse their power, particularly in some fringe areas where service may be scarce. Andrew Schwartzman, interview by author, Washington, D.C., March 1995. Others argue "market dysfunction," "intrusion," "pervasiveness" and "invasiveness."

24. Donahue, *The Battle to Control Broadcast News*, pp. 161–74; *Variety*, November 30, 1988.

25. Spear, *Presidents and the Press*, p. 175. Some broadcasters supported the Fairness Doctrine since compliance helped ensure license renewal. *Broadcasting*, March 1996. Also, the grant of unregulated spectrum might require broadcasters to pay for their use of the spectrum instead of providing public service programming "in exchange" for the license grant.

26. James C. McKinney, Chief of the Mass Media Bureau, FCC Hearings on the Fairness Doctrine, Panel IV (February 8, 1985), 102 FCC2d 145 (1985), p. 191n. 174. The FCC fought to maintain its regulatory power over broadcast news. For example, NBC reported that some pension plans were not providing pensions to retirees who learned of this only after they retired. Legislation was then being considered to remedy this injustice. Accuracy in Media, a special interest group, complained to the FCC, which ordered NBC to broadcast the opposing view, that is, that the pension system was working. NBC refused. The FCC found NBC in violation of the Fairness Doctrine. On appeal, the court upheld NBC, noting the adverse effect of the Doctrine on the broadcast press. The FCC then asked the full appellate court to dismiss the case, arguing that the issue was effectively moot since in the meantime corrective legislation had been passed. On remand, the FCC dismissed the case as moot and the Doctrine was saved. *Accuracy in Media, Inc. Against National Broadcasting Co.*, 44 FCC2d 1027, 1043 (1973), *rev'd sub nom, National Broadcasting Co.* v. *FCC*, 516 F2d 110 (D.C. Cir. 1974), *reversal vacated and hearing en*

banc granted, 516 F2d 1155 (D.C. Cir.), *rehearing en banc vacated*, 516 F2d 1156 (D.C. Cir. 1975), second reversal vacated as moot and remanded with direction to vacate initial order and dismiss complaint, 516 F2d 1180 (D.C. Cir.), *cert. denied*, 424 U.S. 910 (1976); FCC dismissed as moot, *Accuracy in Media, Inc. Against National Broadcasting Co.*, 58 FCC 2d 361 (1976).

27. Fred W. Friendly, *The Good Guys, the Bad Guys and the First Amendment: Free Speech vs. Fairness in Broadcasting* (New York: Random House, 1975), pp. 41–42. In *Red Lion*, the Supreme Court quoted a Stanton statement that the Doctrine would not impair CBS news, but this was exhortative and made before the FCC tightened its enforcement.

28. Friendly, *The Good Guys, the Bad Guys and the First Amendment*, pp. 41–42. Cook quarrels with some of Friendly's description and minimizes the DNC help. Powe, *Broadcasting and the First Amendment*, pp. 113–17n. 22.

29. Recent public opinion polls suggest some censorship of the mass media would be acceptable today. The Center for Media and Public Affairs, in consultation with Louis Harris & Associates, found that 84% of those responding wanted a "Fairness Doctrine," and 70% wanted court fines for "irresponsible reporting." November 1996 Survey, distributed December 13, 1996. The trust in news reports has declined. Television Station Association Bulletin, Report Sponsored by the Pew Foundation, February 1977, *New York Times*, March 21, 1997. In a Newseum/Roper Center survey, only 15% of those polled could name press freedom as part of the First Amendment and 65% supported some censorship. *The Freedom Forum News* 4:4 (March 10, 1997).

Some academics agree. "Some forms of harm normally associated with speech may well be magnified by mass communications," says Frederick Schauer, Professor and Academic Dean of the Harvard University Kennedy School of Government, who would apparently consider reducing First Amendment protection of news. Cass R. Sunstein, Karl Llewellyn Professor of Jurisprudence at the Law School and Department of Political Science at the University of Chicago, would have what he describes as a small government bureaucracy make news coverage, in effect, pro-social to help develop better citizens and a better democracy. Cass Sunstein, "A New Deal for Speech," Preliminary Draft for Columbia Institute for Tele-Information Conference, February 5, 1994; Sunstein, *Democracy and the Problem of Free Speech* (New York: Macmillan, The Free Press, 1993).

Yale Law School professor Stephen Carter would support extensive regulation of new technologies, including news service. Carter writes, "Left unregulated, the modern media could present serious threats to democracy," and he urges that the government play an active role in news. Carter also observes the media will likely become concentrated in fewer hands. Powe, *Broadcasting and the First Amendment*, pp. 248–55. However troubling this prospect, placing news oversight in the hands of one centralized government agency holds little promise for diversity and a likelihood of political censorship as the history of broadcasting has repeatedly demonstrated.

As one appellate judge said of the FCC Commissioners, "Even if a Commissioner makes every effort to remain impeccably neutral, it is nonetheless possible, especially in presidential campaigns, that his partisan and political affiliations might subconsciously influence his decision-making." *CBS, Inc.* v. *Federal Communications Commission*, 629 F2d 1, 32–33 (D.C. Cir. 1980), *aff'd*, 453 U.S. 376 (1981) (Tamm, J., concurring) (footnotes omitted).

30. Ford Rowan, *Broadcast Fairness, Practice, Prospects* (New York: Longman, 1984). Dick Salant said that content regulations "create a brooding omnipresence, which limits robust journalism. . . . [Section] 315 and the fairness doctrine constrict, not expand, the flow of information. They put in the hands of government the coercive power, which history has shown government has sought to use, to manipulate and control" (pp. 121–23).

The NAB said broadcasters "are subjected to a subtle, continuous and strong incentive to avoid the [FCC] investigations . . . by sticking with the safe and the bland, depriving the public of the kind of journalism that a truly free press is able to provide." The Radio Television News Directors Association said broadcasters are "unable to present as forcefully as they should the great issues of our time."

The FCC Fairness Report concluded (August 23, 1985): "The fairness doctrine, in operation, inhibits the presentation of controversial issues of public importance; this fact impels the dual conclusion that the doctrine impedes the public's access to the market-place of ideas and poses an unwarranted intrusion upon the journalistic freedom of broadcasters."

Judge David Bazelon of the Washington, D.C., Circuit Court, which reviewed much broadcast regulation, said, "[T]he fairness doctrine has not fostered wide-ranging debate spanning the full spectrum of political and social ideas. Rather, it has contributed to suppressing programming on controversial issues almost entirely." He continued, [T]he "print model" of the First Amendment, the "hands off policy," has proven more durable and more congenial to our national political values than the different First Amendment standards endorsed in *Red Lion*. We should hesitate to stray from it in the name of diversity. If past efforts are any indication, government intervention is as likely to suppress diversity as to promote it." Judge David L. Bazelon, Address to the UCLA Communications Law Symposium—1979, "The Foreseeable Future of Television Networks," Los Angeles, February 2, 1979; Article, "The First Amendment and the 'New Media'—New Directions in Regulating Telecommunications," pp. 201, 205, 212.

Professor Monroe E. Price, in *Television, The Public Sphere, and National Identity* (Oxford, England: Oxford University Press, 1995), wants to preserve national identities and cultures which may be harmed by pervasive new mass technologies. But he also points to the inescapable interests of all governments: "In this environment, governments never loathe to censor, will be surprisingly resilient. And those passionate enough to press for general conformity to their views will employ the machinery of the state to aid them in their crusade. The more concentrated the press (and other aspects of the entertainment and information industry), the easier it is for the government to affect, sometimes subtly, their behavior. . . . A highly decentralized press . . . can be a greater mark of a free society than a market-place dominated by a few multinational corporations. But if the thousands have to pass through the eye of a single needle, the effect may be similar" (p. 241).

Powe points out in *American Broadcasting and the First Amendment*, "We fear broadcasting because we don't understand it as well as we do print. . . . [This] does not justify regulation, but it does explain it. It also explains why we can expect that as newer technologies become available to the public there will be an immense desire to keep them under control" (pp. 214–15). Donald V. West, editor of *Broadcasting & Cable*, has long defended broadcast press freedom. He points out that the government now has even more restraints on entertainment programming because, in this new age, broadcasting and cable have "sold out their constituents' birthrights for a mess of potage." Only Robert C. Wright, President of NBC, finally refused to agree to increased program content labeling. *Broadcasting & Cable*, July 14, 1997, p. 78; *Wall Street Journal*, July 11, 1997.

31. *Brandywine-Maine Line Radio, Inc.* v. *FCC*, 27 FCC2d 565 (1971) *aff'd on other grounds*, 153 U.S. App. D.C. 305, 473 F2d 16 (1972) (Judge Bazelon dissenting), pp. 78–79, *cert. denied*, 412 U.S. 922 (1973).

32. Jack Fuller, *News Values: Ideas for an Information Age* (Chicago: University of Chicago Press, 1996). The Supreme Court has seen the need for some leeway for the press to do its job: "For better or worse, editing is what editors are for; and editing is selection and choice of material. That editors—newspaper or broadcast—can and do abuse this power is beyond dispute, but that is no reason to deny the discretion Congress provided. Calculated risks of abuse are taken to preserve higher values." *CBS Inc.* v. *DNC*, 412 U.S. 94, 124–25 (1973). But press regulation is insidious because it is usually attractively labeled and, on its face, is directed to desirable social goals. Increased content regulation on the Information Superhighway will be difficult to resist and, once in place, even more difficult to remove. It is simply too easy, even prudent from a business point of view, to accept such government regulation.

At the same time, the need for mass media news to inform the public is increasing. As television "image" commercials and "spin doctors" become accepted purveyors of information, "propaganda" becomes more likely. Anthony Pratkanis and Elliot Aronson in *Age of Propaganda: The Everyday Use and Abuse of Persuasion* (New York: W.H. Freeman and Company, 1991) warn: "The consequences for democracy can be dire . . . the competitive urge to use simpler and simpler persuasion increases. . . . (and) the propagandist must use even more simplistic persuasion devices. The result is an ignorance spiral—a cynical populace bombarded with more and more thoughtless propaganda that they have less and less skill and inclination to process and ability to understand" (pp. 100–101, 265). As it becomes more and more imperative to the propagandist that nothing interferes with the desired portrayal (Spear, *Presidents and the Press*, pp. 88–89), this will increase government's interest in shaping electronic news and will require greater commitment by the press to report actuality and freedom from government oversight to do so.

As Pen American Center points out, concerned at the loss of information because of government and private barriers: "Providing access to information is a major part of maintaining democratic values and ensuring that people can play a meaningful role in political decision-making. The price society pays for failure to remove restrictions on information is an apathetic, ill-informed, and vulnerable citizenry." Donna A. Demac, *Liberty Denied: The Current Rise of Censorship in America* (New York: Pen American Center, 1988), p. 124.

33. *Denver Area Education Telecommunications, Inc.* v. *FCC*, 116 S. Ct. 2374 (1996). Of course, if the point of the First Amendment is to see that the press on which the public relies is free of government interference, then the Amendment should apply to a "pervasive" media more than any other. In *Red Lion*, the Court itself said that it would reexamine its rationale for regulation if proved wrong. Yet even with channel abundance and the FCC finding of a chilling of the broadcast press, the Court continues *Red Lion*. It even upholds regulation on speech and press on cable, a pervasive system important to public knowledge in the next century. In the *Denver* decision, the Court restricts "indecency" on cable, which can be found in museums, theatres, bookstores, magazines and newspapers delivered to the home and in schools and libraries.

Cable systems may refuse to permit "indecent" speech on channels leased by others, speech impossible to define with cultural consensus. The effect can only be suppression, often the purpose of such legislation. Again, the broadcast experience demonstrates the censorial results of such legislation. See Milagros Rivera-Sanchez, "How Far Is Too Far? The Line Between 'Offensive' and 'Indecent' Speech," *Federal Communications Law Journal* (Indiana University School of Law–Bloomington, Federal Communications Bar Association) 49:2 (February 1997): 327–366.

34. *Turner Broadcasting System Inc.* v. *FCC*, 117 S. Ct. 1174 (1997).

35. *ACLU* v. *Janet Reno*, F. Supp. 824 (E.D. Pa. 1996), *aff'd sub nom*; *Janet Reno* v. *ACLU*, 65 LW 4715 (1997); *New York Times*, July 11, 1997; *Wall Street Journal*, July 11, 1997.

36. *New York Times* v. *U.S.*, 403 U.S. 713, 717 (1971).

37. *Olmstead* v. *U.S.*, 277 U.S. 438, 479 (1928), Justice Louis Brandeis dissenting.

38. *U.S.* v. *Associated Press*, 52 F. Supp. 362, 377 (S.D.N.Y.), 1943.

39. *Washington Post*, January 5, 1995.

40. *Wall Street Journal*, June 14, 1994; Reuven Frank, "Turning Knowledge into Profit," *The New Leader*, March 13–27, 1995.

41. Gerald M. Levin, Address to Detroit Economic Club, February 1997; Powe in *American Broadcasting and the First Amendment* concludes that, "As the belief in the uniqueness of broadcasting necessarily evaporates, there

will come a tension about how to deal with an unknown future. The claim will be made that keeping the Constitution up with the times requires a newer tradition, one looking to, rather than away from, the government. As we hear this claim, we should recall the lessons of licensing, whether in seventeenth-century England or twentieth-century America."

We can also recall what it took in 1971 to free the editorial judgment of television news coverage from the continuing oversight of the American government. At that time, Dick Salant said: "It takes an awful lot of guts for management to ignore these attacks, because they can literally mean their economic life." The decision "not to do the story" was the problem. The First Amendment was being lost, "a little each day." Fred Powledge reminds us that "The First Amendment does not belong to the press, but to the people, and they must not allow it to be given away or traded for a little respectability, or a little immunity from a politician's criticism." Fred Powledge, *The Engineering of Restraint: The Nixon Administration and the Press*, a report of the American Civil Liberties Union (Washington, D.C.: Public Affairs Press, 1971), pp. 33, 41.

42. Joan Konner, Dean, The Columbia University Graduate School of Journalism, "Is Journalism Losing Its Professional Standards?" address presented at the conference "Ethics and Standards: New Rules for Journalism Assuring Quality Through Self Control and Leadership," Hamburg, Germany, July 3, 1995. She says that the electronic press lacks leadership in its role of informing the public, and she is concerned that high professional standards are not objectives of the developing media.

CHAPTER 15

1. Bill Leonard, CBS News Executive, interview by author, Washington, D.C., March 15, 1995; Leonard, *In the Storm of the Eye*, p. 177. Stanton's industry recognition included election to the Hall of Fame of the Academy of Television Arts and Sciences and to the Radio Hall of Fame, five George Foster Peabody Awards, and the First Amendment Award of the Radio-Television News Directors Foundation.

Selected Bibliography

Colson, Charles W. *Born Again*. Old Tappan, N.J.: Chosen Books, 1976.

Cronkite, Walter. *A Reporter's Life*. New York: Alfred A. Knopf, 1996.

Demac, Donna A. *Liberty Denied: The Current Rise of Censorship in America*. New York: Pen American Center, 1988.

Donahue, Hugh Carter. *The Battle to Control Broadcast News: Who Owns the First Amendment*? Cambridge, Mass.: The MIT Press, 1989.

Frank, Reuven. *Out of Thin Air: The Brief Wonderful Life of Network News*. New York: Simon & Schuster, 1991.

Friendly, Fred W. *Due to Circumstances Beyond Our Control* . . . New York: Vintage Books, 1968.

———. *The Good Guys, The Bad Guys and the First Amendment*. New York: Vintage Press, 1976.

Fuller, Jack. *News Values: Ideas for an Information Age*. Chicago: University of Chicago Press, 1996.

Isaacson, Walter. *Kissinger: A Biography*. New York: Simon & Schuster, 1992.

Kalb, Marvin. *The Nixon Memo*. Chicago: University of Chicago Press, 1994.

Kessler, Richard. *Inside the White House*. New York: Simon & Schuster, 1995.

Kissinger, Henry. *White House Years*. Boston: Little, Brown and Company, 1979.

Klein, Herbert. *Making It Perfectly Clear*. New York: Doubleday & Company, 1980.

Krasnow, Erwin G., Laurence D. Longley and Herbert A. Terry. *The Politics of Broadcast Regulation*. 3d ed. New York: St. Martin's Press, 1982.

Leonard, William. *In the Storm of the Eye: A Lifetime at CBS.* New York: G.P. Putnam & Sons, 1987.

Nixon, Richard. *The Memoirs of Richard Nixon.* New York: Grossett & Dunlap, 1978.

———. *Six Crises.* New York: Doubleday & Company, 1962.

Porter, William E. *Assault on the Media: The Nixon Years.* Ann Arbor: University of Michigan Press, 1976.

Powe, Lucas A., Jr. *American Broadcasting and the First Amendment.* Berkeley: University of California Press, 1987.

Powledge, Fred. *The Engineering of Restraint: The Nixon Administration and the Press.* Report of the American Civil Liberties Union. Washington, D.C.: Public Affairs Press, 1971.

Pratkanis, Anthony and Elliot Gronson. *Age of Propaganda: The Everyday Use and Abuse of Persuasions.* New York: W.H. Freeman and Company, 1991.

Price, Monroe E,. *Television, the Public Sphere, and National Identity.* Oxford, England: Oxford University Press, 1995.

Rowan, Ford. *Broadcast Fairness, Practice, Prospects.* New York: Longman, 1984.

Safire, William. *Before the Fall: An Inside View of the Pre-Watergate White House.* New York: Doubleday & Company, 1975.

Schorr, Daniel. *Clearing the Air.* Boston: Houghton Mifflin, 1977.

Smith, Sally Bedell. *In All His Glory: The Life of William S. Paley.* New York: Simon & Schuster, 1990.

Spear, Joseph C. *Presidents and the Press: The Nixon Legacy.* Cambridge, Mass.: The MIT Press, 1984.

Strober, Deborah and Gerard Strober. *Nixon: An Oral History of His Presidency.* New York: HarperCollins, 1994.

Sunstein, Cass R. *Democracy and the Problem of Free Press.* New York: Macmillan, The Free Press, 1993.

Walker, Daniel. *Rights in Conflict.* New York: Bantam Books, 1968.

Index

About the Author

CORYDON B. DUNHAM was Executive Vice President and General Counsel of NBC for many years. Currently he is Counsel to Cahill Gordon & Reindel and has served as Guest Scholar at the Woodrow Wilson International Center for Scholars. He is the author of numerous articles on issues related to free press and communications.